Eating Out in AUSTRIA

Gretel Beer was born in Austria and is the author of *Exploring Rural Austria* and several cookery books, including *Austrian Cooking, The Sunday Express Cookbook* and *The Diabetic Gourmet* (with Paula Davies). Contributor on travel and food to *Vogue, Taste, The Sunday Express, The Daily Telegraph* and a variety of Swiss and Austrian newspapers and magazines. BBC broadcasts. She was awarded the *Goldenes Ehrenzeichen* (Knight's Cross, first class) for services to the Austrian Republic and is the holder of the Duchessa di Parma award.

Eating Out in AUSTRIA

GRETEL BEER

With line drawings by
Bill Martin

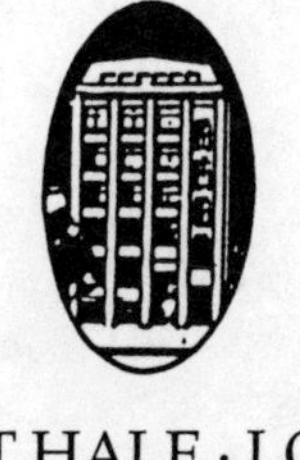

ROBERT HALE · LONDON

First published in Great Britain 1992

ISBN 0 7090 4580 8

Robert Hale Limited
Clerkenwell House
Clerkenwell Green
London EC1R 0HT

Photoset in North Wales by
Derek Doyle & Associates, Mold, Clwyd.
Printed in Great Britain by
St Edmundsbury Press Ltd, Bury St Edmunds, Suffolk.
Bound by WBC Bookbinders Ltd, Bridgend, Glamorgan.

Contents

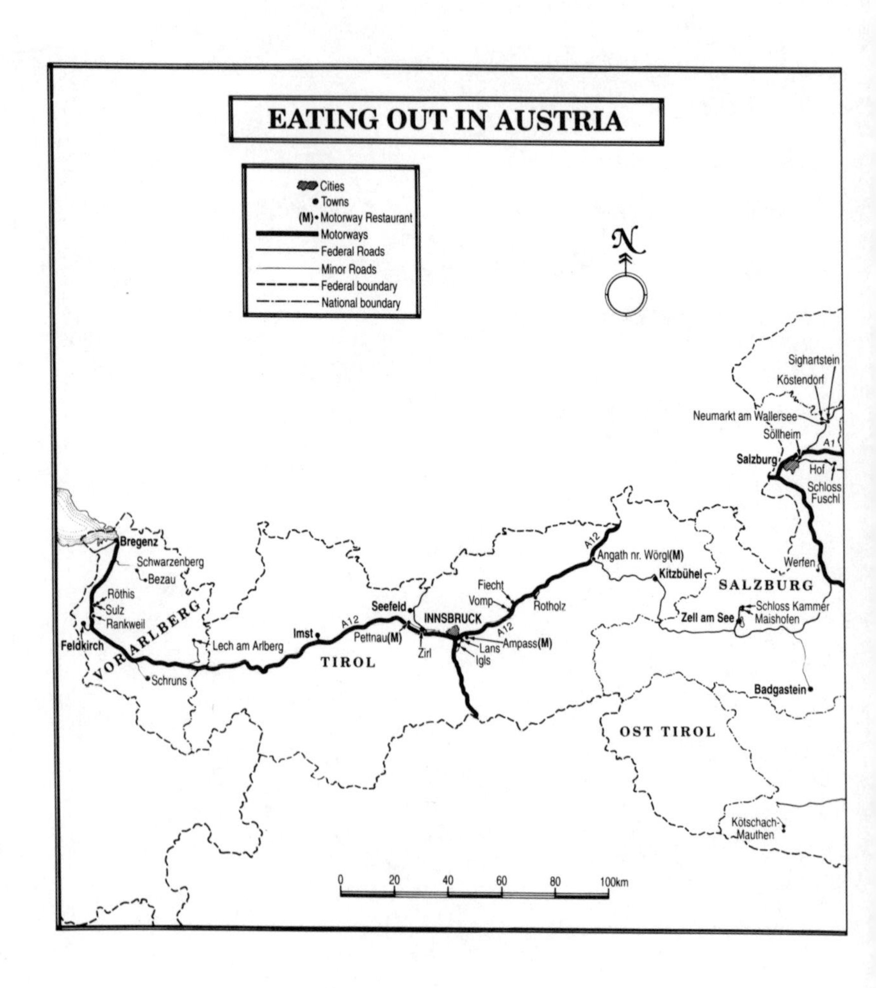
EATING OUT IN AUSTRIA
Cities
Towns
(M) Motorway Restaurant
Motorways
Federal Roads
Minor Roads
Federal boundary
National boundary
N
Sighartstein
Köstendorf
Neumarkt am Wallersee
Söllheim
A1
Salzburg
Hof
Schloss Fuschl
Bregenz
Schwarzenberg
Bezau
Röthis
Sulz
Rankweil
Feldkirch
VORARLBERG
Lech am Arlberg
Schruns
Imst
A12
Pettnau(M)
Seefeld
Zirl
INNSBRUCK
Lans
Igls
Ampass(M)
Fiecht
Vomp
Rotholz
Angath nr. Wörgl(M)
Kitzbühel
Werfen
SALZBURG
Schloss Kammer
Maishofen
Zell am See
TIROL
Badgastein
OST TIROL
Kötschach-Mauthen
0
20
40
60
80
100km

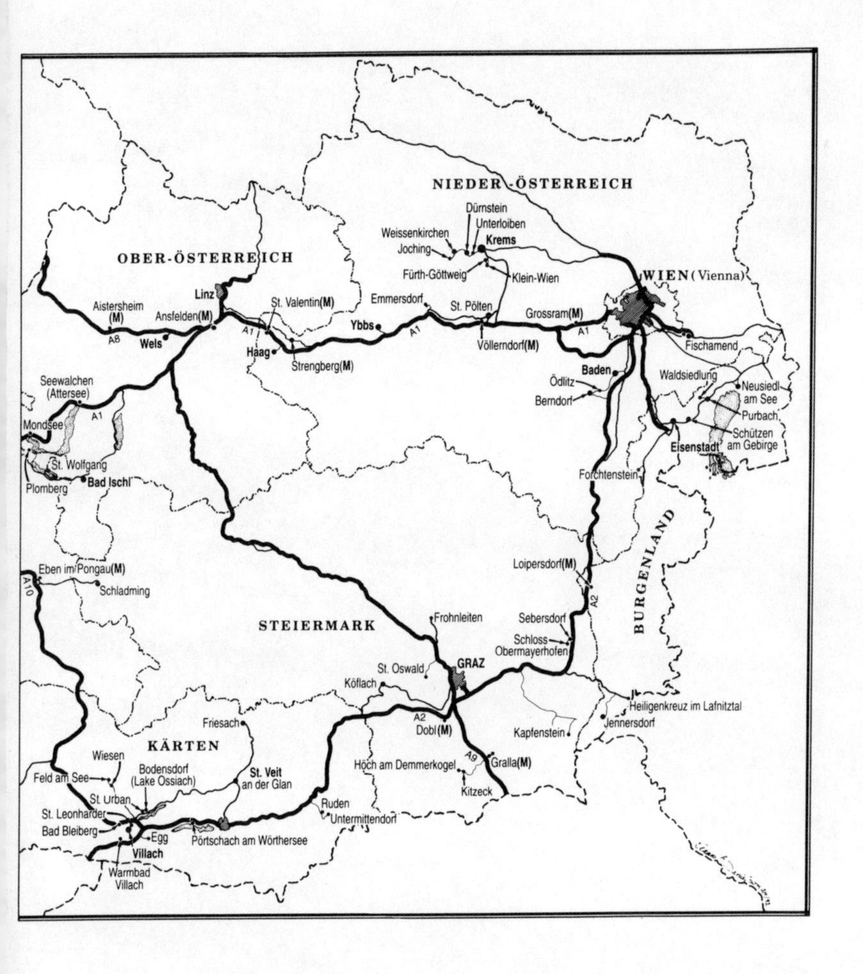
NIEDER-ÖSTERREICH
OBER-ÖSTERREICH
STEIERMARK
KÄRTEN
BURGENLAND
WIEN (Vienna)
Dürnstein
Unterloiben
Weissenkirchen
Joching
Krems
Fürth-Göttweig
Klein-Wien
Linz
Aistersheim (M)
Ansfelden(M)
St. Valentin(M)
Emmersdorf
St. Pölten
Grossram(M)
Ybbs
Wels
Haag
Strengberg(M)
Völlerndorf(M)
Fischamend
Baden
Ödlitz
Berndorf
Waldsiedlung
Neusiedl am See
Purbach
Schützen am Gebirge
Eisenstadt
Forchtenstein
Seewalchen (Attersee)
Mondsee
St. Wolfgang
Plomberg
Bad Ischl
Eben im Pongau(M)
Schladming
Loipersdorf(M)
Frohnleiten
Sebersdorf
Schloss Obermayerhofen
St. Oswald
GRAZ
Köflach
Heiligenkreuz im Lafnitztal
Jennersdorf
Friesach
Dobl(M)
Kapfenstein
Wiesen
Feld am See
Bodensdorf (Lake Ossiach)
St. Veit an der Glan
Höch am Demmerkogel
Gralla(M)
Kitzeck
St. Urban
St. Leonharder
Bad Bleiberg
Egg
Villach
Warmbad Villach
Ruden
Untermittendorf
Pörtschach am Wörthersee
A1
A2
A8
A9
A10

Acknowledgements

with grateful thanks

It would have been impossible to compile this book without the help and encouragement of the Economic Chamber of Austria and Austrian Airlines who transported me and my ever-increasing and heavyweight documentation. Special thanks are also due to Professor Norbert Burda of the Austrian National Tourist Office in Vienna for his untiring support and to my many friends who shared my feasts (or otherwise), assisted, guided and unfailingly pointed my nose in the right culinary direction and particularly to Count Peter Esterhazy, to Victor Juza, great gastronome in retirement at Graz, to Ferdinand Schreiber, food photographer extraordinary at Hof near Salzburg and to Gergely-Werner Szücs (and the sound of his violin).

Introduction

You will eat well in Austria: at inns small and large, more often than not in a garden well-shaded by trees when the scent of linden blossoms will vie with that of the cool wine grown in a nearby vineyard; at elegant restaurants where the cooking is on par with the best in Europe (at prices which may well be agreeably lower); at ancient coffee houses where you may sit for hours consuming nothing more than a cup of coffee for the waiter to bring you countless glasses of iced water (and on your second visit your preferred newspapers) without asking; at pâtisseries which are better in Austria than anywhere else in the world, many of which will serve you a delectable light lunch as well as pastries and luscious gâteaux and all of which, like coffee houses, are fully licensed; at places like the wonderful old delicatessen which is like a private club at certain times of the day where you can choose from fine vintage wines to drink with your delicious snacks.

This book is a personal choice of eating places, some famous, others relatively unknown and including some 'hidden treasures', all of which I have visited, tried, tested and tested again. Some I have known and loved since childhood – marvellous old family inns where a new (and sometimes third) generation now tends the stoves, others I have come to know and love over more recent years. This is not a comprehensive selection (although I have tried to be comprehensive as well as selective), rather a cross-section of inns, restaurants, pâtisseries, coffee houses and places where you can get a snack – a culinary bouquet if you like, gathered to please your palate. My criterion for selection has been simple: would I go back there again and – most important – would I take a guest there? You may notice some rather obvious omissions and this can be due to a variety of reasons: I may not know the restaurant – or not know it well enough (it may have been closed at the time of my numerous visits and in particular at the time of my final testings); there may have been a recent change of ownership or chef or I did not consider it suitable for inclusion because (after several visits) I did not think the food and service were right in relation to the price charged or quite simply because I did not enjoy the food and therefore did not think it right to recommend the place. Nor have I included a restaurant simply because it was inexpensive if the food was not of a commendable standard.

I have deliberately not graded or rated restaurants in any way, because I think that personal ratings are always arbitrary, too personal and therefore often boring and in any case, how do you relate ratings between a simple inn serving top-rate food of its kind and a gourmet restaurant? Hopefully you will like the places I have recommended as much as I do – some possibly less, others perhaps even more. You should certainly not have a bad meal at any of the restaurants listed here, but that does not mean that you can't and it is always possible that you might. Chefs can have an 'off' day and accidents will happen (as they are so fond of saying in Austria 'even a machine is only human'). I have confined my selection almost entirely to restaurants serving typically Austrian food – albeit with accents of an empire on which 'the sun never set'. Austrian and Viennese cooking (there is a difference) are worth exploring and to know what to order (and where to order it) is as important as finding the right restaurant. If the head waiter or the menu suggested that you should start with *Biskuitschöberlsuppe* followed by *Beinscherzl* with *Heurige* and *Fisolen* and finished with *Ribislschaumtorte* you would look in vain for these in a German/English dictionary, for these are strictly Austrian culinary terms. And you would probably not be able to make sense of abbreviations on the menu of a modest inn, some of which read like a knitting pattern – or would you have known that 'm. gem. Slt.' stands for '*mit gemischtem Salat*' (with a mixed salad)? And if the waiter in a coffee house asked whether you wanted a portion of '*Doppelschlag*' with your coffee, would you reconcile this with a double portion of whipped cream? The glossary should help you with all these problems – stating the difference between *Heurige* (new potatoes) and *Heuriger* (new wine as well as the place where it is drunk), between *Kipfel* (croissant) and *Kipfler* (a special kind of potato). It explains the mysteries of such strictly Austrian specialities as *Powidltatschkerln* and should guard you from getting half a pair of Frankfurter sausages (or a carriage drawn by one horse to the door of the coffee house) when you really wanted a glass of black coffee with whipped cream (all three are called *Einspänner*!). I hope it will encourage you to order dishes which have hitherto been unknown to you and which – like the restaurants – you would not have found except for this book. And above all, I hope that you will enjoy *Eating Out in Austria*!

Gretel Beer

How to Use This Book and Other General Information

Listings
Restaurants, inns etc. are listed in alphabetical order according to the name of the town and each listing gives the following information: name of town or village; province (e.g. Styria, Carinthia, etc.); name of the establishment; full postal address including postal code; telephone number; opening and closing times (and dates where applicable); price guide; how to get there (for places other than towns and well-known resorts).

Telephone Numbers
Telephone numbers include local codes (except for Vienna). If telephoning from outside Austria, leave off the first '0' after dialling code for Austria.
Please note: The telephone system throughout Austria is at present being changed to digital and some of the numbers given in this book may have been altered.

Public Holidays
As a rule restaurants which are closed on Sunday also close on public holidays. In Austria these are as follows:

1 January
6 January
Easter Monday
1 May
Ascension Day
Whit Monday
Corpus Christi Day
15 August
26 October (National Holiday)

1 November (All Saints)
8 December
Christmas Day and Boxing Day

Most restaurants – hotel restaurants excepted – are also closed on Christmas Eve evening. If a restaurant is open on Sundays, but a public holiday coincides with its weekly closing day, it will stay open on the public holiday, but close on another day of the week.

Opening Times
Subject to frequent changes and practically a science of its own, inns and large restaurants are usually open all day, some offering *'ganztägig warme Küche'* or *'durchlaufend warme Küche'* meaning that hot food is served throughout the day, though not necessarily a full menu. Some establishments offer a *'kleine Karte'* (limited menu), but food will still be freshly cooked and *'klein'* does not necessarily mean 'small' as far as the dishes are concerned which may well include a *Wiener Schnitzel* or a freshly prepared pasta dish. Speciality restaurants, particularly those with a star chef are usually only open at meal times. Some restaurants, particularly in holiday areas are open all day during the season and only open at meal times during the rest of the year. Where a restaurant's opening times are for instance given as 8.00 – 24.00, giving meal times in brackets, this means that it is open for breakfast and snacks throughout the day, but lunch and dinner are served only during the times specified. It is also quite usual for a restaurant to be open for lunch from say 11.30 – 15.00, but for the kitchen to close at 14.00 and I have given kitchen closing times in brackets (please note that some kitchens close comparatively early, whilst the restaurant may stay open late).

Reservations
In view of the foregoing (if nothing else) reservations or at least a telephone call to check are necessary. This applies particularly to out-of-town places. Opening and closing times are 'flexible' to say the least and restaurants are likely to change their closing times and dates (weekly and annual) quite often and without warning. Always check before making a special journey.

Dining Hours
Austria lunches early (as you will see from the opening hours of restaurants) and though restaurants may stay open until midnight, some kitchens also close early. There are, however, late opening times in restaurants near theatres and at festival times, and I have listed these where applicable.

Licensing
In Austria practically all establishments are licensed to sell alcoholic drinks and this includes coffee houses as well as *pâtisseries*. There are no restrictions as to licensing hours – alcoholic drinks can be sold as long as the establishment stays open.

Price Guide
The price range of restaurants listed in this book goes from inexpensive to expensive. In each case the price guide represents a meal for one person including first course, main course and pudding (or cheese) as well as the service charge and often a quarter litre of wine as well.

inexpensive – up to S200. (in this category this usually also includes a glass or quarter litre of wine or a G'spritzter or a beer)
moderate – up to S350.
upward – up to S450.
expensive – over S450.

It is, however, usual for even quite expensive restaurants to offer a reasonably priced set menu, particularly at lunch (see text for details).

Tipping
You will usually find the words *'Inklusivpreise'* or *'inklusive Steuern und aller Abgaben'* on the menu which means that service charges and VAT are included. Theoretically you are not required to pay more than the final total on the bill, but it is in fact customary to add an additional 5% to 10%.

Credit Cards
Practically all restaurants in this book take credit cards and travellers cheques, but there are frequent and constant changes

as to which establishment takes which credit card and it is therefore best to check details when making your reservation. If a restaurant does not take credit cards, this is stated next to the general information, such as address and telephone number. You would obviously not expect to be able to pay with a credit card in a pâtisserie or a very small country inn which is more of a farmhouse than an inn, though some do accept them as well.

Cover Charge
The price for cover charge (*Gedeck* or *Couvert* is usually marked on the menu. In some restaurants, particularly in country inns, this may be followed by *auf Wunsch*' (on request). This means that the cover charge (if requested) includes bread, butter, sometimes an *amuse gueule* (or some spread as well as butter) and a cloth napkin. If you do not 'request' you pay for the bread or rolls as consumed (you'll have to try and remember how many rolls or slices of bread you've eaten) and the butter and you get a paper napkin.

Measures for Drinks
These may well be changed if and when Austria joins the EEC, but at present the following measures are being used:

BEER
Pfiff – 'whistle'. Old Viennese measure now only used for beer. Usually ⅛l, though sometimes generously extended to 2 dl (Grauer Bär, Innsbruck)
Seidel (*kleines Bier*) – ⅓l
Krügel (*grosses Bier*) – ½l
Bottled beer is sold as '*kleine Flasche*' ⅓l and '*grosse Flasche*' ½l

WINE
Offene Weine (house wine)
House wines which may be served in a glass or a jug are not usually ordered per glass but as follows:
Achtel, Achterl, Achtl – ⅛l
Viertel, Vierterl – ¼l (some restaurants sell wines from ¼l upwards only)
Halber – ½l
Liter – 1l
Note: At a Heuriger the wine is usually served in glass tankards.

BOUTEILLENWEINE (VINTAGE WINES)
Many restaurants offer *Bouteillenweine 'per Glas'* or *'glasweise'* and these appear on the wine list and often on the menu as well, the glass usually containing ⅛l.

Apart from the conventionally sized bottles and half bottles, some Austrian wines are sold as 'Stifterl' varying in size between ⅓l, ¼l and I have even found one containing ½l, but ⅓l is the most usual content.

SCHNAPS (SLIBOWITZ, OBSTLER ETC.)
Stamperl 'einfach', 'klein' – 2 cl
'doppelt', 'gross' – 4 cl
Frackerl, Frackale – a cut-glass bottle usually containing about twelve small *'Stamperl'*, a round of drinks. (Just to confuse matters, the term *Frackale* is sometimes also used for a small glass of *Schnaps*, a *Stamperl* in fact)
Budl, Buderl – a small bottle, usually containing $\frac{1}{16}$l (6cl)

Some Austrian Specialities

SPECIAL OCCASIONS
Most restaurants have special menus during holidays such as Easter, Christmas, etc. as well as a New Year's Eve dinner (Sylvester) which often includes a *'Katerfrühstück'* on the following morning (*Kater* being a Viennese term for hangover). During the carnival season (6 January – Ash Wednesday) some coffee houses stay open late (or reopen in the early hours of the morning) to offer hot *Gulasch* soup and/or breakfast to revellers.

Heringschmaus (herring feast) on Ash Wednesday is a huge hot and cold buffet at a fixed price which usually goes on until the early hours of the morning. Depending on location it varies from a good country inn buffet to an elaborate banquet with caviar and oysters and it is of course priced accordingly. Restaurants often advertise their *Heringschmaus* in the newspapers, stating the price and booking is recommended. (In case you're wondering about the herrings, the buffet always includes at least one and often several dishes with pickled herrings, a Viennese herring salad being *de rigueur* – all said to be splendid cures for a carnival hangover!)

Tea

Tea in Austria, even if served in a pot, usually means a tea bag. The following serve properly made tea (except for herb teas no tea bags are used). I am not suggesting that this list is complete – just a selection I compiled during my travels:

Tennerhof – Kitzbühel
Sheraton – Salzburg
Post – Lech am Arlberg
Hotel Schloss Dürnstein – Dürnstein
Sir Richard – Seefeld
Bleibergerhof – Bad Bleiberg
Schloss Fuschl – Hof bei Salzburg

Eaux-de-vie

They may be listed as *Schnaps, Brand* or *Geist,* always preceded by the fruit from which they are distilled or listed simply as *Obstler* (mixed fruit) or *Slibovitz* (plum brandy) – eaux-de-vie in Austria are generally excellent. In the country you may come across *Bauernschnaps* (farmer's *Schnaps*) or simply *Klarer* which can be distilled from anything ranging from gentian roots to fir tips – worth a try, but go carefully for they are usually very potent.

Wines

Austria produces excellent white wines, some reasonable (and above) reds and outstanding dessert wines. Forget about the wine scandal – Austrian wine laws are stringent now – and drink the wines of the country (and the region whenever possible). This book does not set out to be a wine guide, so I recommend you to beg, borrow or steal *The Wines and Wine Gardens of Austria* (Argus Books 1979) by S.F. & F.L. Hallgarten. Please note that there is a vast difference between '*offene Weine*' and '*Bouteillenweine per Glas*'. The former are 'house wines' offered in fractions of a litre (usually from ⅛l upwards), the latter fine vintage wines sold by the glass. (French, Italian and other imported wines are of course available and you will find excellently stocked cellars on occasion even in remote country restaurants, but Austria is not a member of the EEC – yet – and they will be priced accordingly).

Coffee
You do not simply order a cup of coffee in Austria – you order by name and then specify some more. (I am not sure I believe the story of pre-war Vienna when one of the legendary waiters at the equally legendary Cafe Central kept a chart of numbered shades so that when a guest ordered say a 'number 5' he knew exactly the right mixture of coffee and milk).

Here are just a few of the Viennese specialities:

Melange – goes back to the seventeenth century when the first coffee house was opened in Vienna (sacks of coffee beans having been left behind by the beleaguering Turks) and the Viennese found the black coffee too bitter. A mixture of coffee and hot milk, originally half and half which can however be ordered *'mehr licht'* (lighter) or *'mehr dunkel'* (darker).

Schale Gold – version of the above ('golden' rather than dark).

Schale Braun – also version of Melange ('brown' rather than 'golden').

Einspänner – a large glass of black coffee with whipped cream.

Espresso – needs no explanation, but Vienna would not be Vienna if there were not special rules for Espresso as well. Thus you order an Espresso *'kurz'* or *'verlängert'* (also known as *'gestreckt'*), depending on the amount of water being used, *'verlängert'* (stretched, lengthened) being the weaker version. Espresso can of course also be ordered as *Melange, Brauner* (*Schale Braun*) or *Schwarzer* (black coffee), large small, *kurz, verlängert* or *gestreckt*!

Kapuziner – black coffee with a dash of milk (or cream) so that the coffee is the colour of a Capucin monk's habit.

Schwarzer – black coffee, small or large (*klein* or *gross*)

Türkischer – Turkish coffee prepared in a small copper pan which can be ordered *'passiert'* (strained).

Kaisermelange – goes back to the First World War. Coffee without milk, but strengthened with an egg yolk (and sometimes a dash of brandy). *Kaisermelange* at motorway and other Rosenberger restaurants however is a large mug of coffee with whipped cream and you are given the mug (or rather a new one) as souvenir.

Sweet Pasta
Austria – as you will notice in no time at all – has a very sweet

tooth and meals consisting solely of soup and pudding are by no means unusual, particularly in rural regions. The pudding may be a fluffy *Kaiserschmarrn, Marillenknödel* (apricot dumplings) or *Topfennudeln* (noodles with curd cheese) thereby introducing you to 'sweet pasta'. There are small gnocchi sprinkled with crisply fried breadcrumbs (or walnuts) and sugar, served with stewed fruit or noodles with ground poppy seeds, sugar and cinnamon – the variations are many and once you've got over the shock of having pasta paired with a sweet rather than a savoury accompaniment you may well acquire the taste.

Diabetics
Many restaurants in Austria offer dishes suitable for diabetics and these are usually listed separately on the menu. Most *pâtisseries* also have at least one – and often several – cakes or gâteaux in that category as well. If you cannot see them at the counter, ask for details.

Useful Addresses
Austrian Embassy & Consular Section
18 Belgrave Mews West, London SW1X 8HU Tel: 071–235 3731
Austrian Airlines
50 Conduit Street, London W1R 0NP Tel: 071–439 0741
Austrian National Tourist Office
30 St George Street, London W1R 9FA Tel: 071–629 0461
Anglo–Austrian Society
46 Queen Anne's Gate, London SW1H 9AU Tel: 071–222 0366. Founded in 1944 to promote friendship and understanding between the peoples of Great Britain and Austria. Provides a year-round travel service with low-cost fares on scheduled flights, car hire, hotels and travel insurance, at excellent value for money. Membership £8.

Although every care has been taken in compiling this guide and all information, particularly that concerning opening times, annual holidays and prices, has been carefully checked, no guarantee can be made or responsibility be taken as to their still being correct.

Vienna

List of Restaurants, Pâtisseries, Cafés, etc.

Vienna

CAFÉ FRAUENHUBER
Himmelpfortgasse 6
1010 Wien
☏ 5333323
Open: 7.30–23.00 Monday/Friday
8.00–16.00 Saturday
Closed: Saturday evening and all day Sunday
Prices: inexpensive/moderate

'Nowhere in the world will you find coffee as excellent as that at Jahn's in the Augarten', exclaimed an eighteenth-century traveller. Franz Jahn, an excellent cook, was made *'traiteur'* at Schönbrunn Palace by the Empress Maria Theresa when he was only twenty-nine years old and later on she entrusted him with the same post at the Augarten as well. After the Augarten was opened to the public in the late eighteenth century, morning concerts were held there – Mozart was not only the instigator of these concerts but also a frequent performer. The public attending the concerts was described as 'exclusive' (ordinary people not being free in the mornings to attend concerts) and breakfast as supplied by Mr Jahn – to quote old records – 'consisted of coffee, chocolate, tea, almond milk and lemonade. Hot dishes were served at lunch and Austrian as well as foreign wines, ice-creams, liqueurs and mineral waters'. Jahn opened his own establishment at Himmelpfortgasse 6 in 1788 where Mozart as well as Beethoven played *'Tafelmusik'*. It has been the Café Frauenhuber 'only' since 1891 and although there'll be no 'Tafelmusik', everything else is pretty much as described in that eighteenth-century report (I won't guarantee the almond milk, but given due notice I am sure that the Frauenhuber would provide that as well!) You can however have a splendid Viennese breakfast which might well include *'zwei Eier im Glas'* (two soft-boiled eggs shelled and served in a glass goblet) after which you may linger for as long as you like, reading the numerous newspapers provided by the café. From time to time a small glass of ice-cold water will be placed before you as has been the custom in Vienna ever since the first coffee house was opened in the seventeenth century.

Hot dishes are not only served 'at lunch' as described in that old report, but throughout the day. If you decide to lunch at the Frauenhuber a starched white tablecloth will be spread over the marble-topped table and you'll be able to choose from a menu which covers several pages. I happen to be particularly fond of their

'*Schwammerl mit Ei*' (mushrooms cooked in butter into which an egg has been scrambled), but the choice is quite extensive. You could of course always order ham and eggs (pronounced in Vienna and sometimes even written thus '*hemmendex*' though of course never at Frauenhuber's!). In the afternoon there will be freshly made pastries and suppers are served until 23.00 (excellent *kalte Platte* – assortment of cold meats – for a late snack). Frauenhuber's is of course fully licensed – Viennese coffee house culture at its very best.

CAFÉ KONDITOREI L. HEINER
Wollzeile 9
1010 Wien
☏ 5122343
Open: 8.30–19.00 Monday/Saturday
10.00–19.00 Sunday
Kärntnerstrasse 21–23
☏ 5122284
Open: 8.00–19.30 Monday/Saturday
10.00–19.30 Sunday
Prices: moderate

Heiner first opened in Wollzeile in 1840, when Franz Josef was ten years old and eight years before he became Emperor. Duly appointed 'k. & k. Kofzuckerbäcker' (*pâtissier* to the Royal and Imperial Court) Heiner is a household name in Vienna, not only for the small and not-so-small delicacies consumed on the premises, but also for the goodies to take home, particularly their *Teebäckerei* (small biscuits and *petits fours*) and few Viennese would dream of buying their edible Christmas tree decorations elsewhere: tiny meringues in pink and white, or their special sweets wrapped in pink and white paper, the edges carefully fringed, all ready for hanging on the Christmas tree. To me no shopping spree in Vienna's famous Kärntnerstrasse is complete without a visit to Heiner's branch there, the excuse always being that it is a convenient spot at which to rest, survey one's shopping list (or the temptations one has seen in the windows *en route*) – but in reality because Heiner's is irresistible. The downstairs room is small and a little cramped – there's much more space upstairs (Wollzeile is more spacious altogether), but I always pretend that it is 'just for a few minutes'. Sometimes it really is only for one of their delicious open sandwiches and a drink, but I have been known to go there at lunch-time 'just for a salad' and then stay on for one of their wonderful puddings: *Mohr im Hemd* (the ultimate in chocolate puddings) or their winter speciality *Maronitöpfchen* (hot chestnut pots) and their featherlight *Topfennockerl* (curd cheese gnocchi) with strawberry purée in summer.

At all times there are, of course, their delicious pastries and gâteaux – some with wondrous names like *Gänsefusstorte* and *Walzersoufflée*.

Like all *pâtisseries* in Austria, Heiner is fully licensed – they'll serve you a Remy Martin to revive you after a particularly tiring (or trying) day, as well as a refreshing non-alcoholic raspberry syrup (with soda or with water).

CH. DEMEL'S SÖHNE
Kohlmarkt 14
1010 Wien
☎ 53517170, 53355160
Open: 10.00–19.00
Prices: upward/expensive

Shop and Sektbar
Kohlmarkt 11
☎ 5336020
Open: shop 10.00–19.00
Sektbar 11.00–19.00

Demel's is a legend and should be treated as such: Vienna's best known *pâtisserie* which is a cross between a stage-set and a museum, where the waitresses never address you personally ('Have already ordered?' is the oft-quoted phrase which they actually use). Frequented more by visitors than by Austrians in recent years and you will have to disregard the occasional bout of tourists bursting in, camera at the ready for snapping the buffet (together with Figlmüller's *Schnitzel* probably the most photographed culinary exhibit in Austria) and disappearing again with rapid speed. This having been said, a visit to Demel's is still a 'must' (look on their prices as the entrance fee to a rather delightful museum) for their offerings are superb. Not only the glorious gâteaux the likes of which you are unlikely to find elsewhere, but for 'simple' pastries like their delicious '*Schneeballen*' (huge mounds of sugared pastry), the delicious cold buffet with tiny open sandwiches and unusual savouries (what looks like a very small roasted poussin turns out to be pâté wrapped in light, flaky pastry) and hot dishes like *Schinkenfleckerl* and *Milchrahmstrudel* at lunch. Demel's ice-creams are famous (ask for the Crème du jour) and their ice-cream coupes wondrous blends of unusual flavours. Excellent hot chocolate (of course) and particularly good quality wines sold by the quarter litre. Demel's has recently been sold (after a few unsettled years) and the new owners have promised not to change anything (hopefully they will change the quality of the coffee) except for opening a shop across the road to sell some of the delicacies for which customers now crowd around an already overcrowded counter: all Demel's specialities from savoury biscuits to gâteaux (Demel lost the lawsuit against Sacher, but they still make an excellent Sachertorte) and some 'specials' which you can only get at Demel's such as coffee beans dipped in bitter chocolate and chocolate couverture for making marvellous chocolate icing. The Sektbar at the back of the shop is the place for Demel's savoury snacks accompanied by a selection of wines, but standing room only.

ECKEL
Sieveringer Strasse 46
1190 Wien
☎ 323218
Open: 11.30–14.30 and 18.00–22.30 Tuesday/Saturday
Closed: Sunday and Monday, also two weeks in August and from 23 December to mid January
Prices: moderate

If you want to savour one of Vienna's most famous wine villages – Sievering – but wish to avoid the rather touristy *Heurigen* with which the area abounds, Eckel is exactly the right place. In summer you sit in a shaded old garden in daytime or dine under the stars at night, with a soft breeze wafting over from the Vienna woods – in winter the panelled dining-rooms are comfortably old-fashioned. And at all times atmosphere and cooking are soundly – not to say resoundingly – Viennese in the best possible way. If you arrive a little late you may find that some of the dishes have already been crossed off the *Tageskarte*, yet there will still be plenty from which to choose. Eckel's cooking is strictly seasonal – there are strawberry and asparagus weeks, game and mushroom festivals (and if nature leaves a gap, there will be a special *Mehlspeiswoche* – a week when you wallow in Viennese puddings). All the good old favourites can be found at Eckel's, and some only at Eckel's, like *Kalbseinmachsuppe* (creamy soup based on veal stock), roast knuckle of veal (*Kalbsstelze*) as well as vegetables such as *Kochsalat* (braised lettuce) which hardly any restaurant seems to bother with these days. (If anyone tells you that this is the surest way to lose vitamins, tell them to take a vitamin pill). When in season try the *Eierschwammerln* (chanterelles) either as a main dish or as a first course (in which case ask for a small portion). Above all, 'leave room for a sweet ending' – Eckel's speciality. Iced pear with chestnut purée and chocolate sauce is a splendid combination, but if you follow my advice you'll 'bespeak' one of their pancakes, preferably a 'Marie Louise' – they are superb. Prices are moderate, unless you order a lobster from the tank (in which case they are commensurate).

Very good selection of wines, many of which are sold by the glass.

FIGLMÜLLER
Wollzeile 5
1010 Wien
☎ 5126177
No credit cards
Open: 8.00–22.30 Monday/Friday
8.00–15.00 Saturday
Closed: Sundays, also 1 August–31 August
Prices: inexpensive/moderate

Figlmüller's *Wiener Schnitzel* are over-sized (they usually overlap the plate on which they are served), over-written and over-photographed. Figlmüller's is also the place where you are most likely to encounter a visiting celebrity or visiting head of state. All reasons for avoiding the place like the plague, yet I go as far as saying that no visit to Vienna would be complete without a meal at Figlmüller's. Why? Because it's good and genuine, that's why. From the dishes chalked up on a blackboard (there is in fact a printed menu, but I've never known anyone ask for it) to the quality of the meat, everything is absolutely first class, and reasonably priced. True, the *Schnitzel* is made with pork instead of the traditional veal, but that does not stop it from being perfect (crisp golden coating enclosing succulent meat) and you can slip your knife easily between the coating and the meat – the true test of a *Wiener schnitzel.* (Another test is that you should be able to sit on the plate where a properly cooked *Schnitzel* has rested, wearing a silk dress without staining it. I have never tried, but Figlmüller's *Schnitzel* are so deliciously crisp and dry that I'm sure they'd pass that test as well!) There's an unusually good selection of salads to go with your *Schnitzel* and if you can't finish it, they'll wrap it up for you to take away (it tastes surprisingly good cold, too).

Figlmüller is not strong on starters – there's usually only the soup of the day, but their *Fischbeuschelsuppe* (thick fish soup made with roe and served around Christmas) is memorable.

Of course, your choice of main dish does not have to be limited to *Wiener Schnitzel.* As befits a restaurant with its own butchery, all meat dishes are excellent – from calves liver sliced and fried like *Schnitzel* to delicately cooked sweetbreads or sautéd kidneys with brains (a Figlmüller speciality), there are excellent steaks (and very good steak tartar), *Tafelspitz* (of course) and marvellous home-made sausages. (Thursday is black pudding day!)

They do not serve beer at Figlmüller's, but all the wines are from their own vineyards (at one time an underground passage connected their wine cellars to St Stefan) and there are no less than ten wines sold from ⅛ litre upwards as well as a marvellous selection of their vintage wines which you can also buy to take away.

Perfectly good puddings, all very Viennese – a variety of pancakes, *Kaiserschmarrn* and even Salzburger *Nockerl* – but you may prefer to walk two doors down the road to No.9 Wollzeile and relax at Heiner's *pâtisserie* (q.v.)

N.B. Although the 'official' address is Wollzeile 5, Figlmüller is in fact in a passage between Wollzeile and Bäckerstrasse, entrance from either side, just follow your nose.

GASTHOF ZUR LOTTE
Heiligenstädter Strasse 179
1190 Wien
☎ 374125
Open: 11.30–midnight (kitchen until 22.30)
Prices: moderate

When the Viennese take a liking to a fairly out-of-the-way restaurant within a short time of its opening, they do so with a vengeance and for good reasons. Zur Lotte is not so much out of the way as on the way – to Heiligenstädt where you go for wine and to wander in Beethoven's footsteps – but the reasons for its quick rise to popularity are quite obvious. The ambience is '*gut bürgerlich*' (good bourgeois), there's the typical garden well-shaded by old trees, and the food is first-rate and moderately priced. The kitchen is operative throughout the day – you can order a *Gulasch* in sizes small or large at any time – and the food is cooking at its best: stuffed breast of veal, *Tafelspitz* (which is proper *Tafelspitz* and not an obscure cut of beef taking the name in vain) is served with creamed vegetables as it should be, there's roulade of beef (*Rindsroulade*), and deliciously fried sweetbreads with a salad of lamb's lettuce and *Kipfler* potatoes, roast lamb with broad beans cooked with bacon as well as a few excursions into the higher regions of culinary art. Puddings once more conform with the '*gut bürgerlich*' ambience – it is the sort of restaurant where *Strudel* and gâteaus are proudly proclaimed as 'home-made' – and where a lavish slice of gâteau is a very acceptable 'pudding', but if you want to go for something a little lighter, choose *Schneenockerl* (floating islands) or *Kastanienreis*.

Small selection of good Austrian wines and excellent beer.

How to get there: Tram D from the centre of Vienna stops almost opposite the house.

GROTTA AZZURRA
Babenbergerstrasse 5
1010 Wien
☎ 5861044
Open: 12.00–15.00, 18.30–24.00 (kitchen 23.00) Monday/Saturday
Closed: Sunday
Prices: upward

I do not think that the Grotta Azzurra was Vienna's oldest Italian restaurant, but it has always been known as 'the' Italian restaurant, even without mentioning the name. A little musty, a good deal old-fashioned and very much a fixture of Vienna, but in urgent need of some drastic renovation. All this has now happened – the restaurant is under the same ownership as 'Zu den 3 Husaren' and 'Hietzinger Bräu' and the new owners have waved the proverbial magic (and very expensive) wand: the restaurant has been completely refurbished and though there have been voices declaring the new décor as unfashionable (what precisely is 'fashionable' in a restaurant decoration?) and Kitsch. I rather like the clear new look which makes the restaurant appear very much lighter and brighter – and more luxurious which in view of all the money that has been spent on it is just as well! And I certainly like the food – good, genuine Italian with not even a whisper of Viennese. There's a large table of excellent cold hors-d'oeuvres (no, not shades of the famous hors-d'oeuvre trolleys at the 3 Husaren and you are not charged by the portion – you select either a small or large platter or leave the selection to the waiter). Excellent pasta dishes (all pasta is home-made) and particularly good risotti – freshly made to order, of course. My *fegato alla Veneziana* was absolutely authentic and the sea bass with red peppers and polenta ordered by my companion was rated 'superb'. Puddings – though simple by Viennese standards – are equally good, even judged by the same exacting Viennese standards and I was particularly taken by the chestnut meringue.

Large selection of Italian wines only – except for Austrian Sekt and French champagne.

HALALI
Neuer Markt 2
1010 Wien
☏ 5129202
Open: 9.30–24.00
Prices: moderate

In summer there are a few tables on the pavement outside – in winter the restaurant tends to get crowded in a rather comforting way and you might well find singers from the nearby Staatsoper as well as some from the not-so-nearby Volksoper at the more secluded end of the restaurant. Excellent food and late opening hours make it a much-favoured rendezvous after performances at either house. As the name implies (Austrian for Tally Ho) the restaurant specializes in game (the 'game' page in the menu is marked with a pheasant's feather), but do not let that deter you from choosing some of their other specialities. *Waldviertler Rahmsuppe* (soup made with sour cream and a regional speciality of the 'forest' region of Lower Austria) is a great favourite, as are the Viennese potato soup and the Matjes Herring Fillet. Halali's *Tafelspitz* (the famous boiled beef of Vienna) far exceeds in quality that of many more expensive restaurants and there are many other Viennese specialities like *gefüllte Kalbsbrust* (stuffed breast of veal) or *gebackene Kalbsleber* (calves liver dipped in eggs and breadcrumbs and fried) which are worth trying. Good, typically Viennese desserts too such as plum dumplings (*Zwetschkenknödel*) and *Powidltascherln* (no need to try and pronounce this – if they are on the menu you could just point! Small 'pockets' of pasta in fact, filled with thick dark plum jam and served with melted butter and a thick sprinkling of sugar and cinnamon).

HEDRICH
Stubenring 2
1010 Wien
☏ 5129588
Open: 9.00–21.00 Monday/Thursday
Closed: Friday, Saturday, Sunday
Prices: moderate

To an outsider Hedrich is a bit of a mystery: a thriving small restaurant in the centre of Vienna that stays open on four days of the week only and even on those days shuts its doors firmly at nine in the evening. One visit solves the mystery: Richard Hedrich is a superb chef and the clientele is drawn mostly from the surrounding ministries (always trust the Austrian Civil Service when it comes to food!) which explains the closing times – weekends in Vienna start early on Friday, certainly early enough to skip lunch! The kitchen is operative throughout the day, however – if you want a delicious mid-morning snack of goose liver or a *Wiener Schnitzel* freshly cooked to your order during mid-afternoon (or a quick meal before going to a theatre), Hedrich's the place!

The restaurant is small, sparsely furnished (not to say Spartan) – you will almost certainly have to share a table and if you want a cloth rather than a paper napkin, that'll be an extra S10.-, but the food is impeccable (trust the Austrian Civil Service once again to know where to go and what to choose, when to make a fuss and when to let the occasional slip in the kitchen pass unnoticed – they've got it at their fingertips!). There is a daily very reasonably priced lunch menu (a positive bargain compared to the price of the aforementioned napkin!) and a small, but delectable choice of dishes which changes daily. The chicken liver pâté is first class (served with an apple/pineapple salad) and I am rather partial to Hedrich's *Rindsroulade* which he serves with ceps-stuffed tortellini and a crisp salad. Hedrich is particularly good on puddings – you'll get a *Strudel* filled with green grapes, curd cheese soufflé with a coulis of bilberries, a *gratin* of oranges and lots of other delicacies.

Very good – though necessarily small – selection of wines sold by the glass, bottle or half-bottle.

HIETZINGER BRÄU — No credit cards
Auhofstrasse 1
1130 Wien
☏ 8777087
Open: 11.30–15.00 (14.30 kitchen)
18.00–23.00 (22.30 kitchen)
Prices: moderate/upward

' … she had managed to conjure up a typical Sunday lunch,' Josef Roth relates in his novel *Radetzky Marsch* – 'clear beef broth, *Rinderspitz* (a special cut of boiled beef), followed by cherry dumplings,' but it appears that the host was so preoccupied with family matters that 'he ate the *Rinderspitz* as if it had been an ordinary *Schnitzel*'. Legend has it that the Emperor Franz Josef lunched on boiled beef every day of his long life – all of which goes to show the importance of boiled beef in Austrian cooking. This is no ordinary boiled beef though, and certainly not salted, but carefully selected cuts cooked with infinite care and served with at least two different sauces, *G'röste* (q.v.) and a vegetable cooked in an old-fashioned creamy sauce. The cut of meat is all-important – there are numerous special cuts with typically Viennese names such as *Tafelspitz, Hieferschwanzl* and *Schulterscherzl* (classified as *Gustostückln* – especially delectable cuts) and the more robust *Kruspelspitz* and *Beinfleisch,* each with different qualities appreciated by true connoisseurs of boiled beef. The comfortably elegant Hietzinger Bräu offers no less than ten different cuts – all carefully described as to their special qualities (except for the *Tafelspitz* which they just call 'a Viennese legend'). All impeccably prepared and beautifully served in clear beef broth (for which you can order a typically Viennese addition such as fine noodles or gnocchi, *Schöberl* or *Frittaten*) with poached bone marrow, a vegetable *nach Wiener Art, G'röste* and chive as well as apple/horseradish sauce. There are, of course, other beef specialities as well – ox-tongue, *Alt Wiener Suppentopf* (*pot-au-feu* including chicken), steak in a bone marrow crust and *Fledermaus* which is not only the name of a special cut, but also of a dish – tender cooked beef *au gratin* under a creamy horseradish sauce. Nor do you have to be confined to beef in your choice of a main dish – they roast a delectable duck at the Hietzinger Bräu, offer a selection of *G'röstl* (q.v.) and other specialities, including different kinds of mushrooms when in season, prepared *nach Wunsch* (at your choice).

There are some excellent starters, from good old-fashioned *Ochsenmaulsalat* (ox-cheek salad) and herrings with sour cream and apples to goose liver terrine.

Puddings are as Viennese as the traditional boiled beef – *Kaiserschmarrn* and *Milchrahmstrudel,* splendid *Mohr im Hemd,* but for lightness I would recommend their *Schneenockerl* (floating islands) served with three sauces – vanilla, chocolate and strawberry purée.

Selection of wines is excellent, as befits a restaurant under the same ownership as the famous 'Zu den 3 Husaren'.

Advance booking is strongly advised and do not be surprised at the size of the portions – they are more than generous!

HIMMELSTUBE
Hotel am Parkring
Parkring 12
1015 Parkring 12
☏ 51480417 (for table reservations)
Open: 12.00–15.00, 18.00–23.00 Monday/Saturday
12.00–16.00 Sunday
Closed: Sunday evening
Prices: moderate

The entrance is not on Parkring but in a side street and hotel and restaurant only occupy the top floors of this miniature skyscraper. High enough to guarantee a panoramic view of Vienna from all the rooms, yet not too high for the scent of linden blossoms to waft in through the open balcony windows on a soft summer evening. The restaurant is small and modern (with a panoramic map of Vienna obligingly provided on all tables) and whilst it is a splendid place for a romantic candle-lit dinner, it is equally favoured for a leisurely family lunch on Sunday. The menu is printed in three languages and even if they translate *Röstkartoffeln* as 'mouled potatoes', the cooking is absolutely authentic Viennese with a very slight and perfectly permissible 'international' touch. *Cremesuppe von frischen Kräutern* (cream soup with fresh herbs) and *Gurkencremesuppe* (cream of cucumber soup) were faultless and the Himmelstube is exactly the sort of place where I'd order a *Wiener Schnitzel* or *Tafelspitz* (listed separately under '*aus der österreichischen Küche*') knowing that they would be perfect, but where I would be equally confident to venture a little further afield. Puddings are deliciously Viennese throughout (even if they offer Apfelstrudel with vanilla ice-cream) and include long-forgotten specialities like chestnut soufflé (warmer *Kastanienauflauf*) and *Brioche-Kipferlschmarren* (which they – rather unfortunately – translate with 'browned omelette', but having looked at my glossary you'll know what to expect!). Good selection of Austrian wines with a little support from France and Italy.

HOTEL INTER-CONTINENTAL
Johannesgasse 28
1030 Wien
☏ 711220 (71122143 for table reservations at restaurant)
Open: Vier Jahreszeiten restaurant:
12.00–15.00, 19.00–24.00 (kitchen 23.00) Monday/Friday
19.00–24.00 (kitchen 23.00) Saturday
12.00–15.00 Sunday
Closed: Saturday lunch, Sunday dinner
Brasserie:
6.30–24.00 daily
Bar:
10.30–2.00 daily
Prices: Vier Jahreszeiten restaurant: expensive
Brasserie: moderate
Bar: moderate/upward

To outer appearances the Inter-Continental in Vienna is a starkly modern, rather impersonal hotel – not exactly the place you'd pick for typically Viennese cooking or *haute cuisine*. Give it a miss on outer appearances alone and you'll miss some of the best creative cooking in Austria as well as some of the best Viennese specialities and some 'hidden treasures' – but it is very much a question of being in the right place at the right time (and in the right culinary frame of mind). The *bar* comes strictly under the heading of 'hidden treasures' – except for the time preceding lunch or dinner it is an absolute haven of peace where not only delicious snacks but quite substantial (and no less delicious) *plats-du-jour* can be eaten in great comfort (the atmosphere seems suddenly transformed into that of a Viennese coffee house, only you may have to ask them to turn down the air-conditioning which can be rather ferocious). The *Brasserie* – though a bit impersonal as far as looks go (and presumably unavoidable in a large modern hotel) has anything but impersonal service and the menu includes a large '*ganz Wienerisch*' section with good Viennese favourites such as *Tellerfleisch mit Semmelkren, saure Nierndln* (kidneys in a piquant sauce), braised oxtail (*gedünsteter Ochsenschlepp*) with dumplings and of course, *Wiener Schnitzel* and fried spring chicken (though they fail to add to their English translation that it is served '*ausgelöst*' – boned). The section headed 'Special' includes 'Starburger' claimed as 'Vienna's best hamburger' as well as good soups, steaks and salads and there are good puddings and gâteaux from their own *pâtisserie* (including *Wiener Hofburgtorte,* a luscious chocolate gâteau and 'the' house speciality). There is always a good three-course lunch at around S200.- and a separate menu with seasonal specialities. The *Vier Jahreszeiten* is of course the star restaurant – at lunch it is literally packed (booking strongly advised) mostly with Viennese who know a thing or two – not only where good food but also value for money is concerned – and the five-course lunch (which serves as a Viennese type of brunch on Sundays) at S470.- certainly scores on both counts. There is an excellent array of hors-d'oeuvres – particularly good pâtés and salads (the Viennese are also going overboard for the cold roast beef which can always be found on the hors d'oeuvres table and which I must admit is delicious). Soups and entrées are served at the table, usually good beef broth or a light creamy vegetable soup, followed by fish. The great attraction however is the large hot buffet, featuring all the Viennese specialities from *Wiener Schnitzel* and *Tafelspitz* to roast veal and pork, all absolutely authentic and served in large (or small if you so desire) portions, with proper accompaniments. There is of course a good selection of puddings (if you can still manage!). In the evening the restaurant is *haute cuisine* at its highest. Manfred Buchinger is an inspired chef and although some of his ideas might at first strike you as a little far fetched (*medaillons* of lobster and salmon baked in a crust of popcorn, served with a hot Bloody Mary and polenta!) they are eminently successful. (You'll also find a note on the menu saying that they'd also be delighted to prepare your favourite dish, subject to ingredients being available and that if, after all, you're hankering for a *Wiener Schnitzel* or fried spring chicken, they have not forgotten the recipe!). The menu changes frequently, of course, with seasonal specialities much to the fore – be advised by the experts on the spot. I can however strongly recommend the terrine of pike/perch with spiced cream (*Fogosterrine*), fillet of beef with chanterelles and asparagus (*Rindsfilet auf Eierschwammerln mit Spargel*) and what they call *'Feines von und mit Schokolade'* which I'd describe as a chocoholic's dream. Or you could order the four-course dinner at S595.- which on my last visit included a pale green lobster soup (very commendable!).

Excellent selection of wines as one would expect.

P.S. The Inter-Continental may look vast and impersonal, but when I arrived in my room after a delayed flight there was a bottle of Sekt in an ice bucket and a plateful of Carnival doughnuts (it was carnival time) plus the Emperor's Waltz being played on the radio. When I commented on this to the Managing Director I was told that the welcoming radio is always tuned in to the in-house music, all Viennese 'but I can't guarantee the Emperor's Waltz!' More personally Viennese than that you cannot get!

HOTEL SACHER
Philharmonikerstrasse 4
1010 Wien
☏ 51456 (51457841 for table reservations at the Rote Bar)
Open: Café Sacher: 6.30–23.30
Restaurant: 12.00–15.00, 18.00–24.00
Rote Bar: 12.00–1.00
Prices: upward/expensive

The Hotel Sacher stands on the site of the old *Kärntnertortheater* and the deeds of sale decreed that the building must never house a theatre. This has not stopped Sacher from being a stage where grand entrances were made and many a scene was enacted without written script. Certainly Sacher is legendary and no stay in Vienna would be complete without a visit to the *Café Sacher* at least. There are in fact two separate rooms and for some reason the one to the right of the entrance has always been the one in which to be seen (like the front part of the Concorde). I've always preferred the smaller room to the left of the entrance which is slightly less glamorous (and less prestigious) but has a pretty portrait of a young and handsome Franz Josef surveying the scene. Sometimes both rooms will be crowded, at others there'll be an almost club-like atmosphere – strictly a case of 'regulars' to whom waiters bring their orders with barely any questions asked (Sacher clearly is their home from home, their club and their office). In summer the Café extends on to a pavement terrace, a rather superior *Schanigarten* (q.v.). Now to the food which is after all what you've come for: Café Sacher is definitely the place for a light summer lunch or supper after the opera – they serve a very good *'kalte Platte'*, open sandwiches and the famous *Sacherwürstl* which are larger than ordinary Frankfurter. Coffee and cakes seem almost obligatory and quite apart from the legendary *Sachertorte* (like Madame Sacher I find it too dry and greatly prefer the *Sacherkonfekt* which is almost all chocolate icing) there are marvellous pastries which go exceedingly well with coffee. (Not to be contrary but because they do it so well, I'd order hot chocolate, particularly in winter. Topped with whipped cream – and forget about the calories for onc – this is Sacher's, after all!).

My favourite restaurant at Sacher is the *Rote Bar* (despite the name it is not a bar, but a proper restaurant. Just to be confusing the Bar at the Sacher is called Blaue Bar). The Rote Bar is often considered an evening restaurant and with some justification – it is very elegant, all red silk and gilt and gold and crystal chandeliers (and a piano player in the evening), but when I went there on a sunny Sunday morning last summer, the atmosphere had completely changed. It was suddenly a 'Sunday best' private dining-room with doors wide open on to the pavement terrace where tables had been set as well. It seemed heresy to order anything other than traditional 'Sunday best' Viennese, though I stopped short at ordering *Tafelspitz* for which Sacher are famous and instead of the very traditional *Frittatensuppe* I had a light cream of sorrel soup (*Sauerrampfercremesuppe*). The main course was truly Viennese – *gefüllte Kalbsstelze* (stuffed knuckle of veal). *Schlosserbuben* (prune fritters) with rum sabayon were rather tempting, but in the end I finished with a slice of gâteau – Viennese style. No, not *Sachertorte*, but *Punschtorte*, heavily laced with spiced rum.

There is of course an extensive and well-assorted wine list, but my order for a G'spritzter was accepted with approval and beautifully served – the wine in a crystal jug, accompanied by a miniature syphon (I think Sacher must be the only place who still have them).

KAFFEE KONDITOREI LEHMANN
Graben 12
1010 Wien
☏ 512 1815
Open: 9.00–19.00 Monday/Saturday
Closed: Sunday
Prices: moderate

' ... and then I had a beer in that pavement café on the Graben', a friend recently returned from Vienna recounted and it was not until a little later that I realized he was talking about Lehmann, mistaking it for a mere pavement café and that other visitors to Vienna could make the same mistake. Not that there is anything wrong with ordering a beer or a glass of wine at Lehmann's – like all *pâtisseries* in Austria, it is fully licensed. But it also happens to be one of the most 'serious' *pâtisseries* in Vienna, where they take *pâtisserie* very seriously indeed. A look at their window will confirm this, and that's only a 'trailer' of the delights inside. It's a children's paradise, and a surprising number of adult children find their way to Lehmann. It is a good place for a light lunch or a snack as well – small open sandwiches, salads, and their *Lachsschüsserl* (beautifully arranged platter of smoked salmon) is especially commendable. There's chicken soup for chilly days and, of course, wonderful hot chocolate, with or without whipped cream on top. Their chocolate chestnuts are probably the best in Vienna – 'absolutely pure, no preservatives and they should be eaten the same day' I was sternly told when I bought some to take back to London!

KONDITOREI SLUKA
Rathausplatz 8
1010 Wien
☏ 427172
Open: 8.00–17.30
Closed: Sundays and first week in January
Prices: moderate

Set under the arcades next to the town hall, Sluka is the place where the Viennese go for cakes and pastries, for ice-creams and sorbets, for *petits fours* and, on special occasions such as New Year's Eve, for lucky charms like small pink pigs and four-leaved clover made in finest marzipan. The choice is enormous – there's a printed menu listing the 'basics', but it is much better to make one's selection from the tempting display. Sluka's is a splendid place at which to start the day – with a *Wiener Frühstück*, reading the papers and watching the world go by (in fine weather there are tables under the arcades) – or to drop in for a mid-morning sherry and a delicious *Schinkenkipferl* (small croissant with savoury ham filling). At lunchtime there are always one or two hot dishes – paprika chicken perhaps and a light pasta dish – as well as some good soups, but the great attraction is the cold buffet: trout in aspic, slices of ham twisted into a cornet and filled with pâté de foie, delicious salads ... In the afternoon there will be more pastries, as well as luscious gâteaux and cakes of the type that go so well with coffee and whipped cream: *Yeast Strudel* filled with walnuts or poppy seeds, *Guglhupf* and *Bischofsbrot* (sponge cake filled with raisins, nuts, glacé fruit and small chunks of chocolate). If you are tempted to buy one of their cakes to take home they'll advise you which keeps best and wrap it beautifully for you. And any time between October and April do remember to ask for their chestnut specialities: *Maronitorte* (chestnut gâteau) and chestnuts worked to a paste and then dipped into chocolate. Sluka also have a good selection of cakes as well as ice-cream for diabetics.

LA SCALA (VIENNA PLAZA)
Schottenring 11
1010 Wien
☏ 31390150 (for table reservations)
Open: 12.00–14.30, 19.00–23.30
Prices: expensive

'Do you want to eat or does sir wish to dine?' a Viennese waiter was once overheard to enquire of a guest and it is definitely the latter at La Scala where Werner Matt rules supreme. He is the doyen of Austrian chefs, the grand master of *grande cuisine* and his honours and awards are too numerous to count. 'Officially' the cooking at La Scala is Italian augmented by Viennese specialities – in fact it is pure Werner Matt. Many of his creations have become classics which you may well find in other restaurants (his pupils, like his awards, are numerous), but I happened to be there when he had just perfected his savarin of salmon (modestly described as '*gedämpft auf neue Art*') served with an asparagus vinaigrette. To quote Christopher North it was truly 'a salmon served up in its integrity' – don't miss it if you have the chance. Nor should one miss one of the pasta specialities like *Brennesselnudeln* (green noodles made with nettles) with morels and sweetbreads or one of the star turns, quail '*im Kartoffelmantel*'. There's always a small section headed '*aus Werner Matt's Kochbuch*' (his cookery book *Erlesenes aus Osterreich's Küche* has been a constant favourite since it was first published in 1982) of which *marinierte Beeren im Blätterteigkrokant* have become rightly famous, but I've got a weakness for the *Topfenterrine im Baumkuchenmantel*, a splendid combination of creamy curd cheese terrine wrapped in pastry. Werner Matt's Gourmetmenü (six courses for S790.-, five for S650.-) are very good value and always include his latest creations.

LUKULLUS BAR at MEINL
Naglergasse 1
1010 Wien
Open: 9.00–18.30 Monday/Friday
9.00–12.30 Saturday
Closed: Sundays
Prices: moderate

Julius Meinl are food and wine shops *par excellence*, branches of which can be found throughout Austria. Their flagship (or should it be flagshop?) is on Graben in Vienna and you can walk through the shop to the Lukullus Bar or use the separate entrance in Naglergasse round the corner. It is not the most comfortable place at which to eat (standing room only, and tends to get crowded at crucial times) but it is an absolute must for a delicious, if hurried, snack. Have a glass of Sekt whilst making your selection from a superb array of cold platters and you will not really mind that you have to perch your plate and glass on the least available space. Everything is as fresh as fresh can be for supplies clear fast and are swiftly replenished. Tucked away towards the shop interior there's a small counter providing hot dishes at lunch-time and the bar is, of course, fully licensed. Walk down to Lehmann on Graben afterwards for coffee and *pâtisserie*!

PFUDL
Bäckerstrasse 22
1010 Wien
☎ 5126705
Open: 9.00–24.00 Monday/Friday
9.00–15.00 Saturday
Closed: Sundays
Prices: inexpensive/moderate

Everything about Pfudl is typically Viennese, including the name (and more Viennese than that you cannot get) and the fact that the last time I tried to look it up in the Viennese telephone directory, I looked in vain. Pfudl is listed under the name of the present owner: Bottoli. Typically Viennese too, that it took a lot of 'regulars' – and if you are not a regular, you'll soon become one – a long time to realize that there is a very comfortable – even cosy – room downstairs to which to escape from the invariably crowded room upstairs. Nobody had told them. And most typically Viennese is the food – in the nicest possible way. All the specialities are there – beautifully and freshly cooked. This is the place where you can safely order sweetbreads, egg – and breadcrumbed like *Wiener Schnitzel* or *gebackene Leber* (calves liver cooked the same way). At the right time of the year there'll be wild boar and roast goose (a quarter goose equals one portion) and there will always be inexpensive dishes like pork *Gulasch*, *gelegte Kartoffel mit Salat* (layered potatoes with savoury filling, served with a salad) or *gebackener Leberkäs* (nothing to do with either liver or cheese and best described as a rather delicious cross between meat loaf, pâté and sausage), as well as moderately priced luxuries like beautifully cooked goose liver (*Gansleber glaciert oder gebacken*). Very good puddings too, like *Kastanienreis* (sweetened chestnut purée pushed through a potato ricer), Chestnut roulade (*Kastanienroulade*) or *B'soffene Liesl* (baked pudding moistened with mulled wine) all served with great mounds of whipped cream – unless you just prefer a *Nusskipferl* (croissant with moist walnut filling) with your coffee.

Wines come from their own vineyards and beer from a small, privately owned brewery, both in Lower Austria. As I said before, all typically Viennese.

ROSENBERGER MARKT RESTAURANT
Maysedergasse 2 (Corner Kärntnerstrasse)
1010 Wien
☏ 5123458 No credit cards
Open: Bistro 8.00–23.00
Restaurant: 11.00–23.00
Prices: inexpensive

I am not a great devotee of self-service restaurants, but I'm more than half-way of becoming a devotee of the new Rosenberger Market Restaurant which is not so much a restaurant as a market place where you choose the raw materials which are then cooked for you. The restaurant is spread over three levels and a little conducted tour should help you to get the best – on all levels. The ground floor Bistro which opens early is the place for breakfast, light snacks such as filled baguettes, soups and practically any drink you care to choose – my own favourite choice being a mid-morning Sekt Orange with freshly squeezed orange juice. Take the lift to the huge basement restaurant (the former Mathias Keller which like the rest of the place has been completely rebuilt and refurnished) where you'll find masses of covered stalls piled high with fresh produce: juicy steaks and home-made sausages, vegetables in peak condition. There are seasonal offerings – on one occasion 'new' herrings served in the traditional way with sour cream, chive sauce and new potatoes cooked in their skins, on others, particularly in cold weather, it might be a warming potato *gulasch,* spiced apple punch or – to cheer weary Christmas shoppers – delectable open sandwiches of smoked salmon. The selection of salads is particularly good (with a choice of dressings) and there'll be a terrine of soup (or two) bubbling away gently on a tiled stove. Pasta is freshly cooked, of course and bread and pastries are baked on the premises. What I like almost as much as the food however is the lay-out of the place – full of secluded corners and differently styled areas, as if the whole of Austria (at the time of the Austro-Hungarian monarchy and beyond) had been condensed into a small space. There's a 'sitting-room' complete with tiled stove, a Viennese coffee house as well as an Italian trattoria, a Biedermeier room (dedicated to Josef Mayseder, a noted Viennese musician after whom the street is named), an arcaded gallery from which to survey the scene and one secluded corner which is a genuine Viennese *Heuriger* in miniature.

There's also a gift shop on the ground floor. The lift takes prams as well as wheelchairs and you can deposit your parcels in a locker (for a returnable S10.-).

SCHIMANSZKY
Biberstrasse 2
1010 Wien
☎ 513 4543
Open: 11.00–14.30, 18.00–22.00 Monday/Friday
Closed: Saturdays and Sundays
Prices: moderate/slightly upward

Schimanszky in Vienna is a fairly new restaurant, but the name is not exactly unknown. Whole generations of Viennese have made the trek to Schimanszky at Berndorf (q.v.), first in pursuit of a perfectly fried spring chicken, good local wine (and if they were 'in the know', superlative apricot brandy) and in more recent years for Schimanszky's excursions into higher culinary regions. I am including 'new' Schimanszky not on past Berndorf performances, but based on a single visit to the new restaurant in Vienna, having taken along a discriminating friend likely to find fault where others don't (and I am delighted to say that he did not succeed this time).

Schimanszky is not over-elegant, just comfortable, with a slight, rather pleasant country atmosphere – like the *Extrastüberl* (small private dining-room) of a country inn set for a special party. We went for dinner, but I noted that there was a very reasonable set lunch: cream of beetroot soup, *gekochtes Meisl* (Viennese boiled beef with the exact cut of meat properly specified) with all the traditional accompaniments, followed by orange jelly with rhubarb and a purée of berries (S210.- for three courses, S170.- without pudding).

I started with clear beef broth with *Bröselknödel* (always a good test) – the broth truly strong and the small dumplings featherlight. Not in order to be contrary, but simply because I liked it, I had one of the starters as a main course – *Tafelspitzsulz* (beef in aspic) with pumpkin-seed dressing which was exactly as it should be – light, with the pumpkin-seed oil giving a delicious nutty flavour – whilst my critical companion had started with the same aspic and gone on to venison accompanied by lentils and *Griesstaler* (crisp rounds of semolina gnocchi), all declared perfect. (I tasted the lentils and they were marvellous.) As a rule I am against a selection of puddings, maintaining that the taste of one usually cancels out the other, but in this particular case I was overruled and I finished them to the last scrap (as did critical companion): poppy-seed cream with fruit sauce, *Powidltascherl* (small pasta envelopes filled with dark plum jam), apple fritters with marzipan cream, chocolate mousse and a featherlight curd dumpling dusted with ground walnuts, served with plums marinaded in rum.

Good selection of Austrian wines, careful attention to the beer (critical companion is a singer and asked for his beer to be 'not too cold' and they got the temperature exactly right). Don't forget the apricot brandy!

SCHWARZE KATZE
Girardigasse 6
1060 Wien
☏ 5870625
Open: 18.30–1.00 Tuesday/Sunday
Closed: Mondays
Prices: moderate

Few Viennese refer to it by its proper name 'Schwarze Katze' – it is almost invariably called George Dimou's, after the Greek singer who settled in Vienna to open a restaurant. Much frequented by artists, not only from the nearby Theater an der Wien, but also from much further afield. On my last visit three of the Volksoper's stars were joined by a noted Austrian Cabaretist, to be joined in turn by George Dimou – and a very entertaining time was had by all, including the other guests. At other times the restaurant will be quiet, a little piped background music providing the only entertainment. The food is Greek (with an almost imperceptible Viennese touch which manifests itself in the written menu more than in the actual dishes) – simply, but authentically prepared. Take George Dimou's advice when ordering, particularly if you're dining late (Dimou's stays open until 1 a.m. which makes it an ideal after-theatre restaurant). You'll probably start with an ample assortment of good Greek hors-d'oeuvres, followed by one of Dimou's fish specialities or lamb which has reached perfection point just at this moment and end with a platter of Greek sweetmeats. That way you'll never find out the 'secret of the house' (listed on the menu as such), but you'll have a thoroughly pleasant meal at a moderate price.

P.S. Should you happen to order the 'secret of the house', do let me know. I have tried for ages, but have always been sidetracked by 'you can have the secret of the house any day, but today we have … which you must not miss'.

STEIRERECK
Rasumofskygasse 2
1030 Wien
☏ 7133166
Open: 10.30–24.00 (lunch 12.00–15.00, 19.00–23.00) Monday/Friday
Closed: Saturday, Sunday
Prices: expensive (except for *Gabelfrühstück* and *Wiener Mittagessen*) see description

The name of the Steirereck's chef is Helmut Österreicher – Mr Austria –

which is more than appropriate since the Steirereck, often hailed as the best restaurant in Austria by guests and restaurant critics alike, certainly ranks among the top three (as you will have gathered from the introduction, I am not awarding stars, stripes or any other kind of decoration). 'I cannot fault it,' said my favourite and most critical gourmet and indeed it would be difficult to do so. The Steirereck is impeccable in every way – a combination of superb cooking (very grand cuisine indeed, mingled with absolutely genuine regional dishes) served faultlessly and without fuss, an admirable wine cellar (which may be visited) and a cheese chamber for which alone it should be given a special award. It is a very grand restaurant – all the more remarkable since it was once an ordinary *Gasthaus* in an unfashionable part of Vienna (not far from the centre but 'out of the way') and the conversion, both culinary and as far as the actual building was concerned must have been fraught with difficulty. It is also a very welcoming restaurant – guests are always greeted by the owners, Mr & Mrs Reitbauer, like guests in a private house (due to its previous life as a spacious inn, the restaurant is rather sprawling yet they manage to convey this feeling of warm hospitality).

Steirereck

The Reitbauers have also reintroduced the good old habit of *Gabelfrühstück* (q.v.) which is served from 10.30 onwards and a splendid way of getting to know the Steirereck in a simple – and inexpensive – way.

You can sample cooking in rather splendid surroundings – not just simple dishes like *Gulasch, Kalbsbeuschel* and *Krautfleisch* (and excellent beer from the woods), but also goose liver (served in a small pot), steak tartar and *Eierspeise,* this typically Viennese cross between an omelette and scrambled eggs (made at the Steirereck with green pumpkin-seed oil for the Reitbauers are Styrian to the core), all at very reasonable prices, ranging between S50.- and S125.- per dish.

The Steirereck has the same menu at lunch and dinner (except that it changes so frequently that if you return for a favourite dish you are likely to find that it has been replaced by something even more delicious), but there is also a *Wiener Mittagessen* served at the winter garden at lunch-time which – at S390.- for three courses – is one of Vienna's gastronomic bargains, since it includes such Steirereck 'specials' as their roast duck (voted as 'exceptional' more than once) and half a lobster, to say nothing of absolutely marvellous puddings.

Evening is the time for the full menu (I'd still choose the winter garden which is particularly pretty at night) and for selecting à la carte. Whatever you choose will be memorable, but don't miss the *'kalte und warme Vorspeisenplatte'* a recent innovation, consisting of five different hot and cold starters which are an absolute joy. Be advised about the main course – there are bound to be new specialities, though if *Steirisches Lammkarree mit Basilikum* (Styrian rack of lamb with basil) happens to be on the menu, I'd be tempted to look no further! Puddings are listed on a separate menu (with appropriate wine suggestions) and the *Nougat-Nussknödel* as well as the *warme Schokoladeknödel mit Himbeer* are a dream of chocolate, walnuts and raspberries, but there's also a pudding simply called *'böhmisch-österreichische Mehlspeis'* which just about sums up the Steirereck: Austrian cooking at its most delicious best!

TRZESNIEWSKI
Dorotheergasse 1
1010 Wien
☎ 5123291
Open: Monday/Friday 9.00–19.30
Saturday 9.00–13.00
Closed: Sundays
Prices: inexpensive

Visitors rarely find their way to Trzesniewski – and 'find' is the operative word, for although the name is up high at the corner of Graben and Dorotheergasse, there's no sign at the entrance. In summer one or two high-shelved tables outside point the way, for the rest of the year you just make for the first entrance on the left, coming from the Graben, push open the thick plate glass doors, work your way through a heavy felt curtain to enter what has been known as 'the sandwich bar' in Vienna since well before the last war. In those days there were three tiny tables plus a counter. Now Trzesniewski (no-one has ever tried to pronounce the name) has doubled in size which means that the counter turns a sharp corner and that, with luck, you may find a bit of ledge on which to park your plate and glass. But you do not go to Trzesniewski for comfort (it is usually packed), you go for the tiny crisp rolls, split open and topped with a generous portion of fresh goose liver, the small hot pâté wrapped in flaky pastry and above all, their own type of open sandwich which cannot be found anywhere else. Thick dark country bread spread with their own 'secret' mixture into which ham or herrings, lobster or cucumber, chopped peppers or smoked salmon have been folded. All clearly labelled – there is even one which says *Pfefferoni – scharf* to warn customers that the finely chopped pickled green peppers are rather hot. (People have tried time and again to find the secret of the basic mixture – the daughter of the founder once said that it all rested on the ability to boil an egg. I doubt whether it is as simple as all that, though possibly the basic mixture is based on mayonnaise and hard-boiled egg.) Quality has been constant since the days when a Trzesniewski sandwich cost 40 Austrian Groschen, yet the price is still an unbelievable 7 Austrian Schillings. With your sandwich you can have practically any drink you like, from Vodka to Vermouth, perfectly good Austrian wine and hot Korn with honey in winter, but more often than not I opt for a *Pfiff* (whistle) of beer – a measure which, at least as far as I know, was first reintroduced at Trzesniewski. It is equal to about ⅛l, and after all, you can always order another …

WRENKH
Bauernmarkt 10
1010 Wien
☏ 5331526 5353362
No credit cards
Open: Restaurant 11.00–15.00 (kitchen 14.30)
18.00–24.00 (kitchen 23.30) Monday/Saturday
Bar: 11.00–1.00 Monday/Saturday
Closed: Sunday
Prices: inexpensive/moderate

Wrenkh's vegetarian restaurant at Hollergasse 9 (1150 Wien) set in an old inn with well-shaded garden proved so successful that they have now opened up in the centre of Vienna. The premises once housed one of my favourite old-fashioned and rather staid restaurants, full of plush and dark panelling with a nice turn-of-the-century touch. The décor has been left almost unchanged, but the adjacent small coffee house has now been refurbished and turned into a bar where small and not so small snacks can be obtained. Wrenkh's has rapidly become a favourite restaurant not only for vegetarians but for all those who love beautifully prepared food at reasonable prices and the hors-d'oeuvres (selected from the menu with daily specialities served from the trolley) are star starters (try the Mozzarella with sun-dried tomatoes, herbs, olives and olive oil dressing). One of my favourite main courses is the creamy risotto of wild rice with ceps (*Wildreisrisotto*), but this would not be Vienna if they did not have *Wiener Schnitzel* on the menu (*Glutenschnitzel Wiener Art*) and there's also an excellent *Glutenragout* with almonds for extra flavour. The mixed vegetable platter is not only excellent but it will be prepared with butter or oil according to your choice. Puddings are typically Viennese – featherlight curd cheese dumplings with toasted walnuts and three different sauces (*Topfenknödel*), there's a good *Punschpudding* laced with alcohol and *Rotweincreme* with fresh fruit salad. Small, but particularly good wine list many of which are offered by the glass, excellent fruit juices and digestifs.

ZIMMERMANN
Armbrustergasse 5
1190 Wien
☏ 372211
Open: 17.00–24.00 Monday/Saturday
Closed: Sunday and 22 December/20 January (slightly variable)
Prices: moderate

Zimmermann is a completely genuine and wonderful Viennese world of its own, a *Heuriger* at its very best: a series of old vintners' cottages with small and not-so-small but incredibly cosy rooms, set in gardens that seem to stretch into eternity, yet with an almost impossible number of secluded corners. Visiting Zimmermann's is like being the very privileged guest at a private party (and you more than willingly pay for that privilege) – the only thing it has in common with other *Heurigen* is that you select your food from the hot and cold buffet (the wine is brought to the table). All the wines come from the Zimmermann's own vineyards and the food is of a very superior quality: fried spring chicken and *Wiener Schnitzel* (which come in deliberately smaller than usual sizes to nibble with the wine) are only coated with breadcrumbs immediately before frying and fried to order and the goose liver, cooked very gently and set in its own fat is the best ever. There are of course quite a number of the usual dishes you'd expect to find at a *Heuriger* such as freshly roasted pork, *Schinkenfleckerl*, smoked ox-tongue, *Fleischlaberln* (spiced meat cakes), Liptauer cheese and a selection of salads with particularly mild dressing. Puddings are delicious too and *Kirschenstrudel* as well as *Topfenstrudel* outstandingly good. And if by any chance you are staying in Vienna in private accommodation rather than a hotel and feel like throwing a party, Zimmermann's will take care of this as well (or you can book one of the smaller rooms and give a dinner party there).

Zimmermann

ZU DEN 3 HUSAREN
Weihburggasse 4
1010 Wien
☏ 51210920
Open: 12.00–15.00, 18.00–1.00
Closed: over Christmas and mid July/mid August
Prices: expensive

'Zu den 3 Husaren' is the best traditional and most typically Viennese restaurant in Austria and probably the whole world. Very elegant with its plush and gilt setting and secluded corners to which a pianist in the evening adds the right romantic touch. Concessions to other countries are made only where the wine list is concerned – Ewald Plachutta is a grand master of the classical Viennese cuisine, this delicious mixture of show-off and understatement of which the famous hors-d'oeuvres trolleys (four of them) are a typical example. There's nothing ornate or flamboyant about them, no tricks, gimmicks or unnecessary decorations, just a selection of about forty dishes, each and every one of them a little culinary masterpiece. Choose from their famous pâté de foie gras, calves brains on spinach leaves with a light mustard sauce, delicately composed salads, miniature steak tartar topped with a quail's egg (before you get carried away – you are charged according to portions which is only fair and should stop you from going overboard, leaving no room for other culinary delights Ewald Plachutta has in store for you). I am always amused by the fact that the menu has a special section headed '*Wiener Küche*' (as against '*wir empfehlen*' – we recommend) since the culinary repertoire is totally and utterly Viennese throughout executed with a perfection that is practically unequalled. This is the place in which to order all the specialities which have made *Wiener Küche* rightly famous (even though there was a time when it was 'fashionable' to sneer at it for being old-fashioned), to enjoy *Hechtnockerl* (*quenelles de brochet*) in their Viennese glory with dill sauce, to have *Krautfleckerl* (q.v.) with the pot roast (some of the guests – at least so it is rumoured – order the pot-roast for the accompanying *Krautfleckerl*), to order *Kaiserschnitzel* or the delicately prepared goose liver with *Schupfnudeln*. Puddings are truly excellent as well (you'll be glad you didn't go overboard with the hors-d'oeuvres) – *Kirschenstrudel* with cinnamon sabayon or fried *Strudel* leaves with berry cream, but I always opt for the *Husarenomelette* (pancakes filled with walnuts, topped with chocolate sauce, strawberry purée and whipped cream) in fond memory of the legendary previous owner of the 3 Husaren, Egon von Fodermayer, who created the dish.

If you happen to be in Vienna on Ash Wednesday and in an extravagant mood, reserve a table for the Heringschmaus at 'Zu den 3 Husaren'. It's expensive, booked up to the last available chair and the buffet is sensational.

ZUM BETTELSTUDENT
Johannesgasse 12
1010 Wien
☏ 5132044
Open daily: 10.00–2.00, Friday/Saturday 10.00–4.00
Prices: inexpensive.

Opened in December 1986 and in the same building as the 'Bora Bora' Bar and 'Queen Anne' disco (same ownership), the Bettelstudent (Beggar Student) was named not so much after the operetta, but as a reminder of the owner's hungry student days. The food is hearty, prices are low and portions enormous starting with *Studentenbrote*, giant 'snacks' on bread or toast which range from bacon, onion and fried egg to Styrian *Verhackerts*, the most popular being the garlicky *Bettelstudent*. There's always a good, very inexpensive two-course lunch and a large choice of good hearty dishes, all very reasonably priced. Look under *Hausmannskost* (good home cooking) for all-time favourites such as *Schwammerlgulasch* (mushroom goulash) and *Blunz'n G'röstl* (black pudding) with *Sauerkraut*, but there is also good brown cheese soup and the *Kleine* Beefsteak (served on toast) topped with a fried egg and accompanied by a huge salad, was the juiciest, most tender tournedo I've had for a long time. Puddings too are designed for hungry students, particularly *Palatschinke* Robert Stolz (pancake with curd cheese, chestnut mousse and chocolate) and *Hausg'wuzelte Mohnnudeln* (a rather filling sweet pasta dish with poppy seeds and sugar – possibly an acquired taste, but excellent once you've acquired it).

There are over twenty different kinds of beer, including Budweiser from Bohemia and Hirter from Carinthia, wines sold by the eighth litre and of course spirits and *Schnäpse* for richer students! Although by now the Bettelstudent caters also for a much more prosperous clientele and has been 'discovered' by visiting celebrities, prices and portions have remained at their original generous level – commendable in every way!

ZUM SCHWARZEN KAMEEL
Bognergasse 5
1010 Wien
☎ 638125 (table reservations 638967)
Open: Shop 9.00–19.00 Monday/Friday
9.00–12.30 Saturday
Restaurant 9.00–19.00 (lunch 12.00–15.00) Monday/Friday
9.00–14.00 Saturday.
Closed: Saturday afternoon and evening and all day Sunday
Prices: moderate/slightly upward

'Zum schwarzen Kameel' purveyors of fine foods and wines have been established in the Bognergasse since 1618, the beginning of the thirty-years war. The original owners were called Kameel (the signboard depicting a camel came much later, the first one being painted by Waldmüller, no less) and one member of the family went to the Philippines as a missionary to bring back a rare flower now known as Camelia (named after the discoverer). Beethoven bought sugar and coffee at the shop in the Bognergasse (and did not always pay his bills promptly). In later years the place was known as 'Zum Stiebitz' after the then owners though it was generally thought that the name came from the word '*stiebitzen*' (to snatch) in this particular case 'to snatch a bite' since by then the place was also well known for its snacks and for the excellent restaurant at the back of the shop established about a hundred years ago which has remained unchanged to this day. At that time the Ministry of Defence was just across the road from the Stiebitz and it is said that there was a secret passage linking the two premises. (Always trust the Austrian civil service when it comes to finding the best places for food!) It is also being said that in those golden days large bowls of caviar stood on the counters (rather like salt almonds). 'Zum schwarzen Kameel' (having reverted to its original name, though the telegraphic address is still 'Stiebitzerei') has been in the hands of the Friese family for many years now and although the – probably legendary – bowls of caviar have gone, shop and restaurant have remained virtually unchanged – not just a marvellous shop, but a very superior place for snacks as well as for full meals. At lunch-time there are hot dishes from the buffet – ham on the bone, *Wiener Schnitzel*, roast beef and the like, but it is the small snacks where the 'black camel' surpasses all others: tiny crisp rolls split open and filled with luscious ham, open sandwiches topped with all sorts of wonderful mixtures like finely chopped ham sitting on a small mound of lentil salad or smoked sprats cradled in mayonnaise atop lightly toasted bread (there are some tables at the back, otherwise you perch your plate and glass on the counter). If you walk in around noon, particularly on a Saturday, you could be forgiven for thinking you had strayed into a private party – the place will be packed with people who all appear to know each other, exchanging gossip over bite-sized delicacies and a glass of Sekt.

The restaurant 'proper' adjoins the shop (booking strongly advised), unchanged since the days when it was built nearly a hundred years ago and the interior styled by Portois and Fix who were responsible for the furnishings of so many of the stately Danube cruisers. The food is typically Viennese (in the best possible way) – goose liver in Traminer sauce, smoked ox-tongue with pease pudding, *Schulterscherzl* (special cut for the famous boiled beef), venison with woodruff sauce – as well as some lighter dishes and a good four-course set lunch at S350.-

The wine cellars reach three floors below street level and the wine list is superb (called '*Weinbuch*' since it is indeed a tome) with about half the wines available by the glass.

Lunch at the restaurant is served between noon and 15.00, but the restaurant stays open until 19.00, a wonderfully quiet (and almost secret) place in which to meet during the afternoon for a superb glass of wine and one of the delicious snacks from the counter. (One of the few remaining 'secrets' in this respect – so much so that it almost hurts to give away the information. Treat it with the respect it deserves!)

Cities, Towns and Villages from A to Z

Aistersheim *Upper Austria*

ROSENBERGER AUTOBAHN-
STATION AISTERSHEIM
4676 Aistersheim
☏ 07734 2191
Open: 6.00–23.00 June/October
6.00–22.00 November/May
Prices: inexpensive

A.8 Innkreis Motorway – accessible from both directions

Market Restaurant
No credit cards

For description see under Motorway Restaurants (Rosenberger)

Ampass nr. Innsbruck *Tyrol*

ROSENBERGER AUTOBAHNRESTAURANT AMPASSER HOF
6020 Innsbruck
☏ 0512 46431
Open: 6.00–23.00 June/October
6.00–22.00 November/May
Prices: inexpensive/moderate

A.12 Inntal Motorway – accessible only from one direction

No credit cards

For description see under Motorway Restaurants (Rosenberger)

Angath nr. Wörgl *Tyrol*

ROSENBERGER AUTOBAHNRESTAURANT ANGATH
6300 Wörgl
☏ 05332 7875
Open: 6.00–23.00 June/October
6.00–22.00 November/May
Prices: inexpensive/moderate

A.12 Inntal Motorway – accessible from both directions
Motor-Hotel

No credit cards

For description see under Motorway Restaurants (Rosenberger)

Ansfelden *Upper Austria*

ROSENBERGER AUTOBAHNRESTAURANT ANSFELDEN NORD
4052 Ansfelden
☏ 07229 87166
Open: 6.00–23.00 June/October
6.00–22.00 November/May
Prices: inexpensive/moderate

A.1 West Motorway – accessible one direction only

No credit cards

For description see under Motorway Restaurants (Rosenberger)

Bad Bleiberg *Carinthia*

BLEIBERGERHOF
Drei Lärchen 150
9530 Bad Bleiberg
☏ 04244 22050
Open: 12.00–14.00, 18.00–21.00 (last reservation) Wednesday/Sunday
Closed: Monday, Tuesday, also 2 November–20 December
Prices: moderate/upward

Bad Bleiberg is 892 m above sea level, a fairly 'young' spa (at least by Austrian spa standards, some of which were known to the Romans) at the foot of the Dobratsch (Slav for 'good mountain' since it harbours a number of thermal springs). The Bleibergerhof is a comparatively new hotel, not over large, but massively built with balconies which seem to be suspended in the sky. It is a wonderfully restful hotel – much polished wood has gone into its making and the scent of pine mingles with that of freshly baked bread usually greets you on arrival. An unusual hotel on many counts, last but not least because of the excellent cooking – owner Alfred Süssenbacher is one of Austria's top chefs and is hardly ever seen outside the kitchen (leaving his charming wife Regina to look after the guests). At one time meals were restricted to guests of the hotel, but fortunately this has now been changed and the restaurant is open to non-residents once more who can choose from an à la carte menu as well as select dishes from the menu for house guests. Alfred Süssenbacher's cooking is particularly light, using much local produce and his soups practically deserve a special trip. *Kerbelschaumsuppe* (frothy chervil soup) is a typical example, but there's also a light cream of cauliflower with small crunchy sunflower seed gnocchi and on occasion *Kärntner Kirchtagssuppe* (a 'festival' soup made with three kinds of meat and scented with saffron). Unusual combinations abound – purée of artichokes with smoked sturgeon or a soufflé of calves brains dressed with basil flavoured oil. Accompaniments are particularly good – braised spring onions wrapped in lean ham and *Strudel* filled with a purée of savoy cabbage to go with venison. Puddings are light and delicious like *Erdbeerröllchen* (a marvellous concoction incorporating wild strawberries) or a blackberry and curd cheese *Strudel* and there is always an excellent selection of cheeses, usually including local specialities. Very good wine list, very strong on Austrian whites with support from Italy and France, all available by the glass. Excellent digestifs, including some from Pfau at Ruden.

The Bleibergerhof is a superbly comfortable spa hotel with a variety of available treatments including aromatherapy and the open-air swimming-pool (with thermal water) can be used throughout the year.

How to get there: from Villach on 100 direction Spittal an der Drau. About 4 km outside Villach take the left turning marked Heiligengeist and Bad Bleiberg which leads through lovely woods (there is also a shorter and more direct road from Villach to Heiligengeist which joins this road – if you can find it!)

Baden nr. Vienna ***Lower Austria***

KAFFEE KONDITOREI FRANZ WIEDHALM
Josefsplatz 11
2500 Baden bei Wien
☏ 02252 48428
Open: 7.00–20.00 Monday/Saturday
9.00–20.00 Sunday
Prices: moderate

There are other, more modern *pâtisseries* in Baden bei Wien, but for me there exists only one: Wiedhalm (not to be confused with the coffee house and restaurant of the same name – and same ownership – across the road which is of fairly recent vintage). 'My' Wiedhalm is old and small and not really cosy at all, or even particularly comfortable, but their pastries and confectionery are superb and it has remained virtually unchanged since I was first taken there as a small child and allowed to choose my first cream gâteau. I can even remember my choice: a soft yellow confection which had chunks of glacé pineapple in it. I think Wiedhalm's still make it, as they do most of their specialities, including the famous *Badener Kaffeezuckerln* – coffee-flavoured sweets which come in a toffee and a soft fudge version. (There's another *pâtisserie* in Baden which sells the only 'genuine' *Kaffeezuckerln* as well, but unlike the legal fight over the genuine *Sachertorte* which went on for years, there has been no dispute over these sweets and for me

Wiedhalm's are the real thing – wrapped in brown or pink paper respectively: brown for fudge, pink for toffee!)

There are a few tables outside – perfect for enjoying Wiedhalm's ice-cream and like all *pâtisseries* in Austria, Wiedhalm's is of course fully licensed.

How to get there: Baden bei Wien is about 25 km from Vienna and you can get to Baden not only by car or train but also by bus and by tram. The bus stops just outside Wiedhalm's.

Badgastein ***Salzburg***

VILLA HISS
Erzherzog-Johann Promenade 1
5640 Badgastein
☏ 06434 38280
Open: 12.00–14.00, 19.00–22.30 Thursday/Sunday
19.00–22.30 Tuesday, Wednesday
Closed: all day Monday, lunch Tuesday, Wednesday
also closed June and September
Prices: expensive

Jörg Wörther is acknowledged as one of the top chefs in Austria. ('No doubt he's a genius' I noted after my first visit to his then newly opened restaurant 'I hope he gets the success he deserves'). He produces original and imaginative food, highly personal yet never outrageous and he loves perfection. In fact the term 'simple perfection' applies not only to his food but also to his menu descriptions. There are three separate menus from which dishes can also be chosen à la carte but to head one of these menus simply as *'Gemüse Speisenfolge'* (vegetarian menu) must surely be the culinary understatement of the century. The same modest simplicity applies to his other descriptions: *'Zander auf frischen Eierschwammerl mit Sardellensaft'* it says or *'Saibling auf Artischocken mit mitgerösteten Erdäpfeln'* (pike/perch with chanterelles and anchovies, char with artichokes and potatoes respectively) to describe yet another culinary masterpiece. There's *Lammkeule auf grünen und gelben Bohnen* (leg of lamb with yellow and green beans) and *Kalbskopfragout in Riesling mit Steinpilzen* (*tête de veau* in Riesling with ceps) all very special indeed and as pleasing to the eye as they are to the palate. Puddings are simply marvellous though again called simply *'Mohnmehlspeis'* (poppy-seed dessert) and *Topfenmehlspeis mit Wachauer Marille* (curd cheese dessert) which does not convey how delicious these concoctions are and *Palatschinken mit Griesscreme* (pancakes with semolina cream) sounds almost off-putting, yet I can recommend all of them as well as my own favourite *Nusschmarrn* with honey cream.

Extensive and excellent wine list, also wine sold by the quarter litre.

Villa Hiss is a fitting frame for Jörg Wörther's cooking – a beautifully restored turn-of-the-century villa which is now a very comfortable and luxurious small hotel with its own little spa centre.

Bad Ischl *Upper Austria*

HOTEL GOLDENES SCHIFF
Stifterkai 3
4820 Bad Ischl
☏ 06132 4241
Open: 7.00–23.00 (kitchen 11.30–14.00, 18.00–21.30)
Prices: inexpensive/moderate

There's something infinitely reassuring about the Goldenes Schiff, a solid, thick-walled eighteenth-century house right in the centre of the town, yet facing the River Traun. The rooms are charming – many of them with balconies overlooking the river and small suites are available at a moderate additional cost. The restaurant is good and pleasantly old-fashioned as well, with a rather larger than average menu and three daily fixed-price menus for selection – the most expensive of these being S195.- and the cheapest S82.- for three courses (against this they put – rather endearingly – 'smaller portions' which are still more than adequate). Choosing à la carte I can recommend their fish specialities – they even state which of the nearby lakes the fish comes from! It is also the sort of place where you could – and should – order dishes like *geröstete Kalbsleber* (sautéd calves liver) or *Eiernockerl mit Salat* – good Austrian home cooking which they do to perfection. Puddings are a speciality of the house, from home-made *Apfelschlankerl* (a sort of apple-cake particular to this region), *Nougatcremeroulade* and a good selection of pancakes to that ultimate of chocolate puddings, *Mohr im Hemd*, rated 'best ever' by a friend who makes a pretty good one herself.

Small, but well-chosen selection of Austrian and South Tyrolean wines.

VILLA SCHRATT
Steinbruch 43
4820 Bad Ischl
☏ 06132 7647
Open: 11.30–14.00, 17.30–22.00
Closed: Tuesday all day and Wednesday until 17.30
also beginning January/beginning February
Prices: moderate/upward

The house was the country villa of Katharina Schratt – actress, confidante and friend of the Emperor Franz Josef who visited her every day when staying at his summer residence in Bad Ischl. He was not her only visitor by any means; the inscription on a plaque inside the villa reads like an excerpt from the *Almanach de Gotha*.

There's a lovely hospitable atmosphere about the house – one of the later owners was a much-loved Viennese actor – and it seems more than appropriate that the prettily refurbished villa should now house a restaurant. The food would certainly please the most illustrious guests: light and delicious as in the 'variations' of fish from nearby Lake Fuschl or the frothy leek soup, and nice and sturdy as in the *Sulz vom Schweinsbackerl* (brawn) served with red lentils and pumpkin-seed oil. Rack of lamb is baked in a crust of thyme-scented potatoes and served with polenta and filet of pike comes in a herb sauce with home-made noodles. Sorbets are home-made as well and the small curd dumplings (*Topfenknöderl*) with fruit were as light and delicious as could be.

Very good selection of Austrian wines, with a little support from Italy and France.

Legend has it that Frau Schratt baked a special *Guglhupf* for the Emperor every day and Zauner's (q.v.) at Bad Ischl say that they always had to bake a *Guglhupf* as well – a sort of understudy in case Frau Schratt's did not live up to expectations. With coffee I was given a miniature edition of this *Guglhupf* – a charming thought, but even a miniature was too much to manage at this point (I would have resisted the *Topfenknöderl*, had I known). I was obviously not the first guest who found this to be the case, for the little cake was swiftly wrapped in a special carton for me to take away. It scented my car all the way back to Salzburg and I had it with my breakfast the next morning. Just like the Emperor Franz Josef.

How to get there: On 158 from Salzburg to Bad Ischl. Slow down as you approach Bad Ischl – Villa Schratt is on the left on the main road.

WEINHAUS ATTWENGER
Leharkai 12
4820 Bad Ischl
☏ 06132 3327
Open: 10.00–14.30, 17.00–24.00 Tuesday/Saturday
10.00–15.00 Sunday
Closed: from 15.00 Sunday and all day Monday, also February/March
Note: During June, July and August Attwengers is open throughout the day from 10.00 until midnight
Prices: moderate/upward

Anton Bruckner was a friend of the Attwenger family and spent frequent holidays here, Franz Lehar wrote *The Merry Widow* next door (his villa is now a museum). The house which dates back to around 1600 was a country inn for well over a century, until the Pfliegler family took over in 1974 since when it has become one of the best restaurants in the region, a region well-studded with fine restaurants.

There's something eminently festive about Attwengers where every meal seems to turn into a feast – whether in the charming rustic dining-rooms or in the lovely garden set on the banks of the River Traun. Fish comes from local lakes and rivers, game from the 'Jagdrevier Franz Josef' (hunting grounds of the Emperor Franz Josef who had his summer residence at Bad Ischl) and quail and guinea fowl are reared especially for the restaurant by a local farmer. The menu is comparatively large and you may well be tempted – at least at lunch – to choose the fixed-price meal which is certainly reasonable (S245.- for four courses, S210.- for three), but I have my own fixed favourites from the à la carte menu, like a starter called *Fischwandl* (a selection of local fish in aspic, served with a dill sauce) and the crayfish terrine (*Krebserlterrine*). *Hauspastete* (pâté maison) is made 'nach k. & k. Rezeptur' (according to Imperial and Royal recipe) and it goes without saying that both the beef broth and the *Tafelspitz* are absolutely authentic as well – as is only to be expected with the ghost of Franz Josef, whose favourite dish it was, probably hovering over them.

Some of the dishes may sound rather ordinary like *Schweinslungenbratl* (roast pork fillet) spiced with caraway seeds and garlic – or a little heavy going like the *gespickte Lungenbraten* (larded whole filet of beef) which is

Attwenger

served with a *Griess Strudel* and mushrooms, but any idea of ordinariness disappears when you taste them and the lightest possible hands appear to be at work in the kitchen – everything is delicate and delicious. My favourite pudding at Attwengers has always been their *b'soffene Liesl* (drunken Lizzie), a featherlight walnut concoction crowned with wine sabayon, but recently, a friend raved over their *Mohnknöderl* – the thinnest possible paste wrapped round a rich dark poppy-seed filling, served with a vanilla cream spiced with cranberries – and I can't wait to try them!

Excellent and very selective wine list and good choice of wines sold by the eighth litre – and upwards.

ZAUNER
Pfarrgasse 7
4820 Bad Ischl
☏ 06132 3522
Open: 8.30–18.00
Closed: Tuesdays (only during October/November and January/April)
Prices: moderate

Zauner is legendary – an Austrian *Konditorei* at its most glorious best which has existed in the same spot for over 150 years. Go there either in the morning or in the early afternoon when the magnificent display has just been completed or replenished. The 'build-up' alone is worth noting: it starts with comparatively simple items such as different tea breads and coffee cakes, then leads via *Teebäckerei* (rather elaborate biscuits) and *petits fours* to luscious pastries and ends in a triumph of gâteaux – all arranged on the huge horseshoe-shaped table which takes up practically all of the first room. Impossible to suggest what to choose, but if wild strawberries are in season, the *Erdbeerroulade* is unsurpassed (and unsurpassable), as are the small tartlets filled with wild strawberries. One of my own favourites is the *Nougat Truffle* gâteau, but nothing is less than perfect, from the simplest *Topfenbäckerei* (with a soft curd filling) to a slice of *Guglhupf* (made according to the same recipe as the one once baked for the Emperor Franz Josef). Don't miss the 'savoury' corner though – tucked away on the side – which has excellent salads and tit-bits, perfect for a light lunch and like all *pâtisseries* in Austria, Zauner is of course fully licensed.

Some of the Zauner specialities are beautifully packaged for taking away – *Ischler Oblaten* (very crisp wafers with nougat), *Zaunerstollen* (a mixture of the above with chocolate and shaped into a loaf) and the famous *Zauner Torte*. All would make perfect gifts to take home, if you could bear to part with them.

If you speak even a little German, get a copy of *Die Konditorei Zauner*

(Wilhelm Goldmann Verlag) which should be available at the bookshop across the road. It gives some of their most treasured recipes and the history of the house of Zauner is as good as their gâteaux and that is saying quite a lot!

Berndorf ***Lower Austria***

SCHIMANSZKY
Rosenstrasse 18
2560 Berndorf 111 – Ödlitz
☏ 02672 2320
Open: 11.00–14.00, 17.30–22.00
Open throughout the day on Saturdays and Sundays and until 17.00 on Bank Holiday Mondays
Closed: Monday and Tuesday
Prices: moderate/upward

A small inn nestling in the woods, a garden with ancient chestnut trees and you have the ideal setting for a *Backhendlstation*, a place specializing in fried spring chicken. Like some of the best restaurants in Austria, Schimanszky started as a *Backhendlstation* which grew quickly in popularity, helped by the fact that it is located on the edge of Austria's Thermal wine region and there's a natural affinity between wine and fried spring chicken. Like some of the best restaurants in Austria which started off as a 'fried chicken station', Schimanszky has now graduated to higher culinary spheres. Fried spring chicken (free range) is of course still a speciality and of tip-top quality, as are other more robust dishes like smoked pork, but the menu now includes a *Parfait* of chicken livers with pistachio nuts – one of the most delicately flavoured I've eaten – and a game terrine of equally high standard. There is a cream of potato soup with wild mushrooms and herbs which is more than commendable and I am told by local friends that the fish specialities which I had no chance of sampling, are well worth the journey.

Puddings are a particular delight: from *Nougatterrine* with strawberry purée to Pistachio soufflé with marzipan cream, to pancakes filled with dark plum jam and walnuts steeped in rum – though quite a few of their 'regulars' never look further than the *Malakofftorte* which is also one of the house specialities.

The wine list consists entirely of Austrian wines, many of them sold by the quarter litre and they also have their own *eaux-de-vie*. Do not miss the apricot one – it's sensational!

How to get there: from Vienna to Bad Vöslau on A.2 on 17 and from Bad Vöslau on 212 direction Berndorf. Just before coming to Berndorf there is a sign on the left for 'Waldgasthaus Schimanszky'. Follow the sign and it will lead you straight to the restaurant (on the left of the road).

Bezau *Vorarlberg*

ENGEL
6870 Bezau
☎ 05514 2203
Open: 12.00–14.00, 18.00–21.00
Closed: Tuesday all day, Wednesday until 17.00
also mid November/mid December
Prices: moderate/slightly upward

Bezau was the centre of the *Bauernrepublik* (farmers' republic) for centuries, when meetings were held in the old town hall which stood on four stilts and could be reached only by a ladder. As soon as the councillors had assembled, the ladder was taken away and only replaced when they had all agreed on the issues at stake. The building which houses the Engel dates back a few hundred years as well and had the Engel been established in those days I am sure council meetings would have ended even sooner. It is a charming old building, sturdy and comfortable, with lots of honeyed polished wood in the cosy *Bauernstuben*. The food is a happy combination of good country fare and some excellent and rather inspired additions – *Bärlauchrahmsuppe* (cream of wild garlic soup) comes with small hazelnut dumplings, potato soup with lightly fried mushrooms and there are small celeriac *gnocchi* in the strong chicken broth, but the soups also include hearty *Südtiroler Kutteln* (tripe). Fish dishes at the Engel are particularly commendable, one of my favourites being the *Eglifilets* from Lake Constance which they fry very simply with thyme, but I can also recommend their stuffed breast of guineafowl (*gefüllte Perlhuhnbrust*) with a *mélange* of yellow peppers and, for hearty appetites, the roast suckling pig (*gebratenes Spanferkel*) with beer and caraway glaze, *gnocchi* and white cabbage salad. Leave room for a pudding – the Engel's warmer *Rumauflauf* (rum pudding) served with coffee ice-cream and cinnamon cream confirms that it deserves its 'angelic' name.

Excellent selection of Austrian wines with strong support from Italy.

How to get there: from Bregenz on 190 direction Dornbirn as far as Lauterach where turn left direction Bezau. Drive to Schwarzach and then turn left for Alberschwende where you join road 200 to Egg and Bezau. The Engel is in the centre of the village.

Bodensdorf (Ossiacher See) *Carinthia*

STOFFL
Deutschberg 6
9551 Bodensdorf am Ossiacher See
☎ 04243 6920
Open: 10.00 – 24.00 (kitchen until 21.00)
daily from May/October, closed Monday for remainder of year
Prices: inexpensive

Stoffl sits very comfortably at an altitude of 760m, with wonderful views over lake and mountains. A splendid old country inn where portions are enormous and prices are small (I know of no other place that can match Stoffl's price for a large dish of chanterelles, for instance). *Kärntner Nudelgerichte* are always on the menu – consisting of large pasta envelopes with a variety of fillings (including a sweet version with dried pears) and this would certainly be the place to try them, either as a substantial starter or as a main course. (The sweet version could, of course, be ordered as a pudding, but in most country regions it is quite usual to have a 'sweet' main course, often based on pasta.) Menus are very seasonal – cream of asparagus soup or asparagus with home-cured ham as starters or the aforementioned chanterelles (served with new potatoes as a starter or – a larger portion – with a dumpling and crisp green salad as a main course). Other main courses are simple, but beautifully cooked such as roast shoulder of veal with a sage and basil sauce, spinach noodles and a green salad. Or more substantial like Carinthian escalope with grated potatoes and herbs, cooked *au gratin*. The fixed-price meal is always excellent value, and is available to senior citizens at just over half-price, with reduced, though still fairly large portions. And if you just want to admire the view, there's a long list of small and not so small snacks! A *G'spritzter* would go well with almost any of the dishes, or have some good locally brewed beer from the barrel.

For those who wish to stay longer there are some good, comfortable rooms, reasonably priced.

To get there: from Villach on to 94, direction Lake Ossiach (north shore). At the beginning of Bodensdorf follow the direction of Gerlitzen-Alpenstrasse on the left. This is a toll road – state at the beginning that you are only going as far as Stoffl (about 6 km). The toll fee will be less and it will also be refunded at the restaurant.

Bodensdorf (Ossiacher See) *Carinthia*

URBANI-WIRT
St Urban am Ossiacher See
Bundesstrasse 50
9551 Bodensdorf
☏ 04243 2286
Open: 10.00–24.00 (kitchen 12.00–14.00, 18.00–21.30)
Closed: Tuesday all day, Wednesday until 16.00 (October/April)
Prices: moderate

The hotel building is of this century, but there's been an Urbani-Wirt for centuries – and in the Nindler family since 1795. A family inn by all accounts, directly on Lake Ossiach and one where children are more than welcome, not only if their parents are staying at the hotel, but as guests in the dining-room where young palates soon learn to appreciate the taste of real food. Meat, sausages and potatoes come from the Nindler's home farm, flavoured with herbs from their garden and apple-juice is pressed from apples in their orchards (to say nothing of more potent drinks distilled from fruit of the same orchards). There's always a proper Sunday roast (*Sonntagsbratl*), game in season with all the proper (Austrian) accompaniments like juniper-cream sauce, cranberries, red cabbage and featherlight dumplings – all the dishes they like to call *gut bürgerlich* (good bourgeois cooking) such as pork cutlets with caraway seeds and garlic, but there are also excursions into higher culinary regions such as a mousse of local asparagus with lightly smoked trout and veal sweetbreads on a bed of spinach with chive sauce. Puddings are very seasonal – if you happen to be there during the strawberry season, try the *Erdbeervariationen* (strawberries served in about six different ways) or just order them *mit Schlag* (with whipped cream). Good selection of Austrian wines, with support from France and Italy and splendid local beer (you might care to try Hirter Morchel, a dark malt beer with a centuries-old history).

How to get there: from Villach on 94 direction Ossiachersee Nord and Bodensdorf. St Urban is just before Bodensdorf and the Urbani-Wirt is on the left.

Bregenz *Vorarlberg*

DEURING SCHLÖSSLE
Ehre-Guta Platz 4
6900 Bregenz
☎ 05574 47800
Open: 12.00–14.00, 18.30–24.00 (kitchen 21.30)
Prices: expensive

Until just over a year ago Ernst Huber's small restaurant 'Zoll' on the outskirts of Bregenz was a Mecca for gourmets and you had to book well ahead of time to secure a table. Now the Deuring Schlössle – painted by Turner as well as by Egon Schiele – makes a far more fitting frame for his art. The Schlössle, set above Lake Constance in the old part of the town, has been very sympathetically restored and turned into a superbly luxurious hotel (prices are those of a four-star hotel). Notwithstanding the elegant bedrooms, very romantic garden and beautifully appointed dining-rooms, the main attraction is still (and always will be) Ernst Huber's cooking – in the top hierarchy of chefs in Austria and now joined by his son Heino. Not even the most beautiful room or view could compete with that – it is perfection of the highest order. The only complaint I have is that having tasted some of his dishes, I want to go back to them time and again rather than try one of his more recent creations. I find it difficult to resist the *Parfait vom Räucheraal* or *Parfait vom Räucherlachs* (*parfait* of smoked eel or smoked salmon respectively) accompanied by Krentomate (a peeled, seeded

Deuring Schlössle

and chopped tomato mixed with freshly grated horseradish. Sounds simple, I know, but that's what I mean by perfection). *Bodenseefischsülze* (aspic of fish from Lake Constance) and *Bärlauchcremesuppe* (cream soup made with wild garlic) are also favourite starters which I'll quite happily follow with noodles with ceps and goose liver (intended as a starter but an excellent main course in my opinion). Other favourites are the fried *Eglifilets* (from Lake Constance again) and the venison with juniper cream, but last time I was persuaded to try the *soufflierter Bodenseezander* (pike/perch cooked so delicately with herbs that it defies description) served with wild rice. *Apfelterrine* with caramel sauce and walnut croquant ice-cream was a dream and I did not even miss my favourite chocolate terrine with orange salad.

As expected there's an excellent selection of wines from France, Italy and Austria.

Brixlegg — *Tyrol*

SIGWART'S TIROLER WEINSTUBEN
Marktstrasse 40
6320 Brixlegg
☎ 05337 2358, 3390
Open: 10.00–23.00 (kitchen 22.30) Wednesday/Sunday
Closed: Monday, Tuesday, also beginning June/mid July (variable)
Prices: moderate

Though the building has been used as an inn for centuries – and in the same family for over a hundred and fifty years – it has all the appearances of an old farmhouse: small panelled rooms, a grandfather clock ticking comfortingly and the scent of freshly baked bread permeating the air. Not an illusion – all bread is home-baked and you get a good introductory taste when you spread the *Kräuterschmalz* (dripping with herbs) on oven-fresh *Weggerl* (crusty home-baked rolls). The cooking is splendidly regional, much bound to local produce. Creamy beer soup with herbs and also a clear oxtail soup with nettle-filled wholemeal pasta envelopes, good starters like a terrine of black pudding with ox-tongue, served with a zucchini salad and a hearty oxtail stew, the oxtail stuffed with mushrooms, with a red wine sauce and root vegetables. Sigwart's is particularly good on fish (which comes from nearby Achensee) and quite exceptional on puddings – I particularly remember a small *Guglhupf* with rum-soaked raisins in a light caramel sauce. There are also some very good Austrian cheeses.

As one would expect from a *Weinstube*, the wine list is very extensive with many rarities of which a good number are available by the glass. *Schnäpse* and *digestifs* are exceptional as well – three kinds of apple brandy, including one made from *Grafensteiner* apples, *Schnaps* made from *reineclaudes,* cherries and wild raspberries, all locally distilled and good Wachau apricot brandy. During May when the *'Gauderfest'* takes place in the nearby Ziller valley, *Gauder* beer (brewed especially for that occasion and left to mature for eight months) is also available, served in *'Pfiff'* (⅛l) measures.

As befits an ancient Tyrolean inn, there's a well-shaded garden near the river.

How to get there: from Innsbruck on 171 or A.12 Motorway, exit Brixlegg.

Dobl nr. Graz ***Styria***

ROSENBERGER
AUTOBAHNRESTAURANT GRAZ-KAISERWALD
8143 Dobl
☏ 03136 3972
Open: 6.00–23.00 June/October
6.00–22.00 November/May
Prices: moderate

A.2 South Motorway (*Südautobahn*) accessible from both directions

For description see under Motorway Restaurants (Rosenberger)

Drosendorf ***Lower Austria***

GASTHOF FAILLER (Goldenes Lamm)
2095 Drosendorf an der Thaya
☏ 02915 327
Open: 7.00–23.00 (11.30–13.30, 18.00–21.00)
Closed: Monday, also last two weeks November and first two weeks March
Prices: inexpensive/moderate

The River Thaya winds in a large loop around Drosendorf, surrounding it on three sides. Enclosed by medieval walls – a tiny, well-protected town with a very great past – its once fierce fortress rebuilt into a rich renaissance castle (destroyed by fire and rebuilt once more). Drosendorf's main square is an elongated triangle with some exceptionally pretty houses – and Gasthof Failler, a picture-book type of Austrian inn with its own butchery, a terrace overlooking the river as well as a nicely shaded garden, good accommodation (at more than reasonable prices) and splendid food of the very best country inn type:

Waldviertler Knoblauchsuppe (creamy garlic soup), impeccable *Zwiebelrostbraten*, excellent local fish (all the best carp in Austria to-day comes from the Waldviertel – the forest region in which Drosendorf is situated) and crisply roasted duck. Puddings are particularly good – like their *Kaiserschmarrn* or the *Rahmpalatschinken* (pancakes with a creamy filling) – or you may well be tempted by the *Mohntorte* (poppy-seed cake, poppy seeds being another Waldviertel speciality). Good selection of wines, including Italian and French as well as Austrian, many of which are sold by the quarter litre and some also by the glass.

How to get there: from Krems on 218 to Langenlois, thence on 34 through the Kamp valley to Horn and on 4 to Geras, from Geras on 30 to Drosendorf.

Dürnstein (Wachau) ***Lower Austria***

HOTEL SCHLOSS DÜRNSTEIN
3601 Dürnstein
☏ 02711 212
Open: 11.00–22.00 mid March/beginning November
(kitchen 12.00–14.15, 18.30–21.15)
(snacks, drinks etc. on the terrace also before lunch and during the afternoon)
Closed: Beginning November/mid March
Prices: moderate/upward

The Wachau has often been described as the most beautiful stretch of the Danube and there's no doubt in my mind as to the most beautiful spot in the Wachau: Dürnstein or – to be precise – Schloss Dürnstein, set high above the Danube. It is also one of the most beautiful and luxurious places at which to stay (at surprisingly sensible prices, all things considered). Rooms are sumptuous, the service is perfect, with nice 'extras' which include not only a thick bathrobe, but slippers and a tray of delicious *petits fours* placed at the bedside. There's an outdoor swimming-pool into which a linden tree sheds its blossoms (alas, threatened as the roots of the tree apparently undermine the castle walls) and a very swish indoor pool as well.

My favourite spot, however, is the large terrace overlooking the Danube. On a warm day there's no better place for a leisurely lunch with the Danube obligingly sparkling bright blue beneath – or for dinner in the soft evening air (you will need to book and also to check on the dates of their grill parties which are very popular). For chillier days there is an elegant dining-room, as befits an elegant castle. The food is splendidly Austrian – the sort one would expect to get if staying as a private guest at the castle (generous too – on one occasion there was a good-sized slice of goose liver as *amuse gueule*). There's usually at least one dish *aus Oma's Kochtopf* (from grandmother's kitchen) not a gimmick in this particular case and perfectly genuine, like baked carp on a bed of *Sauerkraut* cooked with Riesling or a homely cream of potato soup. The fixed-price menus are always good value and well worth considering (S280.- for three courses, S350.- for four). If choosing à la carte try the ham platter with melon (*Wachauer* and *Waldviertler Schinken*, the latter being air-dried from the neighbouring Waldviertel region). On my last visit I had river trout as a main course – cooked *au bleu* (to perfection, and this on a Sunday of all days, when every seat on the terrace was taken), but I can also recommend the veal *medaillons* with morel mushrooms and spinach noodles. The *Topfengratin* (curd cheese *gratin* with fresh fruit) was a joy and I was only sorry that I could not manage the Marzipan *Walnussterrine mit marinierten Erdbeeren* (marzipan walnut terrine with strawberries) as well.

Being in the heart of the Wachau wine region and on the edge of the famous Weinviertel there is of course a superb selection of the best of Austrian wines, ably supported by France, Italy and Spain.

How to get there: from Vienna on 3 to Krems and past Krems to Dürnstein. The centre of Dürnstein is closed to traffic except for access. Either drive through the narrow high street to thunderous looks from pedestrians and you will find Hotel Schloss Dürnstein on your left or remain on the main road which runs through a tunnel. At the end of the tunnel take a sharp right turn which leads straight up to Schloss Dürnstein.

LOIBNERHOF
Unterloiben 7
3601 Dürnstein
☏ 0732 82890
Open: 11.00–23.00
Closed: Monday (1 April–31 October)
Monday, Tuesday (1 November–31 March)
also closed mid January/mid February
Prices: moderate

At its very best on a warm and sunny day during the week (like all places in the Wachau the Loibnerhof tends to get crowded at the weekend) when one can sit out of doors, well shaded by vines and fruit trees, though there's much to be said for the cosy restaurant in winter as well. The Loibnerhof is exactly the sort of place to go for a glass or two of their excellent wine – all the wines except for Sekt and Champagne come from the Knoll family's own vineyards – and then stay for the food: good Austrian country cooking with some specialities others have long since forgotten to put on the menu, or considered too mundane. (If you like tripe, look out for *Kutteln in Weissweinsauce*). The

Waldviertel region is just north of the Wachau and this is where duck and carp come from (try the clear fish broth – *klare Karpfensuppe* – or the fried carp) as well as the recipe for Waldviertler *Rahmsuppe* (soup made with sour cream). Goose liver in various forms is nearly always on the menu, as are *Hechtnockerl* in dill sauce (*quenelles de brochet* – in fact a Viennese speciality). There'll be ham on the bone (*Beinschinken*) with asparagus when in season and home-cured wild boar, all the variations of *Schnitzel* (the Loibnerhof is also strong on veal dishes). Very good selection of puddings, including some regional specialities and an interesting choice of – mostly local – cheeses. Splendid eaux-de-vie (this is apricot country after all – pear too, for that matter) and do not forget a *digestif* – like *Veltlinerhausbrand* or the walnut *Schnaps*. And if you have enjoyed the goose liver *parfait*, it can be bought in a glass jar, ready for taking away (you can also buy a bottle of the walnut *Schnaps* and some of their wines).

How to get there: On 3 from Vienna, past Krems. Just before Dürnstein follow signs for Unterloiben to the right and then turn right for Loibnerhof.

SÄNGER BLONDEL
3601 Dürnstein (Wachau)
☏ 02711 253
Open: 8.00–23.00 (kitchen 11.30–21.00, limited menu 14.00–18.00)
Closed: from 17.00 Sunday and all day Monday (May/March)
from 17.00 Sunday and all day Monday and Tuesday (March and April)
Prices: moderate

Blondel is something of a local hero at Dürnstein – after all, this is where he found his captive king, Richard Lionheart, after much searching. A nice, touching story, to say nothing of the four tons of silver which the Austrians collected by way of ransom money! And what better way to honour a local hero than to name an inn after him? I think Blondel would have approved of his namesake; it is a fine inn in the best Austrian tradition – sturdy and welcoming, with a large tiled stove in the dining-room to ward off winter chills and a welcoming shaded garden for the days when a warm wind wafts up from the Danube below and rustles through the chestnut trees. The food is in the best Austrian tradition too – beautifully cooked and nicely served, whether it is a stalwart favourite like *Gulasch* soup or a delicate cream of pike with small spinach gnocchi, roast lamb or tender calves liver (*sautierte Kalbsleberstreifen*), grilled pike/perch with herb butter or a perfect *Wiener Schnitzel*. There's apple strudel fresh from the oven and good local cheese as well as their *Obatzter* (well-spiced cream cheese) with which they serve their own home-baked wholemeal bread.

The best of local wines of course, as well as their own elderberry liqueur. If you stay at the Sänger Blondel (very comfortable guest rooms at moderate prices) the buffet breakfast includes home-made apricot jam – from local apricots of course!

Eben im Pongau ***Salzburg***

ROSENBERGER AUTOBAHNRESTAURANT EBEN GASTHOFGUT
Gasthofberg 23
5531 Eben im Pongau
☏ 06464 8571
Open: 6.00–23.00 June/October
6.00–22.00 November/May
Prices: inexpensive

A.10 Tauern Motorway – accessible from both directions
Market Restaurant
No credit cards

For description see under Motorway Restaurants (Rosenberger)
Note: Eben Gasthofgut is a market restaurant, not to be confused with Eben Süd which is a conventional motorway restaurant.

ROSENBERGER AUTOBAHNRESTAURANT EBEN SÜD
5531 Eben im Pongau
☏ 06464 8404
Open: 6.00–23.00 June/October
6.00–22.00 November/May
Prices: inexpensive/moderate

A.10 Tauern Motorway – accessible from both directions

For description see under Motorway Restaurants (Rosenberger)

Egg (Faaker See) *Carinthia*

TSCHEBULL
Egger Seeuferstrasse 26
9580 Egg am Faaker See
☏ 04254 2191
Open: 8.00–24.00 (12.00–14.00, 18.00–22.00)
Closed: Monday (winter only), also January/February (variable)
Prices: moderate

Tschebull modestly describes itself as a '*Kärntner Gasthof*' (Carinthian inn) and 'an inn which also lets rooms'. The description is perfectly correct – Tschebull has all the makings of a typically Austrian inn such as its own home farm supplying meat and home-cured ham, its herb garden and home-brewed *Schnaps*, but the rooms are rather more comfortable than one would expect of a simple inn. Tschebull's is what I'd describe as a generously hearted inn seating about four hundred with two-thirds of the accommodation being in the garden and in summer there's a daily open-air grill in the evenings. Do not let the seating capacity influence you though – the cooking whilst including all the expected (and some rather unexpected) local specialities, is definitely of superior quality (if you probe a little further you'll discover that Hans Tschemernjak has done a 'stage' at the Crocodile at Strasbourg). 'Local' specialities extend not only to Carinthia but further south to the Alpe/Adria region which reaches far into Italy and Yugoslavia. The good country cooking aspect is emphasized right from the start when you find that the S20.- (optional) cover charge includes not just crisp rolls and good Carinthian country butter but home-made pâté with lots of fresh herbs. Some of the soups are served '*im Brottöpferl*' (a hollowed-out mound of bread) and their *Frühlingskräuter-Kassuppn* (spring herbs, young vegetables, cheese and sour cream) is particularly delicious as is their creamy mushroom soup served in the same way. The special section headed '*Vorspeisen und Gustostückerln aus eigener Landwirtschaft*' (hors-d'oeuvres and specialities from our home farm) also deserves consideration, particularly the home-smoked char from a nearby river and the cress and potato salad with bacon or go for the *Kärntner Kosterle*, a selection of home-made salami, pâté, two kinds of home-smoked ham and trout. You'll probably need the glossary when it comes to selecting the main course (unless you know that *Nusslan* is Carinthian for *medaillons* for instance), but I can strongly recommend my own favourite at Tschebull's *Schweinsschnitzel Kärntner Gasthof* which consists of pork escalopes in a creamy cheese sauce with spiced plums, gnocchi and ground walnuts. The menu changes frequently of course and there are many other specialities yet to be discovered. Puddings at Tschebull's have long since been famous (their small apple dumplings in wine sauce proved so popular that they've had the recipe printed and it is now available on request) and the honey-cake served with warm chocolate sauce, walnut ice-cream and whipped cream is worth every single calorie and so is the *Nougat Marzipanparfait* with raspberry purée and cream.

The wine list is quite exceptional and the very personal selection by Hans Tschemernjak – the very best of Austria and Northern Italy (ask also for the special list of '*Spitzenweine*' sold by the glass), a very small selection of Bordeaux wines ('a deliberate weakness on our list' it freely admits) plus a few selected Californian and Spanish wines.

How to get there: from Klagenfurt on A.2 past Velden, exit at Villach (Faakersee) on to 84. Drive past Drobollach and you will find Tschebull on your right. OR from Villach on 84 direction Faakersee to Drobollach as before.

Eisenstadt ***Burgenland***

G'WÜRZSTÖCKL (Hotel Burgenland)
Schubertplatz 1
7000 Eisenstadt
☏ 02682 5521
Open: 11.30–14.00, 18.00–22.00 Monday/Friday
18.00–22.00 Saturday
11.30–14.00 Sunday
Closed: Saturday lunch and Sunday evening
Prices: moderate

Hotel Burgenland is part of a large building complex which also houses a big conference hall (large that is by Eisenstadt standards which is the smallest provincial capital in Austria with all of 9000 inhabitants and completely dominated by Schloss Esterhazy). The G'würzstöckl is on the first floor, rather modern, but bright, spacious and comfortable. Sunday lunch-time brings sizeable family parties, but the cooking is in fact far above average – what I'd describe as 'elevated regional' with a strong Hungarian influence (Eisenstadt is very close to the border). Most of the main courses and even some marked '*Schmankerln für den kleinen Appetit*' (specialities for the small appetite) can be ordered in what they call '*Probierportionen*' (sample portions) which quite frankly are still more than adequate given a normal appetite. *Glasierte Putenleber mit buntem Nudelauflauf* (turkey liver with noodles *au gratin* and zucchini) or *Schwammerlterrine* (terrine of wood mushrooms) both from the '*Schmankerln*' section would make good light luncheon dishes. Soups are particularly good and again rather regional, like *Kukuruzcremesuppe mit Paprikaschoten* (cream of corn soup with green or red peppers) or the mushroom ravioli in potato soup (*Schwammerlravioli in der Erdäpfelsuppe*). Choosing from the 'full-size' main courses I was very taken with the *Gulasch von österr. Fischen* (*Gulasch* of Austrian fish with strips of green pepper) and with the rack of lamb (*glasierter Lammrücken*) served with a broccoli purée and potatoes cooked with tomatoes, a typically local mixture. *Schaumröllchen mit Calvadoscreme* (small rolls of puff pastry filled with Calvadoscream) served with an apple sorbet was a rather inspired pudding, as was the honey-cake soufflé (*Lebkuchen Auflauf*) with iced vanilla sauce.

Exemplary wine list (with the exception of French champagne exclusively Burgenland wines). Ask for the *Tageskarte* for a list of *Prädikatsweine* sold by the glass.

Emmersdorf (Wachau) — ***Lower Austria***

LANDGASTHOF PRITZ 'ZUM SCHWARZEN BÄREN'
3644 Emmersdorf
☏ 02752 7249
Open: 8.00–23.00 (kitchen 11.00–21.00)
Closed: Tuesday
Prices: inexpensive

The original inn dated back to 1670 when the licence extended to 'dealing in salt and iron'. Burned down during the Napoleonic Wars and faithfully restored, the 'Black Bear' has remained a family inn in the best Austrian tradition, serving good, heart-warming food throughout the day. One of the places where you can get what is fondly known as a *Frühstücksgulasch* (breakfast in this case meaning a mid-morning snack!) in sizes small and large and a freshly cooked *Wiener Schnitzel* during mid-afternoon, should you have missed lunch and feel peckish by then. There are good local specialities like *Weinlandschnitzel* and *Wachauer Knödelreindl*, a slight misnomer since it is not just 'a panful of dumplings'. It consists of black pudding, ham, speck, as well as a sliced up dumpling with lightly scrambled egg – you will certainly not need a starter and hardly have room for a pudding! The *Tagesmenü* is quite extensive, ranging from the typical *Bauernschmaus* or *gebratener Lammschlögel* (roast leg of lamb) both served with *Waldviertlerknödel* (potato dumplings) and *Speckkraut* to nicely garnished cold roast beef and exemplary Steak Tartar. Nice local touches too, like the *Hausweckerl* – particularly good crisp rolls – and if there's room left for pudding, try the *Wachauer Mohntorte*, a lovely moist cake with crushed poppy-seeds. Good Wachau wines, of course, as well as beer from the woods and *Wachauer Marillenbrand* (apricot eau-de-vie).

There are some comfortable, moderately priced rooms at the Schwarzen Bären and a brand-new, rather elegant hotel at the back which fits into the landscape perfectly. Complete with garden, terrace and heated swimming-pool. A hidden treasure – which it will not remain for long – and still very reasonably priced.

Feld am See ***Carinthia***

HUBMANNHOF
Wiesen 8
9544 Feld am See
☏ 04246 2667
Open: 8.00–22.00
Closed: some time in November (variable)
Prices: inexpensive

Once the property of the princely Porcias, a centuries-old farmhouse set on a hill, with scented meadows sloping down to the valley. You can drive right up to the front door, but it might be prudent to walk at least the last stretch to work up an appetite, for the food is certainly hearty. Everything is home-produced – milk, butter, meat – and of course home-made sausages. The surprisingly large menu contains many local specialities like *Gegentaler Gelbe Suppe* (a rich soup which is not often found on restaurant menus) and *Kärntner Ritschert*, a thick stew with barley and home-smoked pork. The set lunch is very good value; the last time I was there it consisted of clear broth with meat strudel, followed by a large *Wiener Schnitzel* with salad and a purée of local apples for about S100.-. There are good snacks too such as local cheeses and home-cured pork, but if you just care to order a glass of milk (or buttermilk or sour milk) they'll be perfectly happy as well. Alternatively, you could try one of the rather fierce spirits like *Latschengeist* (fir), *Enzian* (gentian) and *Wacholder* (juniper).

The Hubmannhof is a lovely, peaceful place at which to stay – comfortably and reasonably – a genuine, 'away from it all' spot, yet within a stone's throw of towns such as Villach and near several lakes (hardly surprising since there are 1,270 lakes in Carinthia!) and lakeside resorts.

How to get there: On 98 from Villach direction Radenthein, through Afritz and past Lake Afritz. At the end of Lake Afritz turn left at the petrol station and the Hubmannhof is about 300m further up the hill.

Feldkirch ***Vorarlberg***

TREFF
Mühletorplatz 2
6800 Feldkirch
☏ 05522 28746
Open: daily from 10.00–1.00 (limited menu between 14.00–16.00)
Prices: inexpensive/moderate

'Treff' which means meeting place is small and bright and modern, yet it fits in beautifully with small and ancient Feldkirch – an ideal meeting place whether it is just for drinks or a large or small meal. Excellent soups – not only as starters, but to round off a late night out: *Bodenseefischsuppe* (fish soup from Lake Constance) is practically a meal in itself and the same could be said of the onion soup. Very good light salads and substantial baguettes filled with ham and herbs or with cheese, fried egg and onion or – my own favourite – mushrooms in a light cream and wine sauce. Cassoulet is another speciality, usually giving a choice of goose and pork. The *Tageskarte* is short, but very seasonal and everything is absolutely fresh. The traditional *Tafelspitz* (boiled beef) comes with an untraditional cucumber sauce and Swiss *Rösti* (Feldkirch is border town to Switzerland), but a large dish of *Pfifferlinge mit Rahm und Speck* (chanterelles with cream, bacon and a dumpling) could not be more Austrian. Good light puddings like *Apfelküchle* (*Vorarlberg* for apple fritters) with vanilla sauce and ice-creams including *Wiener Eiskaffee* with a dash of liqueur.

As befits a 'meeting place' the list of beverages is rather extensive, including some unusual non-alcoholic drinks and there are good Austrian and South Tyrolean wines sold by the quarter litre.

Fischamend — *Lower Austria*

MERZENDORFER
Hainburger Strasse 1
2401 Fischamend
☏ 02232 314
Open: all day, hot food from 11.00–14.00 and 17.30–22.00
Closed: from 16.00 Sunday and all day Monday, also during August
Prices: moderate

There's a fish atop the local medieval tower and you could be forgiven for thinking that there might be a connection between this and the name of the little town. Not so – the name is derived from the River Fischa which used to flow into the Danube at this point, i.e. it 'came to an end'. Fish does however feature prominently at Merzendorfer which has been in the same family since 1865 – and famous even before the days of the legendary Hermine Merzendorfer, known as 'Madame Sacher of Fischamend'. Visitors came not only from Vienna, but also from Bratislava – just across the border in Czechoslovakia now – in the days when it was still called Pressburg or Poszony, depending on whether you were Austrian or Hungarian, and when there was no border to cross. Merzendorfer is still immensely popular – I know people who on arriving at Schwechat Airport first turn east for Fischamend and Merzendorfer before travelling to Vienna – and it can get pretty crowded at lunch-time, even in winter. Not a luxurious setting, but a good solid little country inn, particularly pleasant on a warm summer evening when you can sit out of doors and a breeze wafts over from the Danube. It seems almost a sacrilege to order anything except fish, particularly as there are specialities which you are unlikely to find elsewhere: *Fischbeuschelsuppe* for instance, the thick creamy fish soup traditionally served only at Christmas. Try pike with anchovy butter, or pike/perch with a saffron sauce (menus are translated into three languages, except for the specialities of the day). Although there are some good puddings from which to choose, look no further than the *Esterhazy Schnitte* a great speciality of the house. (Quite wrongly described as hazelnut flan on the menu – wafer-thin pastry layered with butter cream and absolutely delicious!) Stick to Austrian wines seeing that they described a Muscadet de Sevres et Maine as 'a wine from Alsace' on one of their menus, but do not let that prejudice you in any way!

How to get there: from the centre of Vienna via Rennweg which leads into Simmeringer Hauptstrasse. Continue on this road, passing Vienna's huge municipal cemetery (*Zentralfriedhof*) on the right. At the fork keep left, signposted 'Hainburger Bundesstrasse 9' and later 'Hainburg/ Fischamend'. Keep on 9 – airport on right, oil refinery on left – until you come to Fischamend. Merzendorfer is on the left on the main road in Fischamend.

Forchtenstein — *Burgenland*

REISNER
Hauptstrasse 141
7212 Forchtenstein
☏ 02626 63139
Open: 8.15–23.00 (kitchen 11.30–14.30, 18.00–22.00)
Closed: Wednesday and for a fortnight following Ash Wednesday
Prices: inexpensive/moderate

Forchtenstein certainly warrants a visit – in spring when the fortress wreathed in cherry blossoms looks more like a fairy-tale castle than the fierce fortress which has withstood invaders time and again, in summer when the air is thick with the scent of wild sage and strawberries ripening in the fields, and at all times of the year for Reisner, one of the more unusual restaurants in Austria. An ordinary village inn on first impression – complete with *Stammtisch* with 'regulars' having a drink or a mid-morning snack in the front room (the rather elegant dining-room lies beyond, though you may well prefer a table on the small terrace outside). One look at the menu will tell you that this is no ordinary village inn, for which ordinary village inn would offer you *marc* and *eaux-de-vie* from no less than six different distillers (and include rarities such as *eau-de-vie* made from vineyard peaches, quinces and morello cherries)? Or air-dried lamb with a delicate salad of apple, cheese and walnuts? Goose liver is cooked with ceps and Sirloin steak served with a delicious bone marrow and herb sauce. Game dishes are particularly good – *medaillons* of venison with goose-liver (this is goose-liver country, after all), small dumplings and rather deliciously cooked marrow. If you like roast suckling pig, it is usually served with a warm cabbage *Strudel* and marjoram potatoes. There are two set menus as a rule and on my last visit I was rather impressed by the lower-priced (S225.-) one, starting with a soup of fresh peas and small gnocchi which took me straight back to my childhood, followed by pike/perch with watercress sauce and ending with *Topfenknödel* (very light curd cheese dumplings) with honey-cake crumbs fried in butter and strawberry purée.

The list of puddings proves once more that this is no ordinary country inn: Rose-hip *parfait* with warm waffles and peach sauce, *Strudel* filled with local grapes, good gâteaux and *brauner Kirschenkuchen* (dark cherry cake made from local cherries).

Excellent wine list which accentuates local Burgenland wines, with many of the special wines sold by the glass.

How to get there: On the S.31 from Eisenstadt, exit to Forchtenstein should bring you straight into Hauptstrasse (which looks like a suburban road rather than the 'high street' of Forchtenstein). Reisner is on the right and there is usually plenty of parking space in the road.

Friesach — *Carinthia*

CRAIGHER
Hauptplatz 3
Friesach
☏ 04268 2295
Open: 7.00–2.00
Closed: Sundays
Prices: inexpensive

Small, medieval and moated, Friesach is not only the oldest town in Carinthia, but also one of its most attractive ones. Parked cars in the main square obscure the Renaissance fountain and you may as well park your car and explore Friesach on foot (call at the very helpful tourist office at Hauptplatz 1 for information and guidance) and return to the main square towards the evening when most of the visitors (and their cars) will have departed. There is no better place from which to survey the scene than Craigher's where the selection of *pâtisserie* may be small, but superb and their Ribislkuchen (pastry topped with redcurrants nestling in clouds of meringue) is one of the best I've ever tasted. The coffee is good and strong and you could, of course, also order a savoury snack and a glass of wine. I am credibly told by the friendly waitress that 'at night' (time unspecified and Craigher's stays open until 2 a.m.) the place is 'more of a bar than a coffee house', whatever that may mean. Night-life in medieval Friesach, with the moon illuminating the fortress ruins and playing on the Renaissance fountain is something yet to be experienced. Perhaps you'll stay on and let me know!

How to get there: from Klagenfurt on 83 direction St Veit an der Glan. Continue on 83 past St Veit to Friesach. Craigher is in the main square on the right.

Frohnleiten — ***Styria***

WEISSENBACHER
Grazer Strasse 2
8130 Frohnleiten
☏ 03126 2334
Open: 9.00–22.00
Prices: inexpensive

Frohnleiten, as seen from across the River Mur looks exactly like a toy town, its multi-coloured houses set down very carefully by a giant's hands – and the best vantage point for seeing it is from the garden and terraced dining-room at Weissenbacher's. It is the best place for food too – an enormous, rather jolly inn with rather robust food of excellent quality (its own butchery supplies meat and sausages) and enormous portions. You know exactly where you are at Weissenbacher's, where a special section on the menu headed '*Jausengerichte*, warm' (hot dishes for a mid-morning or mid-afternoon snack) lists *Gulasch, Tellerfleisch* (literally 'a platter of meat') and *Flecksuppe* (tripe soup, though really more of a stew and practically a meal in itself), as well as the more obvious toasts sausages – and snails in herb butter (Styrian snails are excellent, but mostly exported – you may care to enjoy them whilst you have the chance). Viennese as well as regional specialities are well represented on the menu: *Mastochsenfleisch* (a great dish of boiled beef) is still served in the traditional way with a garnish of different sauces and vegetables. Weissenbacher's carefully list both *Kalbswienerschnitzerl* and *Schweinswienerschnitzerl* on the menu (*Wiener Schnitzel* made with veal and pork respectively), not to be confused with *Kalbsnaturschnitzel* – veal lightly cooked in butter, a pork version also being available, of course, and *Kalbsschnitzerl mit frischen Kräutern* where the veal is cooked with cream and fresh herbs. Home-made brawn comes with a salad of large beans dressed with green pumpkin-seed oil, as is the *Steirische Salatschüssel* which includes strips of beef. There's good Styrian cheese (*Glunken*) with a pumpkin-seed oil vinaigrette, and country ham. You may not want a great pudding after all this, though their walnut soufflé has been much commended (it's enough for three to four people though!). In which case have a *Nusskipferl* (croissant filled with walnuts) with your coffee! (Ice-cream for diabetics is also available).

How to get there: from graz on S.35 direction Bruck an der Mur. Exit at Frohnleiten – Weissenbacher is just before the bridge which leads into the old part of the town.

Gralla — *Styria*

ROSENBERGER AUTOBAHNRESTAURANT GRALLA-OST
(Steirer Rast)
8430 Gralla
☏ 03452 4771
A.9 Motorway – accessible only from one direction
Open: 6.00–23.00 June/October
6.00–22.00 November/May
Prices: moderate

For description see under Motorway Restaurants (Rosenberger)

Graz — *Styria*

CAFÉ KONDITOREI STREHLY
Sporgasse 14
8010 Graz
☏ 0316 813030
Open: 7.00–19.00 Monday/Saturday
Closed: Sunday
Prices: moderate

Sporgasse which rises steeply from Graz's main squares is full of treasures and surprises: a charming courtyard here, a strange doubly twisted staircase there, a fine old jewellery shop, the oldest restaurant in Graz 'Zur goldenen Pastete' (q.v.) and the oldest *pâtisserie* – Strehly's. According to one Austrian writer there was an elderly gentleman who always stopped outside Strehly's, waiting for the door to open, just to get a whiff of that special scent of 'vanilla and raspberry, cinnamon and icing sugar, chocolate and coffee' which took him back to his childhood. Strehly's really is the *pâtisserie par excellence* – glass counters piled high with delicacies of which I rate the wild strawberry gâteau highest. Others swear that the marzipan should top the list and there are, of course, true devotees of the two house specialities, *Schlossbergtorte* and *Schlossbergkugeln*, wondrous confections in which nougat and chocolate cream, walnut marzipan, caramel and toasted almond play prominent parts. You can start your day early at Strehly's – there's a splendid breakfast buffet – have a light lunch (good salads, filled croissants and freshly baked onion tart) or one of their delicious hot puddings like *Milchrahmstrudel* (*Strudel* filled with curd cheese baked with cream), pancakes stuffed with curd cheese (*Topfenpalatschinken*) or one of their excellent ice-creams. Like all *pâtisseries* in Austria, Strehly's is fully licensed and please note that as in all the best *pâtisseries* in Austria yesterday's buns and pastries are carefully labelled thus 'vom Vortag'. Should there be any left over that is, which does not happen often and then only in small quantities.

ELISABETHOF (formerly LAUFKE)
Elisabethstrasse 6
8010 Graz
☎ 0316 33470
Open: daily from 11.30–22.45 ('limited' menu between 14.30–18.00)
Prices: inexpensive/moderate

Well-established and reassuring, you can always rely on Laufke for good food in comfortable, if somewhat staid, surroundings. Special events such as asparagus weeks or Italian weeks (after all, Italy is practically 'down the road') add a touch of festivity to the menu which is much appreciated by Graz 'regulars' as a change from the good local fare which they can enjoy all year round. As a visitor I'd advise sticking to good regional cooking as you are unlikely to find *Grammelstrudelsuppe* (beef broth with a Strudel filled with crispy bits of crackling) or *Steirische Milchsuppe* (Styrian milk soup) anywhere else, and the same goes for their lamb specialities, or Styrian cutlets (*Steirisches Kotelett*) served with a warm potato and chicory salad dressed with Styrian pumpkin-seed oil. There are simple, rather robust dishes such as *Speckknödel auf Kürbismus* (dumplings with creamed marrow – in Styria there are countless delectable ways of cooking that much maligned vegetable), *Steirischer Linseneintopf* (a marvellous lentil stew with sausages) and *Rahmschwammerln mit Heidensterz* (creamed mushrooms with Sterz – the Styrian version of Polenta). Salads are fairly hearty too – *Linsensalat mit Speck* (lentil salad with fried bacon), *Käferbohnensalat* (large dried beans about the size of small chestnuts – and tasting not unlike these), all dressed with pumpkin-seed oil, of course. All this sounds – and frankly is – rather filling food, though you could of course opt for something a little less robust, like trout dusted with buckwheat flour and crisply fried. This doesn't leave much space for puddings, but they have a remarkably light hand with these as their *Schneenockerl* would prove: 'floating islands', this time floating on a 'lake' of blueberry purée. Good wines sold by the quarter litre and of course excellent Styrian beer.

The adjoining foodshop – fully licensed – is open at the same time as the restaurant and much favoured by the worthy citizens of Graz.

ERZHERZOG JOHANN
Sackstrasse 3–5
8011 Graz
☏ 0316 811681
Open: 11.00–14.30, 18.00–22.30
Prices: moderate

A hostelry as far back as the sixteenth century, Archduke Ferdinand – who was later to become Emperor Ferdinand II – arranged for an inspection of the building in 1595 to ensure that it would meet the requirements of 'most noble personages'. It remained one of the few hostelries within the city walls until the beginning of the eighteenth century when the house was rebuilt as town residence for a noble family and noted for the opulence of its interior and splendid ceremonial rooms. The building returned to being a hotel during the nineteenth century, special permission for it to be called Erzherzog Johann having been granted by the self-same Archduke, who rates practically as the patron saint of Styria (he married a postmaster's daughter from local Bad Aussee). It is a marvellous building which has somehow retained both the snugness of an old inn and the leisurely elegance of a noble town residence, one of the great attractions being the arcaded courtyard with its cascades of greenery, now covered with a glass roof and used as a lofty dining-room.

As practically everywhere in Graz, there is always an inexpensive lunch menu, but choosing à la carte gives you the chance of sampling Austrian and particularly Styrian specialities which are not often found elsewhere: *Steirische Krensuppe* (horse-radish soup) and a creamy soup made with pumpkin seeds (*Oststeirische Kürbiscremesuppe*), *Rindfleisch Alt Graz* (an excellent beef salad) and *Steirisches Ritschert* (smoked pork with barley and beans) are nearly always on the menu, with the *Tageskarte* offering further and more seasonal pleasures – *Medaillons* of veal in a snail sauce and excellent game and mushroom dishes. A section of the menu '*Aus der Naturküche*' is devoted to vegetarian specialities.

There's a good choice of puddings – try the poppy-seed pudding (*Mohnauflauf*) with vanilla sauce or the *Wachauer Palatschinke* (pancakes filled with vanilla cream and hot grape sauce), not strictly Styrian, but well worth the excursion into another region.

Good selection of wines, and of course excellent Styrian beer.

Erzherzog Johann

GERLINDE'S GASTHAUS
Bürgergasse 4
(Entrance Abraham-a-Santa-Clara-Gasse)
8010 Graz
☏ 0316 813830
Open: 17.00–24.00 Monday/Saturday
Closed: Sundays
Prices: moderate

Some new restaurants give the impression that they've been there all the time, and Gerlinde's is exactly that sort of place. It feels comfortable, well lived-in and the scene of many happy meals, and if the almost life-size mural of a bearded Franz Josef and his beautiful Empress in one of the dining-rooms could be considered *Kitsch* by some, it is *Kitsch* of a rather endearing kind and the adjoining Jagdstüberl should satisfy the more fastidious tastes. Above all, there's that undefinable aura of good cooking – you know the food is going to be as pleasant as the surroundings before you've even looked at the menu. Try a Grafensteiner Apfelbrand – Styrian apple brandy at its best – whilst you ponder on what to order and note the nice balance between good regional cooking and flights into higher gastronomic spheres: Styrian country pâté, a rather hearty *Bauernsalat* with strips of beef, potatoes and hard-boiled egg as starters, as well as delicate chicken livers in aspic and creamy soup made with smoked trout. Veal *Gulasch* (*Kalbsrahmgulasch*) is properly accompanied with *Nockerl vom Brett* (small gnocchi which are snipped off from a board directly into boiling salt water) and pink rack of lamb roasted with thyme comes with *Rahmkohl* (creamed savoy cabbage which many restaurants have long since forgotten) and potato croquettes. As Styria is apple country try *Mousse vom Steirischen Apfel* (apple mousse) or the *Kürbiskernparfait* (*parfait* made with green pumpkin seeds) – another Styrian speciality which is served with honey.

The wines are mostly Austrian with strong emphasis on Styria and Burgenland, supported by Italy.

HÄUSERL IM WALD
Roseggerweg 105
8044 Graz – Mariatrost
☏ 0316 391165
Open: 6.30–24.00
Closed: Mondays
Prices: inexpensive

Mariatrost, on the outskirts of Graz, is known for its important pilgrimage church and like all places of pilgrimage, it abounds in good restaurants. None friendlier than the Häuserl im Wald (little house in the woods) which sits very prettily on a hill, overlooking Styria's green lands. For all its modern aspects – soft, polished wood, large picture windows and paved terrace – there's a thoroughly old-fashioned (in the nicest possible sense) attitude towards food; everything is fresh, freshly cooked and cooked exactly to the customer's wishes. If you order *Steirisches Backhuhn* (fried spring chicken) you are asked for the exact shade to which you want it fried – from blond to dark brown – and whether you want it 'with' or 'without' skin. As everywhere else in Graz, the set luncheons are particularly inexpensive and one of these might well consist of 'soup and pudding' (on my last visit good clear broth with *tortellini,* followed by a large pancake stuffed with sweet curd cheese and topped with caramel sauce). The standard menu is available in English, but look to the *Tageskarte* (which they will gladly interpret) for seasonal specialities like mushroom dishes, various vegetables such as aubergines, courgettes and cauliflower crisply fried in batter and a whole host of other good things. Cakes and pastries come from their own *pâtisserie,* which makes the terrace a favourite spot for mid-morning or mid-afternoon snacks (breakfast too, for that matter!). Good Styrian beer, of course, plus a fair selection of wines sold by the quarter litre.

Two nearby guesthouses – Cäcilia and Sonne – are owned by the same family – modern, comfortable and very reasonably priced.

How to get there: via Heinrichstrasse, Mariatroststrasse and Hans Mauracherstrasse or by Tram No.1 from Graz (alight at Roseggerweg).

HOFCAFÉ EDEGGER-TAX
Hofgasse 8
8010 Graz
☎ 0316 830239
Open: 7.00–19.00 Monday/Saturday
Closed: Sundays
Prices: moderate

'Hofbäckerei' stands for 'court bakers' and the Imperial double eagle is firmly affixed above the thick wooden portals of Edegger-Tax. It is a marvellous shop, heady with the scent of freshly baked bread mingled with spice, and the only shop I know where you may sample the different kinds of bread before buying. Edegger-Tax proudly proclaim that they were first established in 1569 which makes them the oldest bakery in Graz and their Hofcafé next door a mere fledgling since it opened as 'recently' as 1955! Open in time for early breakfasts when the wonderful scent of baking wafts over from next door and of course you get the very best selection of bread, rolls and croissants. Good for snacks during the day as well – try their crisp *Kornspitz* – an elongated roll – filled with ham. In the afternoon the Hofcafé comes into its own with freshly baked pastries and cakes – absolutely irresistible even if the place tends to get crowded at times.

HOFKELLER (Restaurant Schögler)
Hofgasse 8
8010 Graz
☏ 0316 832439
Open: 11.00–14.00, 18.00–24.00 (kitchen until 22.00)
Closed: Sundays, also three weeks in July and two weeks in December
Prices: moderate

My definition of extravagance is ordering à la carte at lunch in Graz where the choice of fixed-price set meals (*Mittagsmenü*) is about the best in Austria. At inns small and large, stately or secluded restaurants, a rather good three-course meal usually costs less than a main dish from the à la carte menu. The Hofkeller is a shining example: rated as one of the best restaurants in Graz and for years a more or less well-kept secret ('for goodness sake don't tell anyone – otherwise it will get overcrowded'), yet at lunch there's an excellent three-course *menü* for S105.- (If the price goes up before this book is published it will only be a marginal increase). Probably the best value in town – try it to get acquainted with the charming and elegant Hofkeller, to return in the evening when the setting is even more exclusive, not to say romantic, and this will be the time to concentrate on the à la carte selection. You could of course opt for the *Feinschmeckermenü* which is still a remarkable bargain at S350.- for five courses, but I prefer to choose à la carte in the evening, starting perhaps with a smoked tongue salad with celeriac or oxtail soup with small ravioli filled with bone marrow. *Medaillons* of lamb with creamed lentils were a particularly good choice as a main course (as was the roast lamb and the roast quail with duck's liver on other occasions) and when I saw the delicious-looking smoked ox-tongue at my neighbour's table I began having regrets for choosing tongue as a starter. Sorbets at the Hofkeller are outstandingly good, and I was rather taken with the rum *parfait* with caramelized apples.

There is a small but nicely balanced wine list, strong on Austrian and particularly Styrian wines, but also including some interesting choices from Friuli and South Tyrol.

HOTEL DANIEL
Europaplatz 1
8021 Graz
☏ 0316 911080
Open: 11.30–15.00, 18.00–22.30
Closed: 22 December–7 January
Prices: moderate

Station restaurants in Austria's provincial capitals were renowned for the excellence of their food – a reputation that appears to have been transferred (deservedly so) to the restaurants in the hotel nearest to the station – like the Bayrischer Hof in Salzburg and the Daniel in Graz. Graz abounds in restaurants offering excellent cooking at reasonable prices in settings ranging from rural sturdiness to great elegance – if customers (both business and private) crowd into the Daniel's dining-room near the station, the only reason must be the quality of the food. Not that the setting is anything like that of a station restaurant; the dining-room is light and airy, the atmosphere relaxed and the service impeccable. As everywhere in Graz, there's a reasonably priced set lunch (S165.- for four courses) as well as a *Tellergericht* (*Plat du jour*) if you are in a hurry (on my last visit the *Tellergericht* was a good-sized pork escalope with a large mixed salad for S85.-), but the Daniel calls for a more leisurely approach – it is a splendid chance to try some of the Styrian specialities (duly marked with a panther, the Styrian emblem) on the menu such as *Brennessel Schlutzkrapferl* (small pasta envelopes filled with a purée of nettles and farmhouse cheese, served with brown butter), rack of lamb roast with thyme (*Lammrücken in Thymiansaft*) or *Schweinslungenbraten* (roast pork) served with glazed onions and *Schwammerlgröstl* (Styrian version of Tyrolean *Gröstl* using mushrooms instead of meat and served as an accompaniment).

There are always some good vegetarian dishes, like a *Polentastrudel* with boletus mushrooms or wholemeal pancakes with vegetable and cheese stuffing.

Do not miss out on the Styrian puddings – there's a beautiful *Griessflammerie* with egg liqueur and wild strawberries, or light apple dumplings (*Steirische Apfelknödel*) with toasted pumpkin seeds and sabayon.

Very good wine list – mostly Austrian – many of which are available by the glass. Excellent range of eaux-de-vie, including some from Zieser of Riegersburg.

PLABUTSCHER SCHLÖSSL
Göstinger Strasse 149
8051 Graz
☏ 0316 571055
Open: 19.00–24.00 (kitchen 23.00)
Closed: Sundays
Prices: moderate/upward

Towered and turretted and reached by a steep driveway, the Schlössl looks a bit like a mellowed version of Dracula's castle, particularly if first approached on a dark winter's night. It was in fact built at the turn of the century for a rich Italian wine merchant who, for all one knows, had set his heart on settling in a castle in suburban Graz. (Do ask to see the original bathroom which has been left in all its turn-of-the century splendour!) Empty for some years, the ground floor has now been transformed into a rather splendid restaurant. You may disapprove of the setting and some of the furnishings which border on the pleasantly absurd, but there are compensations: the wide spacing of tables giving plenty of privacy without the feeling of being lost in a desert, the attentive service and above all, the truly excellent cooking created by Willi Haider, one of the most imaginative chefs in Austria. (Haider has now left to run his own cooking academy and only acts in a consulting capacity, but the legacy he left is great and on my last visit since his departure there was certainly no lowering of standards.) *Cappuccino* of forest mushrooms – a Haider speciality – was as sensationally good a starter as ever – light, frothy, yet strongly flavoured. Trout came with a cream of fresh red peppers – a particularly good combination – and the rack of lamb – roasted to pink perfection and accompanied by a *gratin* of potatoes and zucchini – could not have been bettered. Excellent cheese board, featuring some interesting Austrian cheeses and, as was only to be expected, marvellous puddings. I thought that my honey-cake soufflé with red wine sabayon could not be surpassed, but my companion raved over the mousse of quinces with elderberries and cinnamon ice-cream. (There had been appreciative murmurs about his light cream soup with smoked trout and the venison ravioli with juniper cream and cranberries).

Outstanding selection of Styrian wines, supported by the rest of Austria, Italy, Spain and France – many sold by the glass. Eaux-de-vie from Zieser of Riegersburg and the Plabutscher Schlössl is not too grand to sell a 'whistle' (*Pfiff* of beer (⅛ litre).

How to get there: take a taxi from wherever you are staying in Graz, otherwise you'll get lost – if not on the way there, certainly on the way back, and there are no guest rooms at the Schlössl!

STAINZERBAUER
Bürgergasse 4
8010 Graz
☏ 0316 821106
Open: 11.00–24.00 and beyond, Monday/Saturday
Closed: Sundays
Prices: inexpensive/moderate

A very 'in' inn, where everybody knows everybody, where the *Stammgäste* (regulars) outnumber casual visitors by far, but where you will be engulfed by the warm family atmosphere in no time. From Monday to Friday there is an excellent, very inexpensive, two-course lunch (usually around S60.-) as well as a daily 'five-minute dish' served between noon and 2 p.m. (If it arrives later than five minutes after being ordered, there's no need to pay) for people in a hurry, and possibly also for those who have no wish to join in the family atmosphere. For those who do, but do not want a large meal, there are some good salads as well as a selection headed *Schmankerl* (specials) which includes spinach gnocchi (*Spinatnockerl*) and Styrian as well as Carinthian specialities. For more leisurely diners there are some good Styrian soups like *Schwammerlsuppe mit Heidensterz* (mushroom soup with crisply fried buckwheat) and *Klachelsuppe* (hearty soup based on pork and possibly more of an acquired taste) as well as the usual clear beef broth with its infinite variety of additions. Good selection of main dishes including *Rindsfiletgulasch* (very rich stew with a creamy paprika sauce, to which chanterelles, strips of pickled cucumber and hot green peppers have been added) being particularly popular. *Figaroteller Dietmar* may not always be found on the menu, but it is always available on request – two minute-steaks with pepper-sauce – named after the best hairdresser in Graz (or anywhere for that matter) who is clearly also a regular. *Besoffene Liesl* (drunken Lizzie) is a rather light pudding, steeped in spiced wine which is well worth trying, as is the *Kürbiskernparfait* made with pumpkin seeds.

Excellent *eaux-de-vie* and, of course, splendid Styrian beer.

ZUR GOLDENEN PASTETE
Sporgasse 28
8010 Graz
☏ 0316 823416
Open: 11.00–24.00 Monday/Friday
Closed: Saturday and Sunday
Prices: inexpensive

'Zur goldenen Pastete' is the oldest inn in Graz and the building has remained virtually unchanged since the sixteenth century. Cosy and comfortable, with a certain sturdy elegance in the upstairs rooms, it is exactly the sort of inn one would expect at the top of Graz's ancient Sporgasse. The food is predictable up to a point and in the nicest possible way. The menu, which has a special section headed *Schmankerln* ('selected specials') contains many of the favourite 'inn' dishes such as *Schinkenfleckerln* (pasta with ham), *Rahmbeuscherl* (q.v.), *Steirisches Krenfleisch* (pork with horse-radish) as well as good vegetarian dishes such as Potato Strudel (*Erdäpfelstrudel*) and *Vollwertspätzle* (gnocchi made with wholemeal flour). Vegetarian dishes also feature prominently on the daily menu: asparagus risotto (*Spargelrisotto*) or a *Strudel* filled with spinach (*Spinatstrudel*), *Kohlrabiragout* or fried aubergines with sauce tartar. The fixed-price menu is incredibly reasonable – even for Graz – on my last visit the two-course lunch was S66.- (good vegetable soup, followed by stuffed breast of veal, Styrian style)! I can also recommend their salad of lamb's lettuce with potatoes and crisped *Speck* (dressed with Styrian pumpkin-seed oil, of course) which was excellent. Good puddings too, like small apple dumplings with wine sauce.

'Zur goldenen Pastete' is owned by one of the best breweries in Austria so try some good Styrian beer if you have not already done so, though of course there's an adequate wine list.

Grossram — ***Lower Austria***

ROSENBERGER AUTOBAHNRESTAURANT GROSSRAM
3033 Grossram
☏ 02773 6651
Open: 6.00–23.00 June/October
6.00–22.00 November/May
Prices: moderate

A.1 West Motorway – accessible from both directions
Motor Hotel

For description see under Motorway Restaurants (Rosenberger)

Haag — ***Lower Austria***

ROSENBERGER AUTOBAHNRESTAURANT HAAG
(Most-Viertel Rast)
3350 Haag
Open: 6.00–23.00 June/October
6.00–22.00 November/May
Prices: moderate

A.1 West Motorway – accessible only from one direction

For description see under Motorway Restaurants (Rosenberger)

Haag Stadt *Lower Austria*

SCHAFELNER
Hauptplatz 11
3350 Haag Stadt
☏ 0734 42411
Open: 12.00–14.00, 18.00–23.00 or later (kitchen 22.00) Wednesday/Sunday
Closed: Monday, Tuesday
Prices: upward

Haag Stadt is about half-way between Vienna and Salzburg, only a few kilometres from the Motorway. Not a particularly exciting little town, yet most of my friends plan their journeys so as to reach Haag in time for lunch or dinner and on days other than Monday or Tuesday, for that's when Schafelner is closed. And Schafelner would warrant a very much larger detour (and even a special journey): a delightful country inn with quite exceptional cooking. The building which has housed a hostelry (as well as a bakery in the olden days) since the eighteenth century has had its beautiful baroque façade sympathetically restored in recent years. The inside is rather rustic, almost like a well-kept hunting lodge and I can never make up my mind whether I prefer the charming green and white Kaiserzimmer or the dining-room panelled in dark polished wood with its secluded tables, each one almost enclosed in its own booth. In summer there's of course the secluded garden without which no real Austrian restaurant would be complete. Schafelner rightly calls itself *'Spezialitätenrestaurant'* for specialities abound like *Mostviertler Mostsuppe* (soup made with the local apple wine) or a delicious dish of broad noodles with mushrooms and sweetbreads (*Pilznudeln mit Bries*) and *Kübel-Speckknöderl mit schwarzem Rettich* (very light bacon dumplings served with black radish). The last two dishes are intended as starters, but would make a good main course. Choosing from the 'proper' main courses I can strongly recommend the saddle of lamb (*Lammrücken*) baked in Rösti and the venison with juniper cream lentils, and morel gnocchi or the more sturdy *Schweinshaxerln mit Grammelstrudel* if only for sake of the latter (thin *Strudel* paste enclosing a savoury filling of crackling) as indeed most of the accompaniments at Schafelners are noteworthy, like their *Grammelkrapferl* (small baked mounds with crackling). Of course all the good stalwart favourites are there as well, beautifully cooked, like *Zwiebelrostbraten*, calves liver in Madeira sauce and *Tafelspitz*. Puddings include lovely long-forgotten Viennese specialities like *Schmankerlparfait* (q.v.) with morello cherries as well as *Schneenockerl* (floating islands), prunes in Armagnac with a caramel sauce and lemon sorbet and the very rural *Mostschober* a sort of culinary homage to the local apple wine.

Outstanding selection of wines many of which are sold by the glass, but if time allows ask to visit the wine cellar.

At the moment there's only limited accommodation at Schafelner's, but additional and very comfortable rooms are planned for next year. I can foresee the 'absolute necessity' of an overnight stop at Haag in the near future!

How to get there: from Salzburg or Vienna on A.1. Exit Haag Stadt – Schafelner is right in the centre of the small town.

Heiligenkreuz im Lafnitztal — *Burgenland*

GIBISER
7561 Heiligenkreuz
☏ 03325 216
Open: 11.00–22.00
Closed: Mondays (December/March only) and 1–15 February
Prices: inexpensive

Close to the Hungarian border and definitely worth a detour and even a special journey for the peaceful setting, pleasant rooms (accommodation is also available in four eighteenth-century vintners' cottages set in the large grounds) and above all, for the excellent food. It is a very seasonal menu, relying much on regional produce as well as specialities (described as Pannonian aka Hungarian) such as *Krautrouladen* (cabbage leaves with spicy meat filling), *Buchweizendalken* (thick buckwheat pancakes) served with creamy mushrooms and puddings such as *Somloer Nockerl,* a featherlight concoction of chocolate and cream on a sponge base. *Pannonischer Bauernteller* makes the best of fresh herbs – a great mound of home-made noodles with curd cheese, ham, strips of chicken breast, all in a creamy herb sauce and served with a crisp green salad. Remembering, however, that most good Austrian restaurants also pride themselves on their Viennese cooking, there's *Wiener Suppentopf* (*pot au feu*) and Gibiser's is the only restaurant I know where they offer *frisches Kohlrabigemüse mit gekochtem Rindfleisch* (a dish of young Kohlrabi accompanied by boiled beef) and not the other way round, keeping their priorities absolutely right. Don't miss out on the *Früchtestanitzl* – cornets of crisp pastry filled with a light cream and fruits of the season – good Burgenland strawberries more often than not. Selection of wines is short, but to the point – practically all Austrian, many of which are served by the quarter litre.

How to get there: from Eisenstadt on 50 (or S.31 changing to 50) to Oberwart, thence on 57 via Güssing to Heiligenkreuz.

Hof nr. Salzburg *Salzburg*

HOTEL SCHLOSS FUSCHL
5322 Hof bei Salzburg
☏ 06229 22530
Open: lunch 12.00–14.00
dinner 19.00–21.30
supper 22.00–24.00 (during Salzburg Festival only)
snacks, drinks and light refreshments served on the terrace throughout the day
Prices: upward/expensive

Schloss Fuschl which sits rather grandly on the shores of one of the most beautiful clear lakes in Austria was once the property of the Prince Archbishops of Salzburg and fish were bred in the lake exclusively for the archbishop's table. Today it is one of the loveliest castle hotels in Austria and additions made in more recent years blend in rather well. Accommodation is luxurious, hospitality lavish (breakfast is a small feast and taken on the terrace on a fine summer morning as near to heaven as you can get – at least in my opinion) and prices are not above those charged by other five-star hotels (rather less than that off-season). The view from the restaurant and terrace (and most of the rooms) is breathtakingly beautiful – in short, Schloss Fuschl is perfection and the cooking is some of the best in Austria, though I must admit that I've

Schloss Fuschl

found it difficult to concentrate on the food on occasion because of the beautiful views which I feel are alone worth the price of the set lunch (S.450.- for four courses, S.350.- for three). On the last occasion this consisted of *Räucherfischmus* (mousse of smoked fish) with sorrel sauce, very Viennese beef broth with small gnocchi, trout baked with herbs and finishing with rather homely *Nussnudeln* with vanilla sauce and wild strawberries. (Schloss Fuschl has its own fishery and smokehouse and the fish served in the restaurant are descendants of the fish which once graced the archbishop's table). Dinner was more lavish, starting with a terrine of smoked eel and sour cream followed by clear oxtail soup, venison with juniper cream accompanied by chestnut potatoes and a savoury *Strudel* stuffed with red cabbage and apples and finished with chocolate mousse with cognac sauce and strawberries.

Excellent selection of wines (and incidentally, also properly made tea).

How to get there: on 158 from Salzburg direction Salzkammergut/St Gilgen. Drive through Hof and about 2 km after Hof you will see a sign pointing to the left and Hotel Schloss Fuschl (the hotel set immediately on the road called Jagdhof is under the same ownership as Schloss Fuschl and more moderately priced).

Igls — *Tyrol*

SPORTHOTEL
Hilberstrasse 17
6080 Igls
☎ 0512 77241
Open: 12.00–14.00, 19.00–21.30
Closed: beginning October/22nd December
Prices: moderate/slightly upward

There's a charming drawing of the Sporthotel in 1870, looking more like a sturdy farmhouse than the hotel which it was even in those days. It is now rather elegant – take the 'Sport' as applying mostly to the fairly new sports and fitness centre complete with large pool. The dining-room is frequented mostly by hotel guests (or other '*Stammgäste*') who return year after year – it is that kind of welcoming hotel. The cooking is outstandingly good with nice original touches – clear beef broth comes with *Strudelsackerl* (spiced meat wrapped in *Strudel* pastry) or with three kinds of small dumplings (bacon, liver and spinach) and the cream of zucchini soup had an addition of cheese pancakes cut into thin strips. I was also rather taken by rather delicate *quenelles de brochet* and excellent sirloin steak with red wine sauce and the raspberry soufflé was truly superb.

Good selection of Austrian wines supported by France, Italy, Spain and California (despite admonition on wine list that one should stick to the wines of the country).

(You may notice that no vintages are given on the wine list – there is however a small note to the effect that this information will be supplied by the *Sommelier*.)

Imst ***Tyrol***

POST
(Schloss Sprengenstein)
Postplatz 3
6460 Imst
☏ 05412 2554
Open: all day, hot food 11.00–15.00 and 18.00–22.00
Closed: 1 November–20 December
Prices: moderate

'*Z'Imscht auf der Poscht da gibt's a guate Koscht*' runs an old ditty, meaning that you'll fare well at the Post. Certainly the reputation of the house as a place where visitors were made welcome goes back a long way. Schloss Sprengenstein, originally a feudal seat, became a coach station and hostelry in 1637. Now a Romantik hotel, family-owned and run, with very good and comfortable rooms, extensive grounds and large indoor swimming-pool, it is an exceptionally pleasant place in which to stay. You'll certainly fare well at the Post – whether it is in one of the traditional dining-rooms or on the lovely veranda, wreathed in flowers and dappled with sunshine. There is usually a well-chosen fixed-price meal which is good value, but you'll do even better if you choose à la carte and pick some of the local specialities. This is certainly the place to sample *Tiroler Speckknödelsuppe* (Tyrolean dumpling in clear broth) or the Spinach gnocchi with ham and sour cream (*Spinatspatzln in Rahm mit Schinken*). In fact there's a whole range of typically Tyrolean pasta worth trying – *Schlutzkrapfen* and *Kasnocken* – or you could order Tries which lets you sample these and *Spinatspatzln* as well. Game is usually excellent and so is the *Imster Rindstasche* (stuffed steak). Or have one of the simpler main courses like sautéd calves liver with a salad in order to leave room for one of the Post's luscious puddings like chestnut mouuse (*Kastanien Mousse*) with fruit.

Note: In 1949 the first SOS Children's Village was established in Imst and the idea spread from there to all over the world. Do go and visit it, if only to see how much one man's determination (with a lot of help from a lot of friends) can achieve!

How to get there: From Innsbruck on A.12 or 171.

Innsbruck *Tyrol*

EUROPASTÜBERL
Brixner Strasse 6
6020 Innsbruck
☎ 0512 5931
Open: 11.00–15.00 (kitchen 11.30–14.30)
18.00–24.00 (kitchen 18.30–23.00)
Prices: moderate

The Europastüberl, though part of Innsbruck's best hotel, the Europa, has always been considered a restaurant in its own right. There's a separate entrance and just to confuse matters a little, it was originally called Europastüberl, re-named Philippine Welser and now, under new owners, the restaurant is called Europastüberl once more. It has been completely refurbished, much mellowed wood from old farmhouses has gone into the panelling and there's great warmth as well as elegance with Philippine Welser's portrait still adorning one of the walls. (Philippine Welser was the beautiful though non-royal wife of Archduke Ferdinand, son of the emperor and a true Renaissance prince. At the time of the marriage wicked tongues wagged that he married her as much for her cooking as for her beauty which was considerable. Probably untrue, but her collection of recipes can be seen at nearby Schloss Ambras). I think she would almost certainly have approved of the cooking at the Europastüberl which is immensely varied, starting with a very moderately priced selection *'aus der regionalen Küche'* which ranges from the Tyrol straight to Vienna. There are good Tyrolean *'Plattln'* with *Sauerkraut* as well as roast rack of lamb with herb crust, accompanied by potatoes with creamed savoy cabbage, Viennese *Zwiebelrostbraten* as well as Tyrolean *Schlutzkrapfen* with Parmesan cheese and brown butter. More elaborate – and 'non-regional' dishes include veal *medaillons* with morel mushrooms in a creamy sauce and at lunch there's always a good roast served from the trolley. As a starter I could not resist one of my favourites, *Terlaner Weinsuppe,* followed by – and staying strictly regional – *Tiroler Gröstl* which they serve *'im Pfandl'* (from the pan) and with *Speckkrautsalat,* another Tyrolean favourite. There are some lovely very regional puddings like the typically South Tyrolean *Bratapfel flambiert mit Kastanieneis* (flambéd baked apple with chestnut ice-cream) and *Kirchtagskrapfen mit Nuischmalz* too good to be missed, but I also noted the well-chosen assortment of cheese, served with roasted pumpkin seeds.

Very good selection of Austrian wines with support from France and Italy, also some rarities from South Tyrol.

GRAUER BÄR
Universitätsstrasse 5
6020 Innsbruck
☏ 0512 5924
Open: 11.30–14.00, 18.30–23.00
Prices: moderate/upward

The Grauer Bär is a marvellous old family hotel – a little staid perhaps, but spacious and elegant with huge rooms in which you do not feel lost, for there's a nice comforting atmosphere. The same applies to the dining-room where tables are spaced well apart; you can enjoy watching a family celebration at the next table, but you are not made an involuntary witness to whispered confidences. It is the sort of restaurant where the head waiter will attend to a woman dining alone with extra courtesy, instead of showing her to a table behind a potted palm. It is also the sort of restaurant where I am inclined to make straight for the *Tagesmenü* (set-price meal) or order *Tafelspitz* or *Wiener Schnitzel* without even looking at the menu, knowing for certain that they will be there, and perfectly cooked. (At the Grauer Bär they are listed under '*Klassische Gasthausküche* which is a slight understatement, together with such other favourites as *Zwiebelrostbraten* and *Ragout* of venison when in season.) In fact, the *Tagesmenü* at the Grauer Bär is always commendable, as are the above-mentioned 'classics', but the kitchen has much to offer besides: good pasta dishes, for instance, seasonal specialities, very good steaks and truly excellent puddings. There is also a section on the menu headed '*leichte Küche*' which is by no means confined to vegetarian dishes, though these are also always included.

Small, but very good selection of wines, mostly Austrian with a little Italian support and local beer which they also serve in a more than generous *Pfiff* (as a rule a *Pfiff* of beer is ⅛l – at the Grauer Bär it is a commendable 2 dl!) Exactly as one would expect at a hostelry which is generous in every way!

Jennersdorf — *Burgenland*

RAFFEL
Hauptplatz 6
8380 Jennersdorf
☏ 03154 6622
Open: 6.30–24.00
Closed: 24 December (evening) and all day 25 December
Prices: moderate

Jennersdorf is close to the Hungarian border in southern Burgenland, where as the Austrian would say 'the foxes bid each other goodnight', meaning that it is as remote as can be and where nothing much happens. It is certainly not on the shortest route between Salzburg and Vienna, yet friends of mine always choose to travel this particular way – to arrive at Raffel's in time for a leisurely drink, dine to the accompaniment of gipsy music and eventually stagger up to one of the comfortable bedrooms. (Bar the gipsy music, Raffel is the nearest Austrian equivalent to a French *restaurant avec chambres*.) Not that I would hesitate to recommend it for lunch, but the whole atmosphere, the enormous portions and the general sense of well-being make it an end-of-the-day pleasure rather than a daytime one. No use pleading for small portions – I tried this once when ordering *Halászle* (Hungarian fish soup which is one of their specialities) with the result that a fair-sized cauldron was put on my table with a sweep of the hand and an invitation to help myself. Not a gourmet's hushed shrine – the atmosphere is much too jolly for that. Do not expect French or other 'would-be' cuisine; the cooking is strictly Austro-Hungarian and lest you should expect otherwise, there's a special section on the menu headed *Aus der Monarchie* (From the Monarchy) as against *Besondere Gaumenfreuden* (especially pleasing to the palate) which I can assure you is not a contradiction *per se*. Listings under the various sections can be a little confusing: *Esterhazy Rostbraten* appears in the 'Monarchy' section, whilst *Filet Andrassy* is listed under '*Gaumenfreuden*', but they will happily advise you and explain their specialities. There's pike/perch (which they correctly call *Fogas*) *nach Art der Pfarrersköchin* with wine and mushrooms, goose liver cooked in several delicious ways and I love the sound of their *Hofratssouper* which is named after a title in the old monarchy (or possibly after one particular holder of that title for whom it was especially created). You could order a wedding feast for four – which would probably feed forty – but there are also some very simple dishes (I had veal sweetbreads cooked so delicately that they all but melted on the plate) and on my last visit the special spring menu featured some particularly tempting asparagus dishes. Pancakes are a Raffel speciality as are *Nussrahmdalken* (a delicious walnut pudding). Raffel are one of the few restaurants who still employ a *Böhmische Mehlspeisköchin* – a Bohemian cook whose sole job it is to produce delicious puddings, but you may prefer, as I did on the last occasion, simply to order a portion of wild strawberries which could not have been more elegantly served – on a huge silver dish and enough for at least four.

Excellent selection of Austrian wines, with support from France and Italy. Raffel is also one of the few places which serve eaux-de-vie from Zieser of Riegersburg – a rare (if expensive) treat, but you have to ask for them.

As for nothing ever happening at Jennersdorf: it has the largest open-air swimming-pool in Burgenland, with its own restaurant, the Lindenczarda – open during the season, also during the evening, complete with outdoor grill and gipsy musicians. The Lindenczarda is under the same management as Raffel. In fact the Kampel-Kettner family appear to have taken over the culinary régime of Jennersdorf: the daughter now presides over the recently opened *Am Spitz* restaurant (Rax 7, Tel. 03154 8920) and son has opened a *Heurigen* across the road from Raffel – all the more reason for booking a room at Raffel's.

How to get there: from Eisenstadt on 50 (or S.31 changing to 50) to Oberwart, thence on 57 via Güssing to Heiligenkreuz. From there take 65 direction Fürstenfeld, but just outside Heiligenkreuz turn left, direction Jennersdorf and follow this direction (the road runs along the Austro-Hungarian border with warnings at some points that the left side of the road is actually in Hungary!) OR from Graz: On A.2. direction Vienna to Gleisdorf, then on 68 to Feldbach and from there on 57 to Jennersdorf. OR from Vienna on A.2 direction Graz to exit for Fürstenfeld, then 65 to Fürstenfeld and Eltendorf. At Eltendorf take right turn on to 57 for Jennersdorf.

Kapfenstein ***Styria***

SCHLOSS KAPFENSTEIN (Schlosswirt Winkler-Hermaden)
8353 Kapfenstein
☏ 03157 2202
Open: *Beginning March/Easter and during November*:
11.30–22.00
Closed: Mondays and Tuesdays
Easter/end October: 11.30–23.00
Closed Tuesdays
Closed: First week June and beginning December/end February
Prices: inexpensive

Schloss Kapfenstein would warrant a visit even without the food. A fortress built in the twelfth century with wide terraces, small secret gardens and magnificent views. Turn to one side and you can see far into Hungary. To the other, Yugoslavia is spread out before you. Wander around and you will want to stay in this lovely tranquil spot – forever, if this were possible.

You will certainly want to eat there, whether on the terrace, with the scent of phlox wafting over in summer or in the cosy panelled dining-room on a slightly chill evening. It does not matter whether you opt for a full meal or just a snack, the welcome will be as warm as the food is perfect. Schloss Kapfenstein is a family business, now run by a third generation of Winkler-Hermadens: the son cooks, mother looks after the guests and father after the extensive vineyards – only wines from these appear on their list (with fully detailed descriptions – alas, in German, but they will gladly elucidate).

The selection of food is not very large, but the portions are – commendably most dishes are available in small portions and these are marked on the menu. Snacks – or starters – include home-made brawn, pâté with cranberries, or just a bowl of their delicious mushroom soup, all served with home-baked bread using fourteen different kinds of grain. Main dishes could include a mixed grill with a casserole of vegetables from the kitchen garden, roast lamb scented with thyme, accompanied by gnocchi and spinach pudding or crisply fried spring chicken with a choice of salads. All pastries are of course home-made and the *Topfenstrudel* (with a curd cheese filling) and *Marillenkuchen* are particularly commendable – or you may opt for good local cheese which they serve with pumpkin seeds. On Thursday evening there is a giant country buffet with home-made sausages, ham and a whole host of hot and cold Styrian specialities. Some of the latter also appear on the menu during the week. Throughout the year there are special culinary events – a small 'culinary calendar' is available on request.

There are six bedrooms, all with private bathroom and/or shower. The poet's room is particularly attractive, as is the knight's room, with lovely old furniture and marvellous views. Breakfast is a joy – buffet-style, but no horrid selection of packets or slices of sweaty ham: free-range eggs, home-made jam in a crystal jar and a big chunk of local ham on a wooden slab, with a sharp knife provided. Prices are moderate, but book ahead if you want to stay.

How to get there: from graz on A.2. direction Vienna, exit direction Feldbach on to 68 and from Feldbach on 66 to Bad Gleichenberg. Continue on 66 at Bad Gleichenberg direction Bad Radkersburg and take left fork (direction St Anna) taking left fork again for Kapfenstein. Drive through Kapfenstein village and then up the hill, variously signposted Schloss Kapfenstein and Schlosswirt.

Note: There is a shorter, more direct road from Bad Gleichenberg to Kapfenstein, but it is rather twisty and you might lose your way, making it the longer route after all!

Kitzbühel ***Tyrol***

RÖMERHOF
Römerweg 3
6370 Kitzbühel
☏ 05356 72565 and 363677
Open: 11.30–15.00, 18.00–21.30
Closed: Mondays (except July and August)
also closed end September/mid December
and end March/beginning June
Prices: moderate

If you spot an elegant and distinguished-looking gentleman dining in solitary splendour at the Römerhof, it's more likely than not the proprietor of the equally elegant and distinguished Tennerhof (same ownership). This is not a slight on the superb cooking or the ambience of the Tennerhof (q.v.), but simply a tribute to the rural excellence of the Römerhof. It is a typically Tyrolean restaurant with pine-panelled walls, simple table settings, a relaxed atmosphere, and good comforting Austrian food. Soups are particularly commendable: *Rahmsuppe mit frischen Kräutern* (sour cream soup with fresh herbs) or creamy cheese soup (*Käserahmsuppe*). *Unsere leichte Seite* lists starters which could also serve as a light main course, like home-made brawn with brown lentil salad and roast beef with toasted country bread and a salad of lamb's lettuce. The menu is entirely Austrian with some nice special touches like rice sprinkled with chopped chives, vegetables such as beans in dill sauce (*Dillbohnen*) and *Gurkenrahmerdäpfl* (potatoes in cucumber cream), all belonging to an era when it was not *de rigueur* for vegetables to be tough and tasteless. Tyrolean specialities – listed separately (*gschmackige Tiroler Gerichte*) are more hearty, but absolutely authentic, like *Tiroler Schlutzkrapfen* (pasta filled with spinach, potatoes and curd cheese) served with brown butter or Tyrolean liver. There's almost a touch of nostalgia about the puddings: *Buchteln mit Vanillesauce* (small yeast buns with vanilla cream), *Kipferlschmarrn, Polsterzipfel* and *Böhmische Topfenpalatschinken* (pancakes with a filling of curd cheese) – old-fashioned specialities which have disappeared from other restaurant menus in favour of far less desirable novelties – there's always at least one of these at the Römerhof.

There are some very comfortable – in fact rather luxurious – apartments at the Römerhof, reasonably priced and complete with small kitchen, though full hotel service is available.

How to get there: On the 161 direction St Johan (and Salzburg) with the centre of Kitzbühel on your left, watch for a sign marked 'Zur Hornbahn' pointing right. Follow that sign, crossing the railway (the road is called Hornweg). After passing the cable car station on your left, turn left into Griesenauweg. Continue on this road (ignoring signs for Tennerhof on your right) and you will find the Römerhof a little further down the road on your left.

TENNERHOF
Griesenauweg 26
6370 Kitzbühel
☏ 05336 3181
Open: 8.00–24.00 (kitchen 12.00–14.00, 18.00–21.30)
Closed: Tuesdays, also beginning October/mid December
beginning April/end May
Prices: expensive

The Tennerhof is a joy – originally a farmhouse built in the seventeenth century which graduated to a country manor and in the same family since the twenties, catering for a few 'paying guests' at first. Fortunate and privileged guests – for such was the care and attention lavished on them that the fame of the Tennerhof spread and soon additions had to be made to the original building. Like Topsy, the Tennerhof 'just grew', resulting in some oddly shaped rooms, all of which greatly added to its charms. It is now a very luxurious hotel of great elegance, yet the family atmosphere prevails and staying at the Tennerhof is still very much like being a guest at a very grand country house. There are invitations to the alpine pasture land belonging to the Tennerhof where the host tends the barbecue, and special cookery courses – yet privacy is preserved should you wish it. Food at the Tennerhof is of legendary quality (vegetables and herbs are organically grown in the hotel gardens, jam is home-made and tea has not been near a tea bag), yet comparatively few outsiders realize that the restaurant also caters for non-residents. Nor is it a question of intruding on the hotel guests – there's plenty of space in the elegant dining-rooms, in secluded corners and above all on the sheltered terrace which is my own favourite place. The food is a delightful example of Austrian cooking both classic and 'elevated' as a typical selection of soups shows: clear broth of boletus mushrooms with *Schlickkrapferl* (filled pasta envelopes), a light frothy lentil soup with oysters and good strong beef broth 'with traditional additions'. One of the excellent starters is a *Tafelspitz* of venison – a cut usually reserved for beef – in this particular case served as a warm salad with walnut-oil dressing. I can personally recommend the tournedos with a bone marrow and chive sauce and the selection of fish from nearby rivers and lakes in a champagne sauce, but the Tennerhof is not too grand to remember its farmhouse tradition by offering *Bauernbratl vom Spanferkel* (farmhouse version of suckling pig) served with a warm horseradish sauce.

Puddings are particularly good and their platter of typically Austrian specialities is well worth considering, but if you follow my advice you'll order *Salzburger Nockerl* which are made according to the Tennerhof's special recipe – mellow golden mounds (not great show-off mountains), lightly caramelized and absolutely delicious.

Excellent wine list – as one would expect.

How to get there: On the 161 direction St Johann (and Salzburg) with the centre of Kitzbühel on your left, watch for a sign marked 'Zur Hornbahn' pointing right. Follow that sign, crossing the railway (the road is called Hornweg). After passing the cable car station on your left, turn left into Griesenauweg. The Tennerhof is on the right, well signposted.

UNTERBERGER STUBEN
Wehrgasse 2
6370 Kitzbühel
☏ 05336 2101
Open: 10.00–24.00 (kitchen 12.00–13.30, 18.30–22.00) Wednesday/Monday
Closed: Tuesday (possibly also Wednesday until 17.00) also closed middle May/middle June and beginning November/beginning December (dates variable)
Note: During the tourist season the restaurant is open throughout the week
Prices: moderate/upward

'Hasi' Unterberger, one of the best chefs in Austria, calls his Unterberger Stuben a *'Wirtshaus'*. This is a typical Unterberger understatement. A *'Wirtshaus'* is generally considered to be more down to earth (not to say primitive or basic) than a *Gasthaus*. Not necessarily rustic or rural – there are *Wirtshäuser* in cities as well. The Unterberger Stuben are certainly down-to-earth, albeit in a rather casually elegant way with polished wooden floors and furniture and there's the typical *'Wirtshaus' Stammtisch*, except that the 'regulars' sitting around it will more likely than not be celebrities of some sort. The Unterberger Stuben are just about the most 'in' place in very 'in' Kitzbühel, but in one respect the *'Wirtshaus'* definition is absolutely correct: it has always been maintained that the difference between a *Gasthaus* and a *Wirtshaus* is that in the former the guest has the say, in the latter the *Wirt* (mine host) and there's no doubt whatsoever about Hasi Unterberger ruling the roost, greatly assisted by his charming wife and that the guests love every minute of it! He is a master of his art, a cook of the classic school to which are added unmistakable Unterberger touches of genius. In true Wirtshaus tradition there is a set lunch at S350.- which unlike any Wirtshaus I know has included cream of spinach soup garnished with strips of gurnard and filet of hare wrapped in *Strudel* pastry with juniper cream. Some specialities are part of the set lunch on specific days of the week – in true *Wirtshaus* tradition again – and Saturday is definitely *'Tafelspitz'* day. Special Unterberger touches are added to quite ordinary dishes and ordering à la carte which is extensive and may need deciphering as well as translating (which they'll do gladly for you) should bring you a small feast. On the last occasion I had very light and frothy watercress soup, followed by venison wrapped in caul before roasting with a red wine and walnut sauce and polenta which was absolutely marvellous. Puddings at Unterberger Stuben are beyond compare – Florentines with marzipan mousse, figs and dates, Hasi Unterberger works wonders with an ordinary *Scheiterhaufen* (Austrian bread-and-butter pudding) and his selection of *'Alt-*

Unterberger Stuben

österreichischen desserts' are worth the journey all the way to Kitzbühel. (I even forgive him for describing them as the dreaded 'dialogue' of desserts!) As one would expect of Hasi Unterberger, though not of a *Wirtshaus*, there is a very extensive wine list, including some lesser known small vintners.

Much comment has been made recently about the difficulty of booking a table at Unterberger Stuben that it seems only fair to report my own experience: On my first visit I telephoned to book a table at very short notice one Easter Saturday (and if there's anything less desirable than an unknown woman trying to book a table for one when every table in Kitzbühel had been reserved for days if not weeks ahead, I have yet to know). A table was found – without fuss – with the sole proviso that I'd have to vacate it at 21.00 when the next guests were due. As it happened, they were early and I ended up eating my pudding at the Stammtisch with a digestif on the house to make up for the inconvenience!

Kitzeck *Styria*

STEIRERLAND
Höch am Demmerkogel
8442 Kitzeck
☏ 03456 2328
Open: 7.00– 'until the last guest leaves'
Closed: from 18.00 on Sunday and all day Monday, also 2 January–15 February
Prices: moderate

Kitzeck is the highest wine village in Europe – the Steirerland sits higher still, above the vineyards with magnificent views right into Yugoslavia. You've probably encountered a *Klapotetz* or two on the way, a curiously spiked wheel which turns in the wind and is supposed to scare away the birds. Some vintners think differently – they say that the birds come at the sound of the *Klapotetz* like being called to a dinner of extra-juicy grapes!

You know you're in Styrian wine country when you meet a *Klapotetz,* and in a typical Styrian restaurant when the suggested aperitif is a glass of sparkling pink *Schilchersekt* or home-distilled apple brandy and, best of all, when the butter served with the good country bread is no ordinary butter but pumpkin-seed butter. The menu at the Steirerland is well studded with regional specialities; *Sausaler Weinsuppe* or *geräucherter Amurkarpfen* make good starters, the latter being a smoked version of the grass-eating carp bred in a nearby lake. My favourite main course is not always listed on the menu, but they will cook it on request: ask for *Haselnuss Medaillons* (*medaillons* of veal or pork dipped in egg and then ground hazelnuts and fried – the ultimate *Schnitzel*!), but do not forget that *Haselnuss* is the operative word. There are of course quite a number of more 'adventurous' dishes on the menu, plus always a very good five-course set meal, but I'll stick to my Hazelnut *Medaillons* which I have never found in any other restaurant. Specialities on a sweet theme are *Kürbiskerntorte* (cake made with the aforementioned pumpkin seeds) and featherlight *Strauben* – deep-fried pastry dusted thickly with icing sugar.

Steirerland is also the ideal spot for a mid-morning or mid-afternoon snack, which could easily serve as a full meal, particularly if you choose the *Sausaler Platte,* (platter of beef, brawn and caraway cheese with a good vinaigrette dressing).

There's an excellent selection of Styrian wines (what else in a noted wine village?) and of course Styrian beer and some very pleasant rooms if you wish to stay longer – or have stayed too long – with very favourable half-board terms.

How to get there: from graz on 67 direction Leibnitz. Just before getting to Leibnitz turn right on to 74 direction Deutschlandsberg. At the beginning of the village of Fresing turn right for Kitzeck. Steirerland is signposted – it lies in fact above Kitzeck.

WEINHOF KAPPEL
Steinriegel 25
8442 Kitzeck
☏ 03456 2347
Open: 10.00–22.00 (kitchen until 21.00)
Closed: February and Thursdays (November/March only)
Prices: moderate

Set amidst vineyards in Europe's highest wine village and a short distance from a little wine museum, Kappel's could not be more ideally, or idyllically, placed. You go to Kappel for the surroundings, the wine and the food – though not necessarily in that order. Much will depend on your mood and the time of day. Relaxing in the pretty garden and enjoying the lovely views (or in the comfort of the old-fashioned dining-room) you may well be tempted to have one of their rather substantial snacks from the 'ordinary' menu – a taste of *Verhackerts* (q.v.) perhaps or *Winzerrösti* (potatoes *au gratin* with ham and cheese), a *Brettljause* (wooden platter with smoked meats and sausages) or even a *Sulmtaler Backhendl* (fried chicken). All these would go well with the wine from their own vineyards, as would a piece of almond cake which, as they proudly state, 'contains no flour' – all very moderately priced. Move on to the 'specialities' menu – which is nearly as long as the 'ordinary' one – and you move into the realms of 'serious' cooking (still moderately priced). Still very regional, but with a rather elegant touch – particularly good on soups and starters (there was a memorable cream of pea pods), home-cured trout with dill yoghurt, a salad of calves brains and asparagus in aspic). Fillet of beef with a mushroom coating and roast veal wrapped in a herbed caul are but two of their recommended main courses. At the right time of year do not miss the chestnut mousse (with local chestnuts, more likely than not) with elderberry sauce or – at any time of the year – the *Türkentommerl,* a delicious pudding made with cornmeal, served with a cinnamon sauce and apple sorbet.

Kappel's wines are for sale for taking away (do not miss a visit to their wine cellar) and there is very good accommodation at reasonable prices – certainly a place at which you may want to stay.

How to get there: from Graz on 67 direction Leibnitz. Just before getting to Leibnitz turn right on to 74 direction Deutschlandsberg. At the beginning of the village of Fresing turn right for Kitzeck.

Klein-Wien *Lower Austria*

SCHICKH
Furth-Göttweig
3511 Klein-Wien
☏ 02736 218 No credit cards
Open: 9.00–24.00 (lunch 11.00–15.00, Dinner 17.30–22.00)
Kitchen operates throughout the day on Saturdays and Sundays
Closed: Wednesday, Thursday
Prices: moderate

To refer to Schickh's as a station restaurant and to Gerda Schickh merely as Lisl Bacher's sister (see Landhaus Bacher at Mautern) would be as misleading as it is accurate. The restaurant is certainly housed in a railway station, dated 1889 (the year Crown Prince Rudolf shot himself at Mayerling) and the St Pölten to Krems train trundles in every now and then to stop at the strictly one-platform station, but it is the most romantically placed station restaurant imaginable, set amidst woods at the foot of Göttweig Abbey. There's a large garden well shaded by ancient trees as befits a proper *Gasthausgarten*, with a spruced-up old railway carriage that has travelled four million kilometres (bearing the legend 'Orient Express – destination London, Istanbul, Klein Wien') now used as a bar and for small parties. Gerda Schickh is certainly Lisl Bacher's sister – the talent obviously runs in the family – but her cooking is highly individual, very Austrian, very regional – though not necessarily confined to any particular region. Visitors come all the way from Vienna to enjoy the good, absolutely genuine cooking – I'd heard about Gerda Schickh's soups long before my first visit to the restaurant (ask for details of whatever is modestly listed as *Tagessuppe* – soup of the day – or consider one of the 'specials', all excellent). *Tafelspitzsülzchen* (very delicate brawn with beef) is another speciality, but Schickh's also serve by way of starter – and only Gerda Schickh would dare – *Gansleberschmalzbrot* (goose-liver dripping spread on dark bread). Schickh's fish and game specialities are another reason why visitors will come to this remote place and there are of course all the good Austrian favourites like *Wiener Schnitzel* and fried spring chicken, all impeccably prepared.

Puddings are listed as *Schleckereien* on the menu and Gerda Schickh's apricot dumplings are legendary, but I can also recommend the *Kastanienreis* (sweetened chestnuts put through a potato ricer) which is served with a strawberry purée and the peach or the caramel *parfait*.

(It would be a pity to visit Schickh's with anything but a healthy appetite, not to say ravenously hungry, but should this be the case, their list of dishes *Fur den kleinen Hunger* includes a warming bowl of onion soup and snails on toast as well as a series of more usual snacks).

Very good selection of wines sold by the quarter litre and superb choice of Wachau wines with a little support from Italy, France and Spain.

Trains trundling past notwithstanding, you can stay very comfortably – and reasonably – at Schickh's (there is even a room affectionately known as the *Zug Zimmer* – the train room!)

How to get there: from Vienna on 3 to Krems and Stein. Cross the Danube to Mautern and follow directions for Furth. At Furth turn right for Steinaweg and from there to Klein-Wien which consists only of a few houses. Schickh is on the left.

Köflach *Styria*

ZUM KLEINHAPL (W. & G. Gussmack)
Judenburgstrasse 6
8580 Köflach
☏ 03144 3494
Open: 8.00–14.00 (kitchen 11.00–14.00)
18.00–24.00 (kitchen until 22.00)
Closed: from 14.00 Sunday and all day Monday
Prices: moderate

It would be quite easy to go past Zum Kleinhapl and dismiss it as just another country inn, or miss it altogether, and thereby miss one of the best country restaurants in Austria. No longer 'undiscovered' though as its fame has spread far beyond the borders of Styria and advance booking is strongly recommended. If at all possible, avoid Sundays – not only does the restaurant close 'officially' at 2 p.m. (though I have yet to see anyone being turned out at that time), but that's the day when dining-rooms and the small courtyard can be filled to bursting point.

Zum Kleinhapl is strictly rural in the best sense – rather elegant, but not overbearingly so – and this is reflected in the cooking. Good local specialities, using good local produce as much as possible with the very light and elegant touch of Gerti Gussmack who rules supreme in the kitchen. Creamy pumpkin or potato soup with forest mushrooms (*Kürbiscremesuppe* and *Kartoffelcremesuppe mit Schwammerl*) are a treat and this is definitely the place to try Styrian *Sterz* (crisply fried polenta) served with clear beef broth. There's excellent home-made brawn with a dressing of local pumpkin-seed oil and if you like tripe, try their version (*Kuttelfleck in Weissweinsauce*). I was particularly taken with their *Medaillons* of pork iin a light caraway and garlic sauce, served with cabbage *Strudel*, whilst fondly remembering a perfect dish of venison from a previous occasion. Accept guidance on the puddings of the day (or order the *Dessertvariationen* which will give you 'a taste of everything'), though if *kleine Palatschinke mit Limonencreme gefüllt* (small pancakes filled with lemon cream) happens to be on the menu, I'd look no further than that – except possibly towards the small apple 'pockets' (*Apfeltascherl*) with a sabayon of Calvados.

Wolfgang Gussmack's wine cellar is well stocked with the best of Austrian wines, with a strong emphasis on Styrian specialities and 'excursions' to Italy and France (for Champagne only).

How to get there: from Graz on 70 via Voitsberg (where the road inexplicably changes to 79) to Köflach (for the same inexplicable reason the road number changes back to 70 after Köflach!) There are two large open car parks near Zum Kleinhapl – Köflach has a somewhat complicated one-way system plus an unexpected pedestrian zone and you may have to ask the way when you get there (no use giving detailed instructions now – they may well be outdated even before the book appears!)

Köstendorf ***Salzburg***

GASTHOF FRITZENWALLNER
5203 Köstendorf
☎ 06216 302
Open: 7.00–24.00 and beyond (kitchen 11.30–14.00, 18.00–22.00)
Closed: Wednesday and Thursday
Prices: moderate

Fritzenwallner is a family inn in the best tradition: open from early morning until late at night, with comfortable dining-rooms, garden with mature trees, and its own butchery. Since there's also an inspired chef who picks mushrooms and wild herbs in his 'spare' time (or gets another member of the family to do it for him), the food is lifted into higher culinary spheres altogether, though still keeping to its Austrian roots. *Bärlauchcremesuppe* (wild garlic soup) and nettle soup (*Brennesselcreme*) are typical starters, as is a salad of 'meadow herbs' (*Wiesenkräutersalat*). There is of course the full range of traditional dishes – as starters or main courses – *Krautfleckerl* (small pasta squares with cabbage), possibly an acquired taste, but this is the place in which to acquire it. Black pudding is sliced, crisply fried and served on a bed of white cabbage (*Blunzenradl*) and home-made noodles come with *meinem Pesto* made with freshly gathered wild garlic. Roast lamb with a red wine sauce and rosemary potatoes was marvellous, but Fritzenwallner also excels in fish dishes and my poached pike/perch with dill was exemplary. Country inns with attached butchery are sometimes less strong on puddings – not so Fritzenwallner. Their chocolate mousse with black walnuts preserved in their own liqueur proved to be one of the best combinations I've had in a long time. Other puddings were equally successful, such as a *parfait* of oranges with elderberries and a curd and poppy-seed terrine with strawberries. Wines are exclusively Austrian, with many sold by the quarter litre as well as by the glass, and beer is commendably sold in *Pfiff* (⅛l) measures if wanted, but do not miss their own eaux-de-vie and the home-made walnut liqueur.

How to get there: from Salzburg on B.1 direction Strasswalchen, turn left past Neumarkt for Köstendorf.

Kötschach-Mauthen — *Carinthia*

KELLERWAND
Mauthen 24
9640 Kötschach-Mauthen
☏ 04715 269 and 378
Open: 12.00–15.00 (kitchen 13.45), 18.30–24.00 (kitchen 21.30) Wednesday/Sunday
Note: during the season the restaurant is open throughout the week.
Closed: Monday, Tuesday (off-season only)
also closed mid November/mid December
Prices: moderate/upward

The Kellerwand is far away from practically everywhere, except the Italian border (the nearest town in Austria is Villach and that's about 80 km distant), yet to be sure of a table you'll certainly have to book well ahead: Sissy Sonnleitner's cooking has put the Kellerwand definitely into 'top league' – it is original, perfectly executed and a joy to behold. The Italian influence is strong, except that you are not likely to find any of the dishes in Italy – they are Sissy Sonnleitner's creations, pure and simple. Pasta dishes and risotti are particular delights, like *Fondutaravioli* with a paprika cream or the nettle risotto with *quenelles de brochet* (*Brennesselrisotto mit Hechtnockerln*) or *Kräutercannelloni mit Artischocken* (cannelloni stuffed with cheese and herbs served with artichokes). Soups too show the Italian influence – *Paprikacremesuppe* with aubergines and courgettes and scampi vegetable soup with ravioli being but two examples. My own favourite main course is the veal escalope stuffed with walnuts (*Kalbsschnitzel mit Walnüssen gefüllt*) but I can also recommend the chicken stuffed with wild garlic (*mit Bärlauch gefülltes Huhn*). Puddings are pure Sissy Sonnleitner/Viennese – try the *Mohntascherln auf karamelisiertem Apfelragout* (small 'envelopes' filled with crushed poppy seeds and served with caramelized apples) or the *Mohn-Apfelterrine* (poppy seed and apple terrine) with Calvados Sauce. There is good Italian as well as local cheese (*Drautaler* or

Lesachtaler Bauernkäse) served with home-baked walnut bread – in fact all bread and rolls are home-baked and you can occasionally find a delicious *Grammelpogatscherl* (q.v.) in the well-assorted bread basket.

Considering the excellence of the cooking and the elegant surroundings, prices are more than reasonable and there is also a daily *'kleines Gourmetmenü'* (four courses for S370.- as well as a 'romantic' menu (seven courses for S540.-).

Excellent selection of wines many of which are available by the glass, as well as wines sold per ¼l.

If you are wise you'll not only book a table but also one of the delightful rooms at the Kellerwand (and having eaten there you may also decide to enrol for one of the cookery seminaries or book ahead for a 'romantic weekend' or at least ask for details).

How to get there: from Villach on A.2 direction Tarvisio as far as Arnoldstein where you change on to 111 direction Hermagor (careful – you could land on the route to Italy). Continue on 111 past Hermagor which will bring you straight to Kötschach-Mauthen. At Kötschach-Mauthen turn left for Mauthen – the Kellerwand is on the right.

Krems an der Donau — ***Lower Austria***

AM FÖRTHOF
Donaulände 8
3500 Krems an der Donau
☏ 02732 83345
Open: 11.30–14.30, 18.00–22.00
Closed: Thursday and mid February/mid March
Prices: moderate/upward

The original Förthof was built by Charlemagne, destroyed during the Turkish wars and rebuilt in the eighteenth century, when it was used as a hunting lodge first and then 'graduated' to a coaching inn. Am Förthof next door is strictly of this century and was built as an inn right from the start – a good, comfortable inn with good, comfortable rooms and a spacious restaurant. There's a small, heated swimming-pool and a large, shaded garden as well as a wide terrace overlooking the Danube and splendid Göttweig Abbey. Hospitality is lavish, starting with a generous buffet breakfast – generous almost to a fault, with its large selection of home-cured meats, good cheeses and fresh fruit. The restaurant is not confined to hotel guests of course, but if the weather is fine opt for a table on the terrace, or in the garden. The *'Winzermenü'* (vintner's menu) is always worth considering, but choosing à la carte I was particularly taken by the quenelles of pike/perch (*Zandernockerl*) in a light paprika sauce and an asparagus terrine on one occasion, whilst on another the fish soup could not have been bettered and the calves liver was done to the exact shade of tender pink. Let yourself be advised when you've reached the pudding stage – there are always seasonal specialities which are too good to miss.

Wines are primarily of the Wachau region (of course!), ably supported by the rest of Austria and some French, Italian and Spanish. Good selection of vintage wines offered by the glass.

How to get there: On 3 from Vienna. Am Förthof is on the main road on the right.

Lans ***Tyrol***

ZUM WILDEN MANN
6072 Lans
☏ 0512 77387
Open: 11.00–24.00 (11.00–14.30, 18.00–22.00)
Prices: moderate

One of the most attractive country inns in the Tyrol – or anywhere in Austria. Charming small dining-rooms, a warm welcome and excellent food – you can be sure of all those, but reserve a table for the Zum Wilden Mann is by no means undiscovered.

The menu is not too extensive and nicely balanced, with separate sections for '*Aus unserer Schmankerl-Küche*' (pasta and dumpling dishes) and *Unsere Hausmannskost* (rather hearty Tyrolean specialities), but the fixed-price meal (four courses) is always worth considering since it is usually good value (with larger than average portions). If you choose à la carte, do try the *Terlaner Weinsuppe* which is particularly good and include at least one of the specialities (half portions of the pasta and dumpling dishes can be ordered) – the *Hausmannskost* is fairly hearty (home-made black pudding, smoked pork with lentils, calf's head) but beautifully cooked. You'll find good game dishes under *Tagesgerichte* (dishes of the day) and this could also be the moment to try Tyrolean liver (Tiroler Leber) of which you'll get a truly authentic version.

All this will probably not leave much room for one of their very good puddings (on a separate menu) – have a sorbet or even their Sorbet platter.

Short, but good wine list – you'll find Austrian and South Tyrolean wines in the same section, simply headed '*Flaschenweine rot*' and '*Flaschenweine weiss*'. No comment.

How to get there: from Innsbruck via Aldrans or to Igls on 182 and follow directions for Lans from there.

Lech am Arlberg *Vorarlberg*

HOTEL GASTHOF POST
6764 Lech am Arlberg
☏ 05583 220623
Open: 8.00–24.00 end November/20 April, 20 June/end September
Closed: end September/end November, 20 April/20 June
Prices: moderate/upward

The Post carries the description *'Gasthof'* like a proud banner in its title though it can hardly be said to apply any longer to this centuries-old inn which the Moosbrugger family have transformed – gradually and lovingly over decades – into a superbly comfortable and luxurious hotel with famous and indeed royal visitors. The atmosphere is not at all that of a 'grand' hotel though, Kristl Moosbrugger is a wonderful hostess in every way which is why it is almost impossible to get a room during the wintersports season unless you book well ahead. Stay at the Post during the summer when 'winter-fashionable' Lech reverts to its true mountain village character and meadows and mountains are more beautiful than ever. This is the time to enjoy the lavish hospitality at the Post (at very favourable off-season prices) and let yourself be thoroughly spoiled. The restaurant certainly warrants a visit – it is spread over several rooms which have kept their true inn character and the cooking is Austrian at its very best with some very light and original touches. *Rehessenz mit Brandteigkrapferl* (clear venison broth with savoury eclairs) certainly came under the 'original' heading and the salmon steak with ceps (*Lachsmittelstück auf überbackenen Steinpilzen*) could not have been bettered. The menu always includes homely dishes such as *Eierschwammerl in Rahmsauce mit Serviettenknödel* (chanterelles in a cream sauce with dumplings) or a simple 'bollito' of calves tongue and knuckle. Do leave room for a pudding (personally, I'd travel quite a long way for their *Topfenstrudel* which is quite unlike any other, creamy and flaky and utterly delicious) – they do a marvellous *Kaiserschmarrn* at the Post as well, but last time I was completely taken by their *Griessomelette mit Rumzwetschken und Pralineneis*.

Excellent selection of wines, very strong on Austria and including Italy, Bordeaux and Burgundy.

HOTEL SCHNEIDER ALMHOF
6764 Lech am Arlberg
☏ 05583 3500
Open: Stub'n: 12.00–24.00
Walser Stuben: 12.00–15.00, 19.00–24.00
mid December/one week after Easter
Closed: one week after Easter/mid December
Prices: moderate/expensive

Hotel Schneider Almhof is open during the winter sports season only – a large, very elegant and luxurious hotel – family-owned and family-run, with a great family atmosphere. The restaurants are of course open to non-residents and you can take your pick according to your mood – a first visit to the Stub'n perhaps, which is cosy rather than elegant, where beer from the barrel and good Austrian specialities are served at moderate prices: *Tiroler Gröstl*, ravioli filled with black pudding (*Blutwurstravioli*) or fried spring chicken, curd cheese dumplings and *Kaiserschmarrn*. Should you be in a more extravagant mood there are the very elegant Walser Stuben with a menu to match – still very Austrian, but definitely elevated to higher culinary spheres: venison with ceps, accompanied by gnocchi with walnuts and red cabbage cooked with cranberries or guinea fowl with Schilcher wine sauce, polenta and salsify – and marvellous puddings such as chestnut mousse in chocolate leaves with hazelnut sauce. Commendably the same menu is available in either restaurant; you can have the simple food at the elegant Walser Stuben or the 'elevated' range of dishes at the Stub'n, according to your mood.

From about February onwards, depending on the weather, you can also lunch on the open-air terrace – surrounded by snow sparkling in the brilliant sunshine. The menu on the terrace is fairly small, but there's always a good set lunch as well as a splendid hot and cold buffet.

Very extensive wine list as befits a lavish hotel.

Linz ***Upper Austria***

ALLEGRO
Schillerstrasse 68
4020 Linz
☏ 0732 669800, 51095
Open: 11.30–14.00, 18.30–22.30 Monday/Friday
18.30–22.30 Saturday
Closed: Saturday lunch and all day Sunday
Prices: upward

The Allegro is small and modern and shines with lots of glass, brass and marble like a well-polished apple. It also exudes a feeling of comfortable well-being not normally associated with starkly modern restaurants, an atmosphere no doubt created by Günther Hager who won his first 'gold' when he was 25 and who has been collecting gold medals for his cooking ever since. His creations are often startling in their simplicity like his 'nobler *Erdäpfelsalat mit Räucherlachs*' which is simply the best potato mayonnaise I have ever eaten (superb quality potatoes locally grown especially for the restaurant) with a 'rose' of smoked salmon (Günther Hager's love of decorating dishes with a great flourish is well-known). The menu is small but contains some unusual combinations like clear beef broth with *Kalbshirnpofesen* (savoury version of poor knights with a creamy filling of calves brains) or *Shrimpsgröstl* (with Kipfler potatoes). Some of Günther Hager's dishes are regional specialities prepared better than anywhere else in or outside the region, like his *Grammelknöderln* (small dumplings with spiced pork crackling) or the Allegro *Kalbsstelze* (roast knuckle of veal). Good selection of cheeses and some unusual puddings like a mousse of *Beerenauslese* served with rhubarb and strawberries.

There is not only an excellent selection of wines with some rare vintages, but the wine list itself should get a beauty prize!

STADTWIRT
Bismarkstrasse 1
4020 Linz
☏ 0732 273165
Open: 11.00–23.00 Monday/Saturday
Prices: moderate

The Stadtwirt is Günther Hager's 'other' restaurant (see Allegro) and the name (inn of the town) is more than apt: a good, solid inn with a huge garden, a vast dining-room complete with tiled stove as well as 'flowering' chestnut tree (the trunk is for real, the leaves and flowers artificial). Do not look upon the Stadtwirt as a kind of 'lesser' Allegro however – of its kind it is absolutely first class, serving first-class food made with first-class raw materials. It is also one of the few remaining restaurants proud to proclaim '*Wiener Küche*' (Viennese cooking). Beef in marvellous quality is used throughout, particularly for the famous boiled beef specialities (not quite the large selection of cuts as offered at the Hietzinger Bräu in Vienna, but remarkable nevertheless). Special cuts include *Schermrippe,* described as '*leicht durchzogenes* (marbled) *Gustostückl*' and '*Ochsenwadl*' (shin) which is offered with *Semmelkren* (bread sauce spiced with horseradish which not that many restaurants offer these days). Starters include an elegant trout mousse as well as local ham with horseradish and pickled cucumbers and 'nobler *Erdäpfelsalat*' ('noble' potato salad) with pickled herrings and chive cream, the quality of potatoes selected by Günther Hager being legendary. Diminutives abound, not to denote size of portions, but as the term of endearment so often applied in Austria for something particularly delectable or desirable. Thus you'll find *'das klassische Kalbs-Wienerschnitzerl'* for a perfect *Wiener Schnitzel* of true and generous inn proportions and *Linzer 5-Kräuter Schnitzerl,* a special creation by Günther Hager. Puddings are exactly as one would expect: home-made *Strudel, Mohr im Hemd* and *Stadtwirt Krapfen* as well as seasonal specialities rather elegantly presented, like strawberries with red wine. Cheese comes exclusively from Upper Austria, including pungent *Mondseer*.

There is a short selection of good Austrian wines, splendid beer and – this being Most (apple wine) country – apple wine from local sources.

Loipersdorf — ***Burgenland***

ROSENBERGER AUTOBAHNRESTAURANT LOIPERSDORF
7411 Loipersdorf/Burgenland
☏ 03359 2572
Open: 6.00–23.00 June/October
6.00–22.00 November/May
Prices: inexpensive/moderate

A.2 South Motorway (Südautobahn) accessible from both directions
No credit cards

For description see under Motorway Restaurants (Rosenberger)

Maishofen nr. Zell am See — ***Salzburg***

SCHLOSS KAMMER
5751 Maishofen
☏ 06542 8202
Open: 11.30–22.00
Closed: Mondays and during November, also sometime during spring (variable)
Prices: inexpensive.

If you had expected to find a 'Schloss' complete with towers and turrets, you'll be disappointed. Schloss Kammer is best described as a cross between a farmhouse and a manor – a fine, centuries-old building set solidly above the lake amidst lush meadows. It has belonged to the same family for generations and except for the large dining-room on the ground floor, most of the building has remained unchanged. The restaurant – owner-run, of course – is a typical country inn, a place to which the locals go for good local food. It may be just for a snack –

lightly smoked venison (*Hirschschinken*) or some home-made brawn with a vinaigrette dressing or one of the robust 'Pinzgauer specials' (Pinzgau being the local region) – the food is absolutely genuine and truly local. Certainly the place for eating a hearty pot of lentils with sausages, *Kasnocken* (cheese gnocchi with melted butter and chives) or *Kaspressknödeln* (cheese dumplings in clear broth). Not exactly food for the faint-hearted, but highly enjoyable if you've worked up a healthy appetite. There are also more conventional dishes, some very good salads and a very light chestnut pudding with cherry sauce (they call that 'dumplings' too – force of habit, I suppose).

You could, of course, just go to Schloss Kammer to sit on the terrace (in fine weather I know of few better places, with the lake shimmering below and the snow-capped mountains in the distance) and sip a glass of wine or a 'Stamperl' (2 cl) or their fiery eau-de-vie – and after a little while you will start feeling hungry ...

A four-hundred-year-old farmhouse – just down the meadow from the Schloss – was recently converted into very attractive apartments which can be rented at equally attractive prices.

How to get there: From Zell am See direction Saalfelden on 311 to Maishofen. Turn right into Maishofen where take left turn for Schloss Kammer.

Mautern (Wachau) *Lower Austria*

LANDHAUS BACHER
Südtirolerplatz 208
3512 Mautern
☏ 02732 82937
Open: 12.00–15.00, 18.30–22.00 Wednesday/Sunday, beginning November/end April
18.30–22.00 Monday/Tuesday
12.00–15.00, 18.30–22.00 Wednesday/Sunday
Closed: Monday, Tuesday beginning November/end April
Monday all day and Tuesday lunch May/October
also closed end January/end February
Prices: upward/expensive

Lisl Wagner-Bacher is the First Lady of Austrian cooking – no doubt about that whatsoever. A superb cook who has not had any 'official' training, cooking exactly according to her personal taste and adjusting and improving traditional dishes and thereby lifting them into hitherto undreamed-of culinary spheres. (She was proclaimed Chef of the Year in 1983, the year the nomination was first made, but I knew she was a genius when – some years before that – I first tasted her blood-orange sorbet. Her specialities are numerous like *Entensülzchen* (duck in aspic) or a delicate salad of zucchini, truffles and goose liver for starters, but on no account fail to ask for details of the *Spezialsüppchen* (special soups of the day) which are quite remarkable. Main courses are of course inspired as well, like the pike/perch with *Senfgurkensauce* (mustard and cucumber sauce) or the filet of veal with mozzarella, Parma ham and polenta, but Lisl Wagner-Bacher's roast goose (served in generous portions) is exemplary and her saddle of venison with morels and potato soufflé as well as her roast pheasant are beyond compare. Puddings are worth the journey to Mautern from wherever (even on a cold winter's day) and I'd travel a long way for the *Apfel-Lebkuchenschmarren* (a marvellous concoction based on honey-cake) or the *gefüllte Miniananas* (small pineapple) *auf Sektsabayon* and *Mandelparfait*.

The wine cellar is one of the best in Austria, containing about 20,000 bottles including the most complete selection of top Austrian wines as well as a superb choice from France and Italy, many of which are available in half bottles. You can stay very comfortably at Landhaus Bacher with very good terms for half-board and there are also special cookery courses (Lisl Wagner-Bacher has also written an excellent cookery book) and wine seminaries. On a recent visit some time during the afternoon I found Lisl Wagner-Bacher earnestly discussing food with a guest staying at the Landhaus. A special dinner? A celebration lunch? Not at all: the newly arrived guest's dog was not feeling very well and Lisl Wagner-Bacher was putting forward menu suggestions for the light supper she was about to cook for the dog, before setting about cooking that evening's dinner for her guests. Now I know the true meaning of 'lucky dog'.

How to get there: from Vienna on 3 to Krems where you cross over the Danube to Mautern. Do not be misled by first impressions – Landhaus Mautern may appear rather stark and plain at first, but it is very elegantly appointed (Klaus Wagner is rather proud of his collection of about 2000 Riedel glasses) and there's of course the typical *Gasthausgarten* well shaded by ancient trees.

Mayerling ***Lower Austria***

HOTEL MARIENHOF
2534 Mayerling 1
☎ 02258 23790

Open: Café Restaurant Marienhof 7.00–1.00 Tuesday/Sunday
Restaurant Kronprinz 12.00–15.00 (kitchen 14.00) 18.00–24.00 (kitchen 21.00) Tuesday evening/Sunday lunch
Closed: Café Restaurant Marienhof: all day Monday

Restaurant Kronprinz: from 17.00 Sunday until Tuesday 18.00
Prices: Café Restaurant Marienhof: moderate
Restaurant Kronprinz: moderate/expensive

The untimely death of Crown Prince Rudolf in 1889 is still referred to as 'the tragedy' or 'the mystery' of Mayerling and the latter it will probably remain forever. There have been plays, films, a ballet (and a proposed musical) as well as literally thousands of newspaper articles, all of which has never ceased to attract visitors. Not that there is very much to see – the famous hunting lodge where it all happened is now a convent with guided tours and a rather sparse exhibition (scraps of carpet, cups from which the Crown Prince may or may not have drunk on his last or any other night), but there's no denying the fact that the atmosphere is rather strange and definitely eerie (I was taken there as a child and fled screaming from the place, not knowing anything about the background. I was fetched back rather smartly, told not to be silly and that if I had any ideas of having been to Mayerling in a previous life, I must have been a chambermaid!) All this notwithstanding, Mayerling is certainly worth a visit if only for the strange attraction it has for visitors more than a hundred years after the event. There is also a charming modern hotel, the Marienhof, nicely set a little further up the hill amidst meadows and woods, with good accommodation (balconies overlooking the Vienna Woods) and two completely different restaurants. *Café Restaurant Marienhof* is a typically Austrian restaurant, '*gut bürgerlich*' to the core, with a wide terrace, comfortable dining-room and moderate prices, open from the early hours of the morning until the early hours of the next day and serving practically everything from breakfast to dinner, including mid-morning and mid-afternoon snacks and anything else you care to order – good country inn food, well prepared and moderately priced. The rather irreverently named *Kronprinz* (Crown Prince) Restaurant is something else again – highly creative cooking in a very luxurious setting (at commensurate prices). To give you the right 'Imperial' feeling you can drink a glass of champagne on the terrace and wines to complement the *menu degustation* are offered at an all-in price. (Shades of the Crown Prince who would sternly admonish his wife, Crown Princess Stephanie, about the right wines to order for dinner, whilst she was forever complaining about the coarseness of Viennese cooking.) In fact even Crown Princess Stephanie could not have complained about the cooking at the Kronprinz – it is light, original with some quite unexpected touches and innovations and the same light creative hand is applied to Viennese specialities. And the Crown Prince would certainly have approved the selection of wines.

How to get there: from Vienna on A.2 or 17, then on to A.21 direction Hinterbrühl and Alland. Exit at Alland, then follow directions for

Heiligenkreuz on to 11 (to the left). After about 2 km turn right signposted Marienhof and you will find Hotel Marienhof a little further on the left. (If you continue on this road you come straight into Mayerling with the famous hunting lodge on your right.)

Mondsee *Upper Austria*

CONDITOREI FRAUENSCHUH
Marktplatz 8
5310 Mondsee
☏ 06232 2312
Open: 8.00–19.00
Closed: Wednesday, except during June, July and August
Prices: moderate

Comparatively small and almost hidden in Mondsee's main square, Frauenschuh is one of the best *pâtisseries* in Austria. Everything is made on the spot, including the confectionery and of absolute top quality. I'd travel a long way for their *Ribislschaumkuchen* (red currant gâteau with a soft meringue) and though it may be considered heresy, I prefer their chocolate log to Zauner's at Bad Ischl (q.v.); it is of a wonderful soft yet crunchy consistency. They serve beautiful hot puddings too – *Milchrahmstrudel* (*Strudel* filled with curd, sugar and raisins) and *Topfenpalatschinken* (curd cheese pancakes) and a host of others. Real *Eiskaffee* which should be soft and creamy is getting rarer and rarer in Austria – Frauenschuh's is the real thing and an absolute joy, as are their ice-creams. In fact when there was no time for a proper visit I've slipped in there and bought a tub of their ice-cream, to be eaten on the shores of the lake a bit further on, where the waters all but meet the road and there's usually a small secluded bay in which to park a car and have a dip in the lake afterwards. Frauenschuh deserves a more leisurely visit – in fact it is well worth a small detour – don't miss it!

How to get there: from Salzburg on A.1. direction Vienna, exit at Mondsee (about 25 km from Salzburg). Frauenschuh is in the main square.

Mondsee/Plomberg *Upper Austria*

LANDHAUS PLOMBERG – ESCHLBÖCK
5310 Mondsee – Plomberg
☏ 06232 2912
Open: 12.00–14.00, 19.00–21.00 Tuesday/Sunday
Open all week from June to end of August
Note: During the Salzburg Festival the restaurant stays open for dinner after performances
Closed: Sundays (September/June)
Prices: expensive

It is not just the position of Eschlböck's – one of the most beautiful in Austria, with a garden bordering the lake – that draws people from far and wide (and makes them drive out from Salzburg after festival performances), it is first and foremost Karl Eschlböck's cooking. Often called the '*enfant terrible*' of Austrian chefs, he's a genius nevertheless – creative, imaginative and yes, temperamental at times. Eating at Eschlböck's will never be dull – he may well invent a new dish or give an unexpected twist of flavouring to an old favourite whilst preparing it. Eschlböck was the first to take homely dishes and ingredients and elevate them to higher culinary regions – to make a *parfait* of plain black pudding, to resurrect an old Tyrolean dish called *Blunzeng'röstl* (much copied by other restaurants throughout the country ever since) and to do wondrous things with *Kalbsbeuschel* (for description look at the glossary) by cooking it with a Riesling sauce. Some of these dishes now take their rightful place on the menu under '*die Klassiker*' where they are listed together with old favourites such as *Rahmkalbsgulyas* and *gedämpfter Tafelspitz* with 'classic' accompaniments. Salmon trout from the lake served with *Krautfleckerl* (q.v.) certainly comes into the category of 'unusual' if successful combinations, but the *parfait* of goose liver (served with home-baked *brioche*) will be exactly as one would expect it – perfect. I'd travel a long way for Eschlböck's fish and game dishes and the puddings are beyond compare: simple dishes like a *Flammerie* with raspberry coulis, chocolate mousse or his *Zwetschkencrepes* (crêpes with a wonderful soft filling of curd cheese and plums, served with a plum and cinnamon sauce) are out of this world.

Splendid wine list – and quite a number of wines are sold by the glass.

You can stay very comfortably – and not too expensively – at Eschlböck's, but don't blame me for any dietary indulgences!

How to get there: from Salzburg on the motorway direction Vienna, exit at Mondsee (name of the lake as well as of a small town). At Mondsee (town) take road 154 for St Gilgen. Drive through St Lorenzen and you will find Plomberg just after that – a tiny village on Mondsee.

Landhaus Eschlböck

Eschlböck is on the right coming from Mondsee (town), with the garden on the left, directly on the lake.

Mondsee ***Upper Austria***

WEISSES KREUZ
Herzog Odilostrasse 25
5310 Mondsee
☏ 06232 2254
Open: 12.00–14.00, 18.30–21.30 September/July
12.00–14.00, 18.30–23.30 end July/end August (to cater for diners after performances at the Salzburg Festival)
Closed: Tuesday, Wednesday, (beginning September to end July) also closed mid November/mid December
Prices: upward

Mondsee is a charming small market town with a particularly attractive main square and a parish church of great Baroque splendour (the former abbey of a Benedictine monastery). The Weisses Kreuz is set in a quiet backwater, a little distance from the lake – like most hotels in Mondsee. It's a good, comfortable country hotel with an exceptionally good restaurant. Not quite as undiscovered as it might appear at first, yet by no means overcrowded, though booking, particularly during the time of the Salzburg Festival, is strongly advised. I love the rural elegance of their dining-rooms, the attentive service and above all, the perfect simplicity of the cooking which seems to get better on every visit. I tend to order their specialities every time (unadventurous, I know, but they are so good) like fresh cucumber soup (*Gurkenschaumsuppe*) which is Georg Lugerbauer's star turn (though I am told that his soup of spring onions is equally delectable), the incredibly delicate mushrooms in aspic (*Pilzsülze*) and the *Flammerie* with a purée of strawberries. I am also rather taken by the fact that the Weisses Kreuz, though by no means unsophisticated where food is concerned, take special pride in their list of *Schmankerln* (selected specials) which always include items such as oxtail with dumplings (*geschmorter Ochsenschwanz mit Knödel*), *eingemachte Kalbsschulter* (*Blanquette de veau*), *Rindsgulyas* and an excellent *Wiener Schnitzel*, all at very moderate prices, as well as a good three-course menu at S285.-.

Excellent wine list, with many wines offered by the glass.

How to get there: from Salzburg on A.1 direction Vienna, exit at Mondsee (about 25 km from Salzburg). Plenty of parking space at the Weisses Kreuz, but it is more or less behind the main square and you may have to ask the way.

MOTORWAY RESTAURANTS (ROSENBERGER)
at:

Aistersheim	Grossram
Ampass nr. Innsbruck	Haag
Angath	Loipersdorf, Burgenland
Ansfelden	Pettnau
Graz-Kaiserwald (Dobl)	St Pölten (2)
Eben im Pongau (2)	St Valentin
Gralla-Ost	Strengberg

Open: 6.00–23.00 June/October
6.00–22.00 November/May
Prices: inexpensive/moderate
No credit cards

My first encounter with Rosenberger motorway restaurants happened about thirteen or fourteen years ago, travelling on the A.1 from Vienna to Salzburg (and on to London). We stopped at the nearest motorway restaurant (I think it must have been Strengberg) for dinner expecting the usual motorway food which at that time in Austria was as mediocre and uninspired as elsewhere (and usually served in pretty grim and dismal surroundings). Surprise followed surprise – the place was light, airy and though very busy it exuded great warmth and comfort. The further you went into the restaurant the more secluded and almost elegant it got (the front though very pleasant is for motorists in a hurry). We found a window table overlooking the lush countryside (no sight or sound of the busy motorway), but the biggest surprise was the food – beautifully cooked, reasonably priced and charmingly served. There was good hot soup and I remember I had glazed calves liver with fresh vegetables (I found out later that everything is market fresh) and the puddings were obviously freshly made as well. There was a good selection of wines (with an interesting wine of the month recommendation) as well as a good choice of non-alcoholic drinks (freshly squeezed fruit juices and some excellent alcohol-free 'cocktails' with motorists in mind). I began to wonder whether all this was a mirage, but at least had the sense to ask the waitress whether there were other motorway restaurants of this kind and was told that there were indeed about three or four others.

On my next visit to Austria I visited all of them, at various times of the day, going back time and again for different meals, alone as well as accompanied and the picture never varied: excellent food, reasonably priced, well served and very pleasant surroundings. I probed further and found that these motorway restaurants were a family business started by the brothers Rosenberger who had felt that hungry motorists 'deserved better' than the usual motorway food and on meeting both brothers later on they confirmed that they had 'simply put their ideas into practice'.

There are now sixteen motorway restaurants (four of them with motels) and two hotels, as well as a restaurant in Vienna. They serve 11 million meals a year which works out to over 30,000 meals a day, yet each of these restaurants has its own character and cooking, with many local specialities. Some of the restaurants though newly built look as if they had stood there for ages (the one at Loipersdorf on the A.2 is particularly attractive and looks like a farmhouse, whilst the one at Ampass in the Tyrol was an old farmhouse and has been cleverly adapted). There are children's playgrounds, changing rooms for babies and very attractive gift shops (not exactly cheap, but everything is first rate – no tawdry souvenirs – and chocolates etc. are top class), but the most important thing is the food: everything is home-made and cooked on the premises and in some of the motorway restaurants they also bake their own bread which is also sold in the gift shops (it is so good that people travel all the way from Innsbruck to Ampass to buy it). The menu is immensely varied with many regional and local specialities and quite a few 'house specials' (lovely warming *Pongauer* potato soup with bacon and mushrooms at Eben for instance and a marvellous moist cake with fresh fruit at Ampass). The Rosenberger potato *Gulasch* (served at most of their restaurants in cold weather) is one of my favourites and they do good homely dishes like *Würstel mit Saft* (Frankfurter with *Gulasch* gravy). There are always some good vegetarian dishes on the menu, but if you want a steak, they will of course provide it, cooked exactly as ordered and their salad bar is famous (they've had to start selling the bottled dressing for taking away as it has become so popular). Throughout the year there are 'special weeks' featuring everything from a selection of *Strudel,* waffles or pancakes to old-fashioned dishes which really do come from grandmother's cookery book.

About 70% of the guests are Austrians, very often locals. On one occasion the very elegant couple at the table next to me were celebrating their wedding anniversary and when the pudding arrived, Madame found a carefully wrapped diamond ring nestling in tissue paper on top of the whipped cream – the presentation having been previously arranged by her husband in consultation with the waitress (and presumably the chef).

Some of the motorway restaurants are now run as *Market Restaurants* which though self-service are as far removed from an ordinary self-service restaurant (let alone a motorway one) as it is possible to imagine. There are a series of market stalls where you choose your food and it is prepared in front of you whilst you wait (nothing takes longer than about four minutes). I called at the Market restaurant at Pettnau on the Inntal motorway on a recent Bank Holiday Monday when – or so it seemed – the whole world and their families were *en route* to somewhere. The only difficulty was finding a parking space, though that too resolved itself, after which everything was simple. I had freshly prepared gnocchi in a creamy cheese sauce, chose a salad from a large buffet that was as good as that in many an expensive restaurant and finished with a large helping of fresh strawberries. As at all other Rosenberger motorway restaurants, there are seasonal events – I was particularly taken with the 'variations on a theme of ham' which included everything from ham on the bone and ham baked in bread dough to traditional *Schinkenfleckerl* and delicious ham croissants. In November there's usually a *Bauernmarkt* (farmers' market) with home-made sausages, *Speck,* farmhouse bread and *Krapfen* as well as apple wine which is also served hot and spiced (*Glühmost*).

Rooms at the motorway motels are very comfortable and surprisingly quiet. I stayed at Grossram on one occasion where my room looked out on to the Vienna Woods and birds came to my balcony to be fed. Hotel prices are moderate.

Neumarkt am Wallersee *Salzburg*

SCHLOSSWIRT SIGHARTSTEIN
Sighartsteiner Strasse 25
5202 Neumarkt
☏ 06216 6715
Open: 11.00–24.00 (hot food 11.30–14.00, 18.00–22.00)
Closed: Mondays
Prices: moderate

The setting could not be more typically Austrian – a sturdy old country with cosy dining-rooms, a spacious *Gasthausgarten* well shaded by ancient trees, plus the best of regional cooking, elevated to lighter – and higher regions. *Spinatcremesuppe* and *rosa Pfefferrahmsuppe* (cream of spinach and pink pepper soup respectively) were outstandingly good, as was the marinaded fish served warm with a salad (fish from the nearby lake, of course). This is the place for venison with wood mushrooms, cranberries and a light dumpling, for lamb specialities as well as for creamy veal *Gulasch* and for sampling that delicious ragout called *Kalbsrahmbeuschel* (do not be put off by the fact that it contains lights. So does haggis). The Schlosswirt is also strong on vegetarian dishes, starting with freshly pressed fruit and vegetable juices and going on to excellent salads and main dishes such as *Krautstrudel* (cabbage *Strudel*) or light gnocchi in a herb sauce (*Weizengriessnockerl in Kräutersauce*). Puddings are a joy: *Topfenterrine* with orange sauce (made with curd cheese and cream) was particularly good and the *Topfenknödel* served with a froth of cranberries and whipped cream were the best I've ever eaten (I wish somebody would think of another name – dumplings is much too mundane a description).

The wine list concentrates on the best of Austrian – and there is of course excellent beer.

How to get there: from Salzburg on 1 (not A.1) direction Neumarkt. At Neumarkt turn right for Sighartstein.

SEEHOTEL WINKLER
5202 Neumarkt am Wallersee
☏ 06216 270
Open: 9.00–24.00 (kitchen 11.30–14.00 and 18.00–21.30)
Closed: Wednesdays except during July/August
Prices: moderate

Lake Waller is one of the lesser known but no less beautiful lakes near Salzburg. Seehotel Winkler which sits right on the lake is a nice family hotel – a little more sleek than most, with its own beach and one of the most beautiful golf courses about five minutes distant. The restaurant at the Winkler has always been a favourite meeting and eating place – visitors come from even further afield than Salzburg. My favourite time for the Winkler is during late afternoon, to sit on the terrace with a drink and watch the sun set over the lake, whilst starting to contemplate dinner and studying the menu (not that there's anything wrong with going there for lunch – it is just that in the evening you usually have a beautiful sunset thrown in as well. The full name Fisch- und Schnecken-Restaurant says it all: a restaurant specializing not only in fish but also in snails, all of which are local. Of course you do not have to choose either – there are some good meat dishes as well, but the fish is exceptional. It is one of the places where I like to pick my main course first and *Wallersee Fischtopf* with garlic bread (a superb fish stew consisting exclusively of fish from the lake) is my favourite, but *Hecht im Speck gebraten* (pike wrapped in bacon and roasted, served with a herb sauce) comes a close second. To start with one could have the aforementioned snails – try their pepper version (*Pfefferschnecken*) as a change from the more usual herb butter. There's always very good fish soup, carp in aspic or marinaded fish from the lake for starters as well or try one of their good pâtés. You may well want to pause before pudding and this could be the occasion on which to order the famous *Salzburger Nockerl* which take about twenty minutes to prepare, though I stick to their *Marzipanmus* (marzipan cream) which is served with black cherries. Good wine list, mostly Austrian, with a little support from France and Italy.

How to get there: from Salzburg on 1 direction Strasswalchen and Neumarkt. Just before Neumarkt turn left Zum See which leads straight to the lake and Hotel Winkler.

Neusiedl am See — *Burgenland*

BARTH STUBEN
Franz Liszt Strasse 37
7100 Neusiedl am See
☏ 02167 2625
Open: 11.00–23.00
Closed: Mondays
Prices: moderate

One of the prettiest restaurants in Burgenland – lots of light polished wood in the airy dining-room and the flowers in tubs dotted about the small garden are matched exactly by the pink table-cloths. Until fairly recently the Barth Stuben were frequented mostly by discriminating locals, but word about the excellent cooking has spread and it is now quite usual to find visitors who have travelled all the way from Vienna. This has not affected the prices (moderate) or the standards (high); in fact the cooking, if anything, gets better every time – but booking is advisable, particularly during summer weekends.

The food is typically Austrian, with a strong Hungarian accent (beautifully spiced *Halaszlé*, the Hungarian fish soup which is practically a meal in itself) and you may well have to resort to my glossary in order not to miss out on some of the best bits (*Ribiselrotkraut* – red cabbage cooked with red currants – makes a wonderful accompaniment to venison, but you'll look for it in vain in any dictionary!). There are some excellent starters such as cream of fennel soup with pistachio nuts, sprinkled with toasted almonds, a light chicken galantine with peppered sour cream and walnut bread, or goose liver (a speciality of the region) with mushroom vinaigrette. Good fish from the lake too: eel in a herb and garlic butter or simply prepared pike/perch. Some of the main dishes are more elaborate such as fillet strips in a green and pink pepper sauce and a particularly good rack of lamb, well seasoned with herbs and roasted in a caul. Good accompaniments too – apart from the aforementioned red cabbage with red currants – green peppers gently simmered with onions to go with the smoked fillet of pork, rice flecked with walnuts, home-made saffron noodles and broccoli purée. Puddings are a joy, though you may need my glossary again for *Kipferlauflauf mit Marillenröster* (very light pudding made with Viennese croissants, accompanied by apricots stewed in their own juice, with added spices) or *Biskottenterrine auf Pralinensauce* (terrine of layered boudoir biscuits with a nougat/chocolate sauce) unless you order their selection of puddings and sample the lot!

The wine list is quite exceptional – the best of Austrian (note also the remarkable selection of Auslesen, Beerenauslesen, Trockenbeerenauslesen, Eisweine, Ausbruch) with 'excursions' to France, Spain and Italy.

Barth Stuben are open all day and they are perfectly happy if you just order a small snack or a slice of their famous *Mohntorte* (poppyseed cake) with your afternoon tea or coffee, but their full menu is available throughout the day. (On occasion you may care to sample *Burgenland Krautsuppe* (spiced cabbage soup) supposedly the best cure for a hangover and a guaranteed 'reviver', like essence of Tokay, only considerably cheaper and more readily available!)

How to get there: from Eisenstadt to Neusiedl am See on 50, changing on to 51 just before Neusiedl. Drive along Neusiedl's very long main street (which is in fact road 51) until you come to the post office (set back a little from the road on the left). Turn left and left again which is Franz Liszt Strasse. Barth Stuben are on the right.

Pettnau *Tyrol*

ROSENBERGER AUTOBAHNRESTAURANT
PETTNAU
6020 Pettnau
☏ 05238 87350
Open: 6.00–23.00 June/October
6.00–22.00 November/May
Prices: inexpensive

A.12 Inntal Motorway – accessible from both directions

Market Restaurant
No credit cards

For description see under Motorway Restaurants (Rosenberger)

Pörtschach am Wörthersee *Carinthia*

SCHLOSS LEONSTAIN
Hauptstrasse 228
9210 Pörtschach am Wörthersee
☏ 04272 28160
Open: 7.00–2.00 a.m. (kitchen 12.00–13.30, 19.30–22.00)
Closed: Beginning October/beginning May
Prices: moderate/upward

Do not be put off by the fact that Schloss Leonstain sits directly on the main road – the walls are thick, the dining-rooms cosy and secluded and there's a magnificent old linden tree in the enclosed courtyard which alone would warrant a visit. (The courtyard serves as an extra 'dining-room' in fine weather, and that is most of the time in the southern climate of Carinthia.) Exactly the right setting for the very reasonably priced set lunch or the rather more expensive four-course dinner which is usually very Austrian indeed. (*Tafelspitz* comes with *Wiener Kohl* – creamed savoy cabbage or *Cremespinat*, as well as with its 'proper' sauces – the semolina gnocchi in the soup are light and fluffy and the nougat pancakes as mother's cook would have made them at a time when mother still employed a *Mehlspeisköchin* – a cook whose sole job it was to produce delicious puddings). Delicious too the choice from the à la carte menu – avocado cream soup or consommé made from dwarf tomatoes with small basil gnocchi, properly roasted duck with morello cherries and red cabbage, roast veal with walnut sauce, excellent game and fish. Dessert variations are definitely worth sampling, and so are the plum dumplings (*Zwetschkenknödel*). There are special dinners on Tuesdays and Thursdays, and on Sunday evening there's a candlelight buffet. (Do not be put off by the various printing errors on the menu – offering 'Mouse' instead of Mousse on my last visit – they do not extend to the kitchens!)

Brahms spent two summers at Schloss Leonstain – even before it became the superbly comfortable and beautifully run hotel which it is now – a recommendation well worth considering.

Purbach *Burgenland*

AM SPITZ
Waldsiedlung 2
7083 Purbach
☏ 02683 5519
Open: 11.00–21.30 (limited menu between 14.00–17.00)
Closed: Mondays and from Sunday before Christmas until end March
Prices: moderate

Ten barrels of the best Purbach wine and forty oxen bought the local castle for a certain Count Nickolaus in the thirteenth century. Worth it for the site alone I'd say. The inn which now stands in place of the old castle and a later monastery could not be more ideally placed: on a small plateau from which you get marvellous views over Lake Neusiedl and far into Hungary, surrounded by vineyards (the road leading up to it is almost completely submerged by vines – so much so that you might begin to wonder whether the sign on the main road saying 'Gasthof am Spitz' had pointed the right way after all). Summers in this part of Austria are exceptionally hot and dry and seem to last forever which makes the garden, full of flowering oleander trees, a favourite spot (you move into the comfortable dining-room when it gets chilly later on – in time for the game specialities).

Gasthof am Spitz started its culinary career – as have some of the best restaurants in Austria – as a '*Backhendlstation*', a place specializing in fried spring chicken. It is still one of their specialities, but nowadays the owners proudly encourage you to 'order your favourite dish, even if you cannot find it on the menu' (except on Sundays). I do not know whether many visitors have done so – except to order one of the specialities which they had previously enjoyed and which may be absent from the menu on that day, for the selection of dishes is exceptionally varied and changes constantly. Mousse of smoked carp and *Quenelles* of local fish (*Poschierte Fischnockerln*) in a light dill cream are favourite starters, as are *Sülzchen von Neusiedlerseefischen* (local fish aspic), chicken liver mousse which comes with Eiswein aspic and Grandmother Hölzl's chicken soup with small celeriac and bone-marrow dumplings. *Schindelbraten* – delicately spiced roast arranged in overlapping slices like tiles (*Schindeln*) or carp baked with smoked ham in a cream sauce are but two of the main course specialities, as is the *Zweigeltrostbraten* (steak with a rich red wine sauce). There are some very light desserts like Orange *Parfait*, excellent *Eiskaffee* or red-currant sorbet, but if you can possibly manage something a little more substantial, this is definitely the place for a good Austrian pudding such as the poppy-seed pancakes with lightiy caramelized apples which my companion declared 'sensational', and in season ask for the cherry specialities – Purbach cherries vie in excellence with those of Donnerskirchen and Schützen.

The wine list is superb, offering only Austrian wines from their own vineyards and there are some remarkable eaux-de-vie and a *Marc* (called Traminertrebernbrand), as well as a digestif made from green walnuts – all their own produce. (If Herr Schwarz Senior is not too busy, ask him to take you to his wine cellar which is all but buried under the vineyards – you will pass it on the way back to Purbach).

Next to the restaurant there's a very pleasant guest house owned by the same family – as moderately priced as the restaurant.

How to get there: from Eisenstadt on 50 direction Neusiedl to Purbach. In Purbach turn left, following poster to Gasthof am Spitz. The road through vineyards will seem endless, but, in fact, it is about 1 km long and completely submerged by vines and when you think you have lost your way you will have arrived at Am Spitz.

NIKOLAUSZECHE
Bodenzeile 3
7083 Purbach
☎ 02683 5514
Open: 11.30–24.00
Closed: Tuesdays and from beginning December to mid March
Prices: upward/expensive

Take a picturesque sixteenth-century building with an enclosed courtyard and flowering shrubs, and you can see why the Nikolauszeche was known as one of Burgenland's most attractive restaurants – even though it had started to crumble in places and 'attractive' or even 'adequate' was hardly the adjective one would have lavished on the cooking. Not any more – the Nikolauszeche is now a 'country cousin' of Vienna's famous Zu den 3 Husaren and prettier than ever after a little sympathetic sprucing up – with a small, but excellent selection of dishes, a superb wine list and what the Austrians would call *gehobene* (uplifted) prices, though by no means out of proportion to what is being offered. The flavour is strongly Austro-Hungarian: *Topfenhaluzka* (curd cheese pasta) with *Paprikacreme* and *Kalbsgulasch* (veal goulash) are offered side by side with delicate home-made brawn (*Haussulz*) which comes with a vinaigrette to which the green pumpkin-seed oil of Styria lends its nutty flavour. I had the best rack of lamb I've ever eaten (sauce scented with thyme) accompanied by small lentil and bacon pancakes and the sauce which

Nikolauszeche, Purbach

went with the fillet of beef had a sharp tang of Rosemary. There was a *parfait* made from local apricots and the light curd dumplings (*Topfenknödel*) were served not, as is more usual, with breadcrumbs, but with ground walnuts browned in butter.

The very extensive wine list features wines from the Burgenland only, 'since – after all – we are in one of the best wine regions in the country'. Precisely.

How to get there: from Eisenstadt on 50 direction Neusiedl am See. Turn right as you get into Purbach and left at the end of this road which should bring you straight to Nickolauszeche.

Rankweil ***Vorarlberg***

MOHREN
Stiegstrasse 17
6830 Rankweil
☎ 05522 44275
Open: 12.00–24.00
Closed: Mondays
Prices: moderate

Good, solid and dependable, this small country hotel with its large restaurant or perhaps it should be put the other way round because the rooms are really just an appendage to the restaurant which is a great gathering point, not only for locals, but also for 'regulars' coming from across the Swiss and German border. Judging by the late closing times of the restaurant, I gather that quite a few are tempted to stay overnight, rather than drive back across the border.

The food is certainly excellent, relying mostly on fresh produce of which there's plenty and you'll even find the name of the local fishery on the menu by way of reassurance. The *Feinschmeckermenü* is particularly good value (choice of four or six courses), starting perhaps with a salad of sweetbreads, followed by asparagus soup and home-made lamb sausages and *Sauerkraut* cooked with wine. The main course could be fillet of pork with ceps and walnut gnocchi. There will always be a pleasant sorbet and a light – or not-so-light but delicious – pudding like strawberry mousse with pistachios or, in the latter category, dark bread pudding with a spiced wine sauce. I suppose the *Feinschmeckermenü* is intended as a *Menu degustation*, but unlike other *Menues degustation*, portions are as large as the dishes are delicate. Larger still – and equally delicate – if you order à la carte: lightly cooked goose liver with apples, and salmon trout with dill cream and asparagus. There are some excellent vegetarian dishes and very good puddings, but be careful when ordering *Apple Strudel* – they serve it with Vanilla ice-cream and cream (which to add insult to injury they call *Sahne*). I know that this is probably what visitors from across the border want and expect, and you can of course always order it without either of these additions. Good and varied wine list which includes local Röthner Blauburgunder and there's also Fraxner Kirsch and Rankweil Grappa by way of aperitif (or digestif).

The hotel rooms are simple, but very comfortable, mostly with balconies.

How to get there: from Bregenz on A.12 (or 190) direction Feldkirch, exit for Rankweil.

Rosenau nr. Zwettl — *Lower Austria*

SCHLOSS ROSENAU
3924 Rosenau bei Zwettl
☎ 02822 8221
Open: 7.30–22.00
Closed: mid January/end February
(Museum open from 26 March–15 November, 9.00–17.00)
Prices: inexpensive/moderate

Schloss Rosenau is a treasure – originally a Renaissance castle, completely rebuilt by Munggenast during the eighteenth century, with ceiling fresco by Daniel Gran (and a ceiling fresco attributed to Paul

Troger in the chapel, now the parish church), it sits serenely amidst dense woods and meadows. Part of the castle was a Masonic temple during the eighteenth century and now houses the only Masonic museum in Europe. The castle has been transformed into a very comfortable hotel, very reasonably priced and the full-board terms are outstandingly good value. The restaurant – open to non-residents, of course, is a typical country inn, offering good robust country food, served in generous portions: *Waldviertler Rahmsuppe* (soup made with sour cream, typical of the region) roast suckling pig (*Spanferkel*) with *Speckkrautsalat* (cabbage salad with crisp bits of bacon) and Waldviertler dumplings, home-made black pudding and good game dishes. Poppy seeds are strongly in evidence throughout the Waldviertel (the 'forest region' in which Rosenau is situated) and you should try at least one of their special puddings – either the poppy-seed soufflé or the *Mohnsterz*. The fixed price lunch and dinner are particularly good value at prices ranging between S90.- and about S150.-. On my last visit Sunday lunch consisted of good beef broth with small herb dumplings, followed by a giant portion of roast duck with red cabbage and potato croquettes and then a choice of strawberry tart or *Eiskaffee* topped with a small mountain of whipped cream, all for S130.-. (The supper on that day was creamy vegetable soup, followed by a huge cold collation and then either chocolate profiteroles or strawberries with ice-cream – at an 'all-in' price of S90.-!). If the sturdy local food sounds too hearty for you, there's a special section on the menu, endearingly headed *'Internationalen Gästen bieten wir'* – ('for our international guests') which includes *Chateaubriand* as well as *Pariser Schnitzel*, a particularly delicious – and strictly Austrian – version of *Schnitzel*.

Very good selection of Austrian wines, many of which are offered by the glass, splendid local beer and some excellent *Schnaps* (try the quince or the *Mostbirnenbrand* (pear).

How to get there: from Zwettl on 38 in the direction of Weitra. About 3 km outside Zwettl take left fork for Schloss Rosenau and follow further signposts.

Röthis — *Vorarlberg*

TORGGEL
Torggelweg 1
6832 Röthis
☏ 05522 44052
Open: 11.00–24.00 (Full menu 11.30–14.00, 18.00–22.45)
Hot and cold snacks between 14.00–18.00)
Closed: Tuesdays and Wednesdays until 18.00
Prices: moderate/upward

Torggel means 'wine press' and an ancient one of these stands in the centre of the restaurant, the only remaining one of ten which were used in the region. It is an exceptionally attractive restaurant – sprawling yet compact, with its corners and crannies, added space and tables placed in such a way that one has the feeling of complete seclusion. It is also an exceptionally friendly restaurant – friendly to children (with a garden as well as a children's playground) and weary travellers alike. On my first visit I arrived late in the evening, not having reserved a table, at what looked like a completely full restaurant (and not an inch of parking space). In no time at all room was found for my car and I was seated at a comfortable table with an aperitif and told to take my time studying the menu. It is a very varied menu with traditional Austrian dishes listed under *bürgerlich* (bourgeois) and a good selection of specialities with a regional yet light touch. This is also reflected in the two fixed price menus: a three-course typically Austrian one (listed as *Österreichische küche*) and a *Feinschmeckermenü* with six courses. (If you think that this is a good chance to sample some of the specialities, this is fine, but be warned: 'sampling' is not the operative word, for the portions are fairly large!) Be advised on the house specialities which are seasonal: Asparagus Mousse with goose liver, salmon with chervil cream, game … and if *Caramelisierte Strudelteigblätter mit frischen Beeren* (caramelized wafer-thin pastry leaves with fresh berries) are on the menu, look no further!

Particularly good selection of wines and digestifs, with emphasis on Austria (including some local Vorarlberg wines) supported by Italy, France, Spain and Switzerland.

How to get there: from Bregenz on 190 direction Feldkirch to Götzis and from there on unnumbered road to Klaus, Weiler and Röthis. In Röthis turn left up Torggelweg – Restaurant Torggel is on top of the hill.

Rotholz — *Tyrol*

ESTERHAMMER
6200 Rotholz bei Jenbach
☏ 05244 2212
Open: 7.30–24.00 (kitchen 11.30–14.00, 18.00–20.30)
Prices: inexpensive/moderate

You can spot Esterhammer from afar – a large, long-stretched building set well back from the main road on a slight hill and definitely 'lording' it over its surroundings. As befits a *landesfürstlich und kaiserlich privilegierter Gasthof* – an inn granted ducal and imperial privileges in 1581, and one which has been in the same family since 1730. The present building, which also houses a very comfortable hotel, only dates back to the last century, but the core is Gothic and some of the dining-rooms have the original Renaissance panelling on walls and ceilings. Very superior dining-rooms too and far more elegant than one would expect of a country inn with damask table-cloths and napkins, fresh flowers and candles. But then, Esterhammer's is no ordinary country inn – you are the much-welcomed and honoured guest of a family for whom hospitality is not a mere word in the dictionary.

Although kitchen hours are restricted, this applies only to main meals. You can always eat at Esterhammer's – from breakfast until late at night. Meet your friends over a mid-morning cup of coffee and a slice of cake in one of the dining-rooms or sit on the sun-drenched terrace for a draught of their own Obstler (a pretty potent eau-de-vie) or a beer to accompany a platter of sausages and cheese with good dark country bread. Like the very best country inns, Esterhammer has its own home farm which makes for superb quality meat. Definitely the place to order a *Schlachtplatte* at one of the main meal times (pork in its varieties from sausages to ham) served with *Sauerkraut* and dumplings or pickled ox-tongue (*Rindspöckelzunge*). Excellent game and very good selection of grills. Portions are of gigantic 'country inn' proportions, but the kitchen has a remarkably light hand when it comes to specialities such as *Spinatknödel* (spinach dumplings served with brown butter and grated cheese) and gnocchi. There is, of course, always a good three-course lunch for around S105.-.

All cakes and gâteaux are home-made (again gigantic portions). Try the almond cake (*Mandelkuchen*) *mit Schlag* if it is on the menu. You have to be early for this, as the chances are that someone has snuffled the last portion with their morning coffee – it sells as fast as the proverbial hot cakes!

How to get there: from Innsbruck on 171 direction Wörgl past Schwaz and the small village of Buch. Signpost for Rotholz to the right (opposite Jenbach). Follow it and it will land you practically outside Esterhammer's.

Ruden nr. Untermittendorf — *Carinthia*

PFAU
9113 Untermittendorf 1
☏ 04234 8221
Open: 11.00–14.00, 18.00–21.00 (kitchen)
Closed: Monday, Tuesday (October/April only) and beginning January to end March
Prices: moderate

Literally in the middle of nowhere in particular – or rather in eight hectares of orchards – this small, modern restaurant is spread fanwise like a peacock's tail (hence the name). Worth the journey for their *Schnaps* alone (the raspberry one in particular is sensational and bottles of the *Pfau* brand can now be found in some of the best restaurants). The menu is fairly short, but in most cases lists the local suppliers, not only of meat and fish, but also of herbs and oil and in some cases even the types of potatoes accompanying a dish. If all this sounds 'too much of a good thing', let me assure you that the cooking is first-rate and does credit to the excellent raw materials. You may well start with *Mostsuppe* (soup made with apple wine) served in a hollowed-out large bread roll (*im Brottopf serviert*) or a mixture of different smoked meats (from different local suppliers) and there are always a number of Carinthian specialities on the menu. This is the place for *Kärntner Nudeln* (pasta filled with curd cheese and fresh herbs), for pork basted with apple wine and *Mastochsenbraten* (pot roast) with root vegetables, herbs and cranberries. Obviously apples are featured prominently throughout the menu and are much used in the cooking and there is a rather special pudding, *Apfelknödel* in *Mostsauce* (apples cooked with spices and a good dash of the Pfau's apple *Schnaps* and served with a cream made of apple-juice and apple-wine). The Pfau is one of the few places where you can choose your apple-juice according to the different kinds of apples used and it is the only place in Austria which offers wine grown in Carinthia. Good selection of Austrian and North Italian wines, many of which are offered by the glass, as well as the famous Villach beer.

The orchards are open for inspection. You can duly admire Williams' pears growing into bottles (basis for their excellent pear *Schnaps*) and 'adopt' an apple tree for S300.- which entitles you to ten years' harvest (to be reaped in fruit or – alas small – quantities of apple *Schnaps*). All excellent reasons for coming back to the Pfau which has a few good, comfortable guest rooms at very reasonable prices.

How to get there: Take the 70 from Klagenfurt to Völkermarkt, about 3 km past Völkermarkt take right fork on to 80, direction Lavamünd. Drive for about 14 km, then take left turning direction Ruden. The Pfau is well sign-posted after that.

Salzburg *Salzburg*

BAYRISCHER HOF
Kaiserschützenstrasse 1
5021 Salzburg
☏ 0662 46970
Open: 11.00–14.30, 18.00–22.30 Monday/Friday
Closed: Saturday, Sunday
and first two weeks in February
Prices: moderate

A restaurant in an hotel close to Salzburg's main station? Precisely. Go there at noon on any weekday and you'll find out why, but book first, because by that time every available table will have been taken! The Bayrischer Hof has been a favourite eating place for Salzburg worthies (business as well as private) for a long, long time. The food is very traditionally Austrian, meaning that it encompasses the culinary repertoire of the former Austro-Hungarian Empire and includes *Szegediner Krautfleisch* (well-spiced pork goulash with *Sauerkraut*) as well as *Wiener Zwiebelrostbraten, Schweinsjungferl im Speckmantel* (roast pork fillet wrapped in bacon) with a sauce based on beer, good Austrian puddings including *Salzburger Nockerl* (of course) and some of the less usual Austrian cheeses, served with home-baked walnut bread. The fixed-price lunch ranks amongst the best value in town: soup, usually good beef broth with some addition such as small liver dumplings or gnocchi, followed by a traditional meat dish (often *Tafelspitz* or *Kavalierspitz,* (the famous 'boiled beef of Vienna' with its classic accompaniments) and then a good, old-fashioned pudding like *Mohr im Hemd* (chocolate pudding topped with whipped cream and chocolate sauce) or Apple *Strudel* fresh from the oven (for about S125.-) being typical examples. In the evening there is a five-course *Menu degustation* – more expensive and more elaborate. Best of Austrian wines, with some Italian, French and Spanish added for good measure, and the wine recommendation of the month is always worth considering. There is also good Salzburg beer.

The Bayrischer Hof is also a very comfortable hotel, fairly recently modernized (soundproof windows).

CAFÉ WINKLER
Am Mönchsberg 32
5020 Salzburg
☏ 0662 8412150
Open: 11.00–24.00 (full menu 12.00–14.00, 19.00–22.00)
Closed: Monday all day and Tuesday until 14.00 (except during Salzburg Festival)
Prices: upward/expensive

There's no better view of Salzburg than from the terrace or a window table at the Café Winkler. Do not be misled by the name however – it is not just a 'mere' Café (though certainly serving drinks and snacks between 'proper' meal-times). The Winkler is one of Salzburg's most luxurious restaurants and probably named Café to avoid confusion with the restaurant of the Hotel Winkler in town (which is in fact called Jedermann) and possibly also to encourage visitors to make full use of its facilities throughout the day. The view, beautiful in daytime, takes on a magic quality at night when most of the principal Salzburg buildings are floodlit and it says much for the food and service that I'd still rate it as one of Salzburg's best restaurants even on a rainy day when the famous Salzburg Schnürlregen (rain as fine as a thread) blots out most of the view! Manfred Brugger is an excellent chef and if he is given to occasional gimmicks and rather elaborately decorated food, this is perfectly understandable – rather like saying 'pay attention to this – Salzburg will still be there later on'. Clear paprika soup with quail's egg is excellent and the potato soup (served in a hollowed-out baked potato) equally commendable and although I'd list what they call '*Der Paprika als Cremesuppe*' definitely under the aforementioned gimmicks, the unusual presentation (cream of red, green and yellow peppers arranged in a swirl in a soup plate) was certainly successful and tasted every bit as good as it looked. There's excellent suckling pig with small dumplings made from pumpkin seeds and *Sauerkraut* (the dumplings can also be ordered as a main course with *Sauerkraut*, crackling and liver sausage) and splendid pheasant with red onions and lentil sauce. Puddings include '*Die Blutorange mit dem besten vom warmen Lebkuchen*' a good combination of blood orange with warm honey-cake and fried ice dumplings (*gebackene Eisknödel*) served with strawberry beignets – rather unusual but delicious.

Good selection of Austrian wines (particularly strong on Lower Austria) with excursions to France and Italy.

How to get there: Café Winkler can be reached by lift from Neumayerplatz (at the end of Griesgasse) next to the 'Haus der Natur'. The return fare is S19.-.

GOLDENER HIRSCH
Getreidegasse 37
5020 Salzburg
☏ 0662 848511
Open: 12.00–15.00 (kitchen 14.30)
18.30–24.00 (kitchen 21.30 – later during Festival time)
Prices: upward/expensive

It is quite true that a lot of people go to the Goldener Hirsch – especially at the time of the Salzburg Festivals (Mozart, Easter and the Summer Festival) – to see and to be seen – it is then packed with celebrities. At that time the kitchens will be overworked, there will be large private parties within and without the Goldener Hirsch who do a fair amount of outside catering as well and although they will do their utmost, you are likely to be disturbed by the frenzied atmosphere (unless you wish to stargaze or be spotted). I go to the Goldener Hirsch when I want to feel cherished – at times other than at Festival times – and for Herbert Pöckelhofer's cooking which I can then enjoy at its very best. I must plead partiality here – some years ago, staying at the Goldener Hirsch just before Christmas, I received an urgent request from my London newspaper for an additional Christmas recipe. Herbert Pöckelhofer took time off from his busy schedule (they had a banquet for 200 in addition to their usual restaurant diners that night) and gave me his own treasured recipe for roasting goose, testing it in the restaurant kitchen that night. I had a score of complimentary readers' letters as a result of that particular recipe – but if you're now thinking, 'Ah, that's why she gets preferential treatment in the restaurant' you'd be wrong: I've been to the Goldener Hirsch unheralded and unsung, without staying at the hotel and the treatment has always been the same: marvellously courteous with impeccable service. And the cooking, particularly outside Festival times, is absolutely first class – elevated Austrian with strong individual touches – one of the few places where I would accept the *menu degustation* without hesitation. (On the last occasion there was a starter of smoked eel in Riesling aspic, followed by a very Austrian cream of cauliflower soup with small herb dumplings, excellent rack of lamb in a herb crust, thyme-scented sauce with *ratatouille* and *Schupfnudeln* – special gnocchi made with potato paste. There was also a selection of Austrian cheeses and finally chocolate mousse with strawberries). Choosing à la carte on other occasions I've greatly enjoyed quail stuffed with goose liver wrapped in puff pastry with a wine sauce and mushrooms and superb saddle of venison, properly served with *Serviettenknödel*, red cabbage and cranberries – which like all the dishes listed under '*aus der Küche unserer Heimat*' was Austrian cooking at its very best. The Goldener Hirsch is one of the few places where they still make old-fashioned *Schmankerlparfait* and serve it with hot morello cherries as well as Rigo Jancsi, that delectable chocolate confection filled with rich chocolate cream named after a gipsy musician who won the heart of a fair princess. Needless to say that the *Salzburger Nockerl* at the Goldener Hirsch are true to form – mountainous and featherlight.

Large wine list, geared to the international visitors at Festival times.

See also 's'Herzl vom Goldenen Hirsch' in the same street.

SCHATZ-KONDITOREI
Getreidegasse 3 (Schatz Durchhaus)
5024 Salzburg
☎ 0662 842792
Open: 8.30–18.30 Monday/Friday
8.30–13.30 Saturday
Closed: Sundays
Prices: moderate

Situated in the passage between Getreidegasse and Universitatsplatz, the Schatz-Konditorei is like a miniature stage set of a *pâtisserie*. Everything appears to be scaled down in size, yet perfect in every detail – from the sugared violets (the best this side of Parma) to the rose petal jam in small jars and the *petits fours* – only the gâteaux are of the usual Austrian giant size. Nothing miniature about the quality though – you can be sure that whatever you choose will be superb. Marvellous for buying presents too and on more than one occasion I have come away with several cartons of their extremely fragile confections, nursing them all the way back on a plane, simply because I could not make up my mind and ended up by buying half the shop.

There are some good savouries as well, like the *Schinkenkipferl* (small croissants filled with ham) which make a perfect mid-morning snack, accompanied by a glass of G'spritzter. Like practically all Austrian *pâtisseries* the Schatz Konditorei is fully licensed.

Just across from the Schatz-Konditorei – still in the same passage – is one of the nicest old shops, 'Weber', selling candles, honeycombs and above all, honeycakes which are freshly made every day. Don't miss it, if only for the glorious scent of honey and chocolate which permeates the shop.

SHERATON
Auerspergstrasse 4
5020 Salzburg
☎ 0662 793210

Open: Mirabell Restaurant 7.00–23.30,
(kitchen: Summer 12.00–14.00, 18.30–23.30
Winter 12.00–14.00, 18.30–22.00)
Bistro: Summer: 9.00–23.30
Winter: 9.00–22.00

Prices: Mirabell Restaurant: expensive (except for fixed-price lunch menu)
Bistro: inexpensive

Terrace and dining-room of the Mirabell Restaurant are a haven of luxurious peace – both overlooking the beautiful Mirabell gardens. Chef Josef Illinger (formerly at the Schlosshotel Fuschl) certainly knows how to spoil his guests, though anyone ordering à la carte at lunch-time must either be very rich or simply too comfortably seated to move to the buffet. At S.275.- (roughly the price of a main course) it is one of the great bargains in Salzburg: a splendid selection of hors-d'oeuvres (game terrine, fish in aspic, cold cuts, *vitello tonnato*, salads – to name but a few) followed by soup, and a choice of at least four hot dishes and good puddings. (In fact, it would be quite easy to select a perfectly good light luncheon from the hors-d'oeuvres table and on one occasion I did precisely that – followed only by pudding – for which I was charged the grand total of S.125.-!) Evenings are the time for à la carte and specialities such as smoked venison with lentil salad, pheasant roasted in vine leaves with a sauce of green grapes or one of the splendid fish dishes. Puddings are commendable too: *Gewürzpudding* with a sabayon of mulled wine, chestnut crêpes with tangerine sorbet and a host of other delectable 'temptations'. Enormous wine list as befits a five-star hotel.

The Mirabell Restaurant and particularly the terrace is also a splendid place for afternoon tea (or breakfast for that matter) open to non-residents. It is one of the few places in Austria where tea owes nothing to a tea bag!

The Bistro (entrance to the left of the hotel entrance) has long been 'discovered' by locals (in and out of season) for inexpensive fixed-price meals without fuss, and Salzburg locals know a thing or two about good value!

s'HERZL vom GOLDENEN HIRSCH
Getreidegasse 35 (entrance also at Sigmundsplatz 7)
5020 Salzburg
☎ 0662 848517/889
Open: daily 11.00–24.00 (hot food until 22.00)
Prices: inexpensive

s'Herzl (little heart) of the elegant Goldener Hirsch next door is a perfectly good inn in its own right – comfortable and comforting, whether you just want a drink, a snack or a full meal. 'Little' dishes are served throughout the day, like *Gulasch* soup accompanied by a *Vinschgerl* (crusty wholemeal roll with caraway seeds) and the selection of sausages alone would warrant a visit: grilled *Nürnberger* with *Sauerkraut* and freshly grated horseradish (smallest order is for six and it goes up to a dozen!), Munich Whites, hot liver sausage, black pudding (*Blutwurst*) and the house speciality *Saure Zipfl* (sausages served in a sharp bouillon with onions). At 'proper' meal times there's an inexpensive set meal as well as a *Tageskarte* when dishes of the day are added to the 'permanent' menu – *Schinkenfleckerl* perhaps (little pasta squares with ham, *au gratin*) or *Medaillons* of pork in a sharp pepper sauce with dumplings, plus – and this is where s'Herzl scores over other inns – about three or four dishes (including puddings) straight from the *Tageskarte* (and the kitchens) of the Goldener Hirsch. At just slightly over half the price! It is not only a question of price – there are times when it is a positive pleasure to enjoy a rather grand dish in a very informal atmosphere (and not have to dress up for the occasion either!). To celebrate you could have a glass of the special Imperial Sekt as poured next door. Also at just slightly over half the price, of course!

ZUM KREBSEN
Paris Lodronstrasse 1
5024 Salzburg
☎ 0662 8816880
Open: 12.00–14.00, 18.00–23.00
Prices: moderate/upward

Built as a princely palace for Prince Archbishop Paris Lodron over 300 years ago, partly destroyed by fire, restored and eventually home of the renowned Zum roten Krebsen where Salzburg lyricist Georg Trakl had his *Stammtisch*, the building now houses the new Austrotel Salzburg. The restaurant – a large, lofty but convivial cellar – now just called Zum Krebsen still has many crustacean specialities. The lobster bisque is certainly delicious, but so is the cheese soup with a good dash of *Kirsch* and the *Wiener Suppentopf* (*pot au feu*) which is practically a meal in itself. In Salzburg, where they count in centuries rather than decades, the Krebsen rates as a 'new' restaurant – which in a sense it is – and they try very hard to recapture the old renown of the restaurant. My pink trout could not have been poached more perfectly (I had the feeling that someone stood over it and snatched it from the stove at exactly the right point!). *Salzburger Schnitzel*, filled with a ragout of mushrooms, was a splendid local choice and the very Austrian puddings have a number of delicious 'refinements' like the *Powidltascherl* (small pasta envelopes filled with dark plum jam) sprinkled with walnuts fried in butter instead of the more mundane breadcrumbs and the pancakes with a Grand Marnier cream filling. If you wanted that mountainous soufflé called *Salzburger Nockerl*, I'm sure they would do it with extra attention to detail.

Good selection of wines and of course splendid Salzburg beer. Should you be visiting Salzburg by car, the restaurant gives parking vouchers to their guests!

St Oswald nr. Graz — ***Styria***

SCHLOSS PLANKENWARTH
8113 St Oswald bei Graz
☏ 03123 2930
Open: 12.00–14.30, 18.00–22.00
Closed: from 17.00 on Sundays and all day Monday, also January and February
Prices: upward

A fortress built to frighten off invaders some 900 years ago, rebuilt into a fairy-tale castle with towers and turrets in the seventeenth century, Schloss Plankenwarth is now a rather luxurious hotel sitting at an altitude of 700 m with magnificent views. Large lofty rooms plus a few apartments – all rather reasonably priced. The restaurant is under entirely separate management, though half-board terms can be negotiated. It is a rather feudal setting – a bit grand, bordering on the ludicrous – but the cooking is imaginative with nice local touches, like a starter of Styrian ewe's milk cheese with tomatoes and lightly roasted pumpkin seeds – a particularly good combination. *Kalbsleberstreifen im Paprikacreme* (strips of calves liver in a paprika sauce) was excellent and the *Medaillons* of pork with chanterelles and a potato *Strudel* were another commendable main course. I liked the *Pralinenmus auf Weichseln* (light nougat cream with morello cherries) so much that I would have begged the recipe in a less severe setting. I sampled the *Griessflammerie auf Waldbeeren* instead and that too was very good. Plankenwarth is a splendid place for special celebrations and there is a six-course *Champagnermenü* at S1450.- for two, including aperitifs and a bottle of Champagne.

The wine list specializes in lesser known Styrian wines, supported by the rest of Austria, France and Italy.

How to get there: About 15 km north-west of Graz, drive direction Bruck an der Mur as far as Strassengel-Judendorf where turn left, direction St Oswald bei Plankenwarth. Schloss Plankenwarth is before St Oswald and is well signposted.

St Pölten ***Lower Austria***

ROSENBERGER AUTOBAHN RESTAURANT
ST PÖLTEN
3385 Völlerndorf
☏ 02749 2755
Open: 6.00–23.00 June/October
6.00–22.00 November/May
Prices: inexpensive/moderate

A.1 West Motorway – accessible from both directions
No credit cards

St Pölten is a conventional Rosenberger Motorway restaurant and there is also a Market Restaurant in the same building. For description see under Motorway Restaurants (Rosenberger)

St Valentin ***Lower Austria***

ROSENBERGER AUTOBAHNRESTAURANT ST VALENTIN
4300 St Valentin
☏ 07435 2002, 2005
Open: 6.00–23.00 June/October
6.00–22.00 November/May
Prices: inexpensive/moderate

A.1 West Motorway – accessible from both directions
Motor-Hotel
No credit cards

For description see under Motorway Restaurants (Rosenberger)

St Veit an der Glan *Carinthia*

PUKELSHEIM
Erlgasse 11
9300 St Veit an der Glan
☏ 04212 2473
Open: all day – snacks and light meals served throughout the day
Main meals: 11.30–14.00, 18.00–22.00
Closed: Sunday evening and Monday
Prices: moderate

A small house painted terracotta, with barely an indication that it is a restaurant. Darkly panelled rooms and masses of potted plants, and a small sheltered garden, Pukelsheim is friendly, warm and welcoming – a real family restaurant in every way. (Only make sure of your table by booking ahead – even the most hospitable families like a little advance notice so that they can look after you properly.) And they'll certainly look after you given half a chance – with good Carinthian food, uplifted into higher regions: try the salmon trout in aspic (*Lachsforellensulz*) or the brawn with smoked calf's tongue (*geräucherte Kalbszüngerlsulz*) or even just the simple warm potato salad with watercress, lamb's lettuce and diced bacon. Pukelsheim is one of the relatively few places offering fresh nettle soup (*Brennesselsuppe*) and if you're early enough (it disappears off the menu with lightning speed) order *gefülltes Bauernhendl* (farmhouse chicken with stuffing). Calves liver cooked with a dash of apple brandy is a treat (*Kalbsleber mit Apfelschnaps*) and there are always new and original fillings for *Kärntner Nudeln*. You could even try them as a pudding by ordering *Kletzennudel* (pasta filled with dried pears and served with honeyed butter). Alternately try their *Mandeleisknöderl* (almond ice-cream with a marzipan centre, served with strawberry purée). Excellent Austrian wines, many of which are served by the glass.

How to get there: from Villach on 94 to St Veit an der Glan. In St Veit look for sign to Schloss Frauenstein to the left which should bring you to Erlgasse and Pukelsheim.

St Wolfgang ***Upper Austria***

HUPFMÜHLE
5360 St Wolfgang am See
☏ 06138 2579
Open: 10.00–22.00 (main meals 12.00–14.00, 18.00–20.30)
mid December/mid January, Easter/end October
Closed: Tuesday
Prices: inexpensive

Ten minutes walk from the centre of St Wolfgang and the shores of the lake, the Hupfmühle is the ideal small country inn, set next to a small stream, with a terraced garden and rather rustic dining-room. The short walk through flowering meadows is pure pleasure (even in winter when the meadows are thickly covered with snow) and though the menu is small, everything is freshly made and highly enjoyable. There are some good snacks, the sort one would welcome after a (longer) walk – sausage on dark bread, a cheese platter or a good (and genuine) *Brettljause*, a bowl of warming soup, as well as main courses such as *Wiener Schnitzel* and pork cutlets. The great house speciality, however, is trout – order them *en bleu* since the fish will certainly be fresh enough to be cooked that way. And the best *Strudel* this side of Vienna, made by grandmother (the *Topfenstrudel* is particularly delectable), though the *Marillenkuchen* (light sponge with fresh apricots) deserves sampling as well.

There are a few simple bedrooms, very moderately priced and a strip of beach on the lake, exclusively reserved for guests of the Hupfmühle (and you can drive up to within 100 m of the house).

IM WEISSEN RÖSSL
5360 St Wolfgang am See
☏ 06138 23060
Open: 8.00–22.30 (lunch 12.30–14.00, dinner 18.30–22.30)
(snacks, grills etc. 14.00–18.30)
Closed: beginning November/mid December
Prices: moderate

Im Weissen Rössl – the original White Horse Inn of operetta fame – is a family hotel, first and foremost. Family owned and run, and by a typically Austrian family at that, with a very large typically Austrian clientele. To stay means becoming completely engulfed in the family atmosphere and even sharing their preferences of which breakfast is a typical example. Served on the covered terrace it is a many-splendoured leisurely meal 'because,' as the owner once confided, 'I like large, leisurely breakfasts.' Altogether the food is very good indeed, whether you stay at the hotel with full or half board or simply visit the restaurant. (I'd try to avoid the afternoon, if possible, for that is the time when the White Horse Inn is most likely to be overrun with sightseers.) There are, of course, all the old and well-known favourites, but also quite a number of lesser-known specialities like Aberseer fish soup (Abersee being another name for Lake St Wolfgang), smoked *Saibling* (pink trout) mousse, a delicious salad of dandelion, tomatoes and hard-boiled eggs with wild garlic and sour cream dressing, smoked pork (*Geselchtes*) with cabbage cooked in white wine, pike roasted with garlic butter and delicious puddings such as *Erdbeercharlotte* (strawberry charlotte) and old-fashioned *Schlosserbuben* (prune fritters) with a red wine sauce and strawberries, and great fluffy mounds of *Salzburger Nockerl*. The White Horse Inn is also a good place for tasting some Austrian cheeses, like pungent Mondseer or Aberseer goat's cheese.

Beer from the barrel, particularly good selection of house wines and an almost entirely Austrian wine list, with a little support from South Tyrol, Spain and Italy and Champagne from France.

Schladming — *Styria*

ALTE POST
Hauptplatz 10
8970 Schladming
☏ 03687 225710
Open: Daily 11.30–14.00, 18.30–22.00
22.00–23.00 limited menu
Closed: two weeks in November
Prices: moderate

You'll see the initials T.P. and the date 1618 engraved in the dining-room beam. That's the date of the great fire which devastated most of Schladming. The initials T.P. stand for Tobias Pröbstl, owner of the house at the time, immensely respected and – as recorded at the time – 'rich enough not only to start rebuilding at once, but to add luxuries like a marble wash basin in the dining-room'. First mentioned as an inn at the beginning of the thirty-year war, the Alte Post has remained true to form ever since – comfortable and comforting, considerate for the well-being of its guests, and that includes complete renovation of the interior a few years ago. Modern plumbing and other comforts in the bedrooms, but the exterior and the cosy dining-rooms have remained unchanged. Splendid and very reliable Austrian cooking, with quite a number of regional specialities – creamy garlic soup (*Knoblauchrahmsuppe*), tender pink smoked pork or a particularly good beef salad, *Steirisches Jägerpfandl* or their *Postreindl* (pork fillet with creamed mushrooms and gnocchi). Followed – if you can possibly manage it – by one of the Post's delectable puddings like *Mohn-Nussauflauf* (poppy seed and walnut pudding) with morello cherries. I am also particularly taken with the Post's *Abendmenu* served between 10.00 and 11.00 p.m. which offers not only *Gulasch* soup and excellent beef aspic, but their special *G'schmackiger Postteller* which includes home-made sausages, ham, Styrian *Verhackerts*, herb cheese as well as *Liptauer* – a selection which goes so well with the famous Schladming beer which must not be missed. The Alte Post also has a well-stocked wine cellar.

How to get there: from Salzburg on 150, 159 and 99 (or Motorway) to Eben and Radstadt, thence on 146 to Schladming. Alte Post is in the main square.

Schruns ***Vorarlberg***

LÖWEN HOTEL
Silvrettastrasse 8
6780 Schruns
☎ 05556 3141
Open: Wellen Bar: 12.00–21.00
Restaurant Barga: 10.00–24.00
Montafoner Stube: 8.00–24.00
Restaurant Français: 18.00–24.00, closed Mondays
Closed: mid October/mid December, mid April/mid May
Prices: Wellen Bar: moderate
Restaurant Barga: moderate
Montafoner Stube: moderate
Restaurant Français: upward/expensive

Everything about the Löwen Hotel is good, solidly luxurious and generously proportioned – rooms, furniture, the modern building – and the hospitality, starting with a large and luxurious breakfast where you are offered as much Sekt with (or without) your orange juice as you care to drink. Hospitality extends to non-residents who can use the equally generously proportioned indoor swimming-pool (for an entrance fee) and the Wellen Bar for 'large drinks and small snacks' as they say at the Löwen. (You can even watch television whilst you relax with your drink). All the restaurants at the Löwen are open to non-residents:

Restaurant Barga with good Austrian and some regional cooking, where *Kaiserschmarrn* is caramelized which greatly enhances the taste and where they serve a diet ice-cream – possibly to make up for having indulged in the preceding courses – and to encourage you to return for coffee and pastries in the afternoon. The Montafoner Stube is a favourite meeting point not only for visitors but also for locals, offering rather hearty local specialities – Mondays and Fridays being Fondue and Raclette evenings. (I'd also recommend their melted Brie served with *Crème Fraîche,* chopped herbs and potatoes). Restaurant Français is frankly a misnomer. As far as I can gather it was originally intended as a French restaurant, but the cooking which has evolved is as much a mixture of various cuisines as it is chef's own – excellent and highly successful and it seemed churlish to change the name at this point. The restaurant is small, very elegant with a minimum seating capacity (booking more than advisable) with a small and very elegant menu. I had *parfait* of smoked salmon with *crème fraîche,* rack of lamb with thyme-scented tomato coulis and courgette gratin, followed by a magnificent curd cheese soufflé with figs that seemed to be no more than a cloud of deliciousness.

Very extensive wine list covering Austria, France and Italy.

How to get there: from Bregenz on A.14 to Bludenz, thence on 188 to Schruns (Montafon valley).

Schützen am Gebirge — *Burgenland*

TAUBENKOBEL
Hauptstrasse 33
7081 Schützen am Gebirge
☏ 02684 2297
Open: 17.30–23.30 Tuesday
11.30–14.30 and 17.30–23.30 Wednesday/Sunday
Closed: Mondays and Tuesday lunch
Note: the restaurant stays open late on Saturday and Sunday from mid July to end August to accommodate visitors to the lakeside operetta festival
Closed: mid January to first week February
Prices: upward

Drive slowly through Schützen as you could easily go past the restaurant. There's rarely anyone around to ask, except possibly a goose crossing the road – it's that kind of a village. The restaurant is signposted at one end, but *Hauptstrasse* (High Street) in this particular case means no more than a minor road without shops. Look out for the number on the house and for the cars parked nearby. Word has certainly got around about the Taubenkobel (advance booking, particularly at weekends is strongly advised), its small garden full of white oleander blossoms, its typical Burgenland ambience and above all, its elegant and country-fresh cooking. Start with tomato soup made from local tomatoes, spiced with chilli and fresh basil, or locally smoked eel from nearby Lake Neusiedl, or be tempted by their equally local goose liver. Goose liver also adds a special touch to the lentils which accompany the chicken, but the local pike/perch with herb butter is worth considering too and so is the marinaded lamb with herbed courgettes. All vegetables are almost startlingly fresh and cooked to perfection, and if it is cherry time, there'll be a large plate of Schützen cherries 'on the house', but do not let that deter you from ordering the *parfait* made from the self-same cherries or the walnut pudding (*Nussauflauf*).

The superb wine list consists only of Burgenland wines – and their wine recommendation of the month is usually worth considering.

How to get there: from Eisenstadt on 50 direction Neusiedl am See. Schützen is about 8 km from Eisenstadt and there is a sign (to the left) for the Taubenkobel. The restaurant is on the left, coming from Eisenstadt.

Schwarzenberg — *Vorarlberg*

HIRSCHEN
6867 Schwarzenberg
☏ 05512 29440
Open: 10.00–24.00 (hot food 12.00–14.00, 18.00–21.00)
Closed: Wednesday all day and Thursday until 18.00 (March/ mid June and September/mid January only)
also closed 1 November–20 December
Prices: moderate

Schwarzenberg is Angelika Kauffmann country. Although a native of Chur across the Swiss border, she always considered Schwarzenberg to be her home (her father was born there) and you'll find her paintings in the local church. An absolute picture-book village with the Hirschen as its most picturesque centre – an elegant eighteenth-century building with immensely pleasing rooms and good old-fashioned comfort. The atmosphere is very much that of a private home (not surprisingly the Hirschen has been in the same family for generations) – whether in the very individually furnished bedrooms, the attractive dining-rooms or the secluded garden – welcome is written very large indeed.

The bill of fare includes many traditional and regional dishes and I am inclined to order those – *Bregenzerwälder Gerstensuppe* (barley soup), a large dish of good sausages (*Rostbratwürstchen*) with lentils or calves tongue with a creamy caper sauce; dishes which are rapidly disappearing from 'ordinary' restaurant menus (some to reappear at more exclusive establishments at twice the price), but do not let my own preference deter you from ordering fish from Lake Constance or nearby rivers served with gently cooked cucumbers and dill potatoes, smoked trout Mousse (*Räucherforellenmousse*) with horseradish and cranberry cream or one of the special game dishes when in season. There are excellent puddings too – and very good local cheeses which should not be missed.

Extensive list of Austrian wines (some available by the glass) and a good regional choice from Italy and France.

How to get there: from Bregenz on 190 direction Dornbirn as far as Lauterach where turn left direction Bezau. Drive to Schwarzach and then turn left for Alberschwende where you join road 200 to Egg. At Egg turn right (between Gasthaus Ochsen and Gasthaus Löwen) direction Bödele and Schwarzenberg. The Hirschen is right in the centre of Schwarzenberg on the main road.

Hirschen, Schwarzenberg

Sebersdorf *Styria*

SCHLOSS OBERMAYERHOFEN
8272 Sebersdorf
☏ 03333 25030 (Goldesel 03333 3107 Hofstüberl 03333 2959)
Open: Goldesel: 10.00–24.00 (11.00–14.00, 18.00–21.30) Thursday/Tuesday
Closed: Wednesday
Hofstüberl: 18.00–24.00 Tuesday/Friday
11.00–24.00 (11.00–14.00, 18.00–21.30) Saturday/Sunday
Closed: Monday
Also closed beginning January/end February
Prices: moderate/slightly upward

Schloss Obermayerhofen is – as yet – one of the great undiscovered treasures in Austria. Once a fortress, transformed into a luxurious castle and described as '*wohlerbauet* (well-built) like few others in the land' and since 1777 the property of the Counts Kottulinsky (the present owner is the great-great-great-great-grandson). A few years ago the castle was transformed once more – into a luxurious hotel this time – yet still retaining most of the original features. The rooms are stunning, there's a beautiful park, a private chapel with a Gothic altar figure (you can even get married there if you wish), the castle is within easy distance of the recently discovered spa at Waltersdorf and there's a nearby golf course, yet the price for staying there is well below that of other far less luxurious hotels, castle or otherwise.

There are two completely separate restaurants in a side tract of the castle, both open to non-residents, both charming and serving excellent food. The Goldesel tends more towards typically Austrian cooking – clear beef broth with pumpkin seed *Frittaten* (pancakes cut into strips, a favourite addition to clear beef broth and in this particular case greatly enhanced by the nutty flavour of the pumpkin seeds), beef in red wine with *Erdäpfelkrapferl* (small potato cakes), cheese from Vorarlberg and apricot dumplings with toasted almonds on a recent visit when there was also a good four-course menu for S375.-. The Hofstüberl which is open only in the evenings (except at weekends) features more regional cooking and there are several set menus from which separate items can be chosen (some of which are available in small portions as well). I had splendid nettle soup with *Entengrammelknöderl* (small dumplings with duck crackling), lamb roasted with herbs and a rosemary scented sauce, young beetroots and stuffed potatoes, followed by ginger and rhubarb compote with a dandelion *parfait*, all very suitable for 'green' Styria in which Schloss Obermayerhofen is situated.

Predominantly Austrian wines, but though the selection from France and Italy is comparatively short, it is well chosen.

How to get there: On A.2 from Vienna (or Graz), exit at 'Heiltherme Bad Waltersdorf' and follow signs for Schloss Obermayerhofen.

Seefeld *Tyrol*

KLOSTERBRÄU
6100 Seefeld
☏ 05212 26210
Open: Bräukeller: 9.00–24.00
Restaurant Ritter Oswald Stube: 12.00–14.00, 18.30–24.00
mid June/mid October, mid December/end March
Closed: mid October/mid December, end March/mid June
Prices: Bräukaller: inexpensive/moderate
Ritter Oswald Stube: upward

The Klosterbräu began life as a monastery. Emperor Maximilian I built the 'Clösterlein auf dem Sevelt' in 1516, a monastery which for centuries was host to emperors and kings. The tradition for hospitality continued unbroken after the monastery was secularized in the eighteenth century and the Klosterbräu has been in the hands of the Seyrling family since 1805. Hospitality is very much in evidence indeed: there's accommodation for about 200 guests and the Seyrlings employ 170 people to look after them! As a hotel the Klosterbräu is very grand and luxurious (even the small sewing kits with which they supply guests are of a superior quality), not to say feudal. The walls are thick, the rooms huge, but incredibly comfortable – and comforting. It is a place where you are made to feel entirely at home and one of the family, and most of the guests are what is fondly termed *Stammgäste* who come and stay there every year, their children practically 'adopted' by the Seyrlings. A visit to one of the restaurants will confirm all this – the Bräukeller, a large vaulted cellar where hearty Austrian dishes are served throughout the day, ranging from quite substantial snacks including various kinds of sausages, *Bierrettich* (large radish) and *Brotzeit-Brettl* (a cold platter) to good grills, roast suckling pig (minimum order for six people) and an excellent fixed-price meal at S175.- (creamy herb soup, stuffed breast of veal with rice and vegetables and pistachio ice-cream with hot chocolate sauce being a typical example). Portions are of typical Bräukeller generosity – a portion of plum dumplings (*Zwetschkenknödel*) consists of four dumplings!

The Ritter Oswald Stube is something else again – a very elegant restaurant with the same friendly atmosphere that permeates the whole house, and food that definitely reaches higher culinary regions: *kaltes Paprikasüppchen* (iced paprika soup) with poached salmon, fried veal sweetbreads with sauce verte and warm potato salad, followed by *Topfensouffle* (curd soufflé) with three kinds of fruit purée being my most recent 'sampling'. You can also order the *Pensionsmenu* (lunch or dinner as served to residents) which is usually around S360.- (or less) for four courses, to give you a true taste of the Klosterbräu.

Beer from the barrel, house wines and a well assorted wine selection from Austria, France and Italy.

SIR RICHARD
6100 Seefeld
☏ 05212 2093
Open: 11.30–15.00 (kitchen 14.30), 18.00–24.00 (kitchen 22.00)
Service on the terrace from 11.00 until evening.
Closed: Monday all day, Tuesday until 17.00
also closed throughout June
Prices: upward/expensive

Richard Rass – 'Sir Richard' to his guests and all Seefeld – wanted his restaurant to look like an English pub and not like an alpine chalet like so many of the restaurants in the Tyrol. He commissioned a British architect and the result is an immensely pleasing mixture of solid comfort, great elegance and charm – not so much a pub but a club atmosphere with a good dash of Austrian *joie de vivre* thrown in for good measure. 'I shop and my wife cooks whatever I've bought,' says 'Sir' Richard – an over-simplification, but absolutely true. He is certainly an excellent shopper (who thinks nothing of going as far as Munich for specialities) and Styrian Hermine Rass is an inspired cook – an ideal team and no wonder the guests arrive from far and wide. I've resolved not to go to Sir Richard on my own next time so that I can order the saffron fish soup – a speciality of the house the fame of which has spread far beyond the boundaries of Seefeld – but the minimum order is for two. Not that I fared badly this time: smoked venison with cranberry cream, followed by *Consomme vom Tafelspitz mit Markknöderl* and pike/perch in a delicate paprika sauce. Puddings have always been Mrs Rass' forte – on this occasion the *Karamelsüppchen* (caramel cream) with strawberries was so good that I wanted to lick the plate. The *petits fours* with coffee were exceptional, which makes the terrace an ideal place for coffee or afternoon tea (and no tea bags either!)

Excellent wine list comprising the best of Austria, Italy and France.

Seewalchen (Attersee) *Upper Austria*

HÄUPL
Hauptstrasse 20
4863 Seewalchen am Attersee
☏ 07662 8300
Open: 7.00–23.00 (12.00–14.30, 18.00–22.00)
Closed: 22/24 December
Prices: moderate/slightly upward

Häupl is an old family inn sympathetically extended, with very comfortable rooms, a terrace with glorious views over lake and mountains and quite exceptional cooking (full-board terms are particularly favourable and deserve a special mention). Ingrid Hâupl has added her own personal touch (and inventions) to strictly regional dishes and nowadays people think nothing of travelling all the way from Vienna or Munich to enjoy it. Always choose at least one item from the dishes headed *'Aus unserer Schmankerl Küche'* which usually include *Innviertler Speckknödel mit Veltliner Kraut* and a delicate soufflé based on black pudding (*Blunzensoufflé*). There's always excellent *Backhenderl* (fried spring chicken) and *Wiener Schnitzerl* (please note the diminutive 'r' which does not apply to size but to the loving care with which it has been prepared), but you'll also find dishes tending towards higher culinary spheres such as very delicate mushroom and curd cheese ravioli (*Topfenravioli mit Steinpilzen*) and *gefüllte Gansbrust* (stuffed goose breast). Puddings have always been a speciality of the house and Ingrid Hâupl's *Rotwein Guglhupf* with orange sabayon is delicious, but personally I never look further than the *Topfenpalatschinken* (if they're not on the menu, ask for them) which in Hans Häupl's own words come with 'a lot of filling' and one portion should be more than enough for two.

Good selection of wines from Austria, Italy and France, many of which are available by the glass.

How to get there: On A.1 from Salzburg direction Vienna. Exit at Seewalchen – Häupl is in the centre.

Söllheim nr. Salzburg *Salzburg*

RESTAURANT PFEFFERSCHIFF
Berg 24
5023 Söllheim bei Salzburg
☏ 0662 661242
Open: kitchen 12.00–13.30, 18.30–21.30
Closed: Sunday and Monday
Prices: upward

News of good food travels fast judging by the number of cars parked outside the fairly recently opened Pfefferschiff. There is, of course, everything that would make for a successful restaurant: a charming old inn sympathetically restored, a secluded *Gasthausgarten* and above all, the cooking of Klaus Fleischhacker whose devotees have followed him from the Salurner Hof on the other side of Salzburg. Advance booking is strongly advised.

The cooking is very Austrian, very regional – with the lightest possible touch. Soups and starters are as imaginative as the rest of the menu – smoked fish in aspic with marinaded asparagus for instance or a warm trout salad (warmer *Forellensalat*) being particularly good, as were the *Spinat-Grammelknöderln* (small spinach dumplings with a filling of crisp crackling) with a *Sauerkraut* and apple sauce – intended as a starter, it made an excellent main course (quite a few of the main courses are available in small portions as starters). There was *Kohlrabi* soup with small trout gnocchi and a cream soup made with red onions – both delicious. *Zander souffliert* (pike/perch) with walnut stuffing was delicious and so were *allerhand hausgem Würstel* (an assortment of home-made sausages with *Rieslingkraut*). But the absolute star of the evening was a dish called *Blunzenguglhupf* (a featherlight soufflé based on black pudding and baked in a small *Guglhupf* shape, served with parsley sauce and potato roulade. At this point I wished that someone would come up with some easier names: *Blunzenguglhupf* is too much – even for an Austrian – and in any case *Blunzen* (black pudding) sounds far too mundane in connection with this sensational dish.

Puddings are delicious too – try the *Dessertvariationen* to have this confirmed.

How to get there: From Salzburg on B.1 direction Strasswalchen as far as Mayerwies where turn left for Söllheim.

Strengberg ***Lower Austria***

ROSENBERGER AUTOBAHN RESTAURANT
STRENGBERG
(Most-Land Rast)
3314 Strengberg
☏ 07432 2274

A.1 West Motorway – accessible only from one direction

Open: 6.00–23.00 June/October
6.00–22.00 November/May

Prices: inexpensive/moderate

No credit cards

For description of restaurant see under Motorway Restaurants (Rosenberger)

Sulz *Vorarlberg*

ALTES GERICHT
Taverneweg 1
6832 Sulz
☏ 05522 43111
Open: 11.00–24.00
Closed: Wednesday
Prices: moderate/upward

The building dates back to the thirteenth and fourteenth century when the county court as well as a tavern were housed under the same roof. Beautifully restored and sympathetically converted, it is now one of Vorarlberg's most attractive restaurants with cooking to match. Very light, very imaginative – using only the freshest of fresh produce and making the best use of it. At lunch there is a very good fixed-price menu (very fresh tomato soup with basil gnocchi or a finely flavoured cream of savoy cabbage, followed by *Medaillons* of pork with young leeks and small potato mounds or fillet of beef with pepper cream and ceps, then a light orange mousse with poppy-seed *parfait* and strawberry purée or a light confection of blueberries and apricots). There is also a '*Kleines* Menu' consisting of four courses and a more elaborate seasonal menu – apart from which the à la carte selection is certainly varied and tempting. I was particularly taken by a dish of *Edelfische* ('noble' fish) with asparagus and rice and just the right touch of fresh chervil. Puddings range from simple apple- or cheese-cakes (both served warm throughout the day) to delicious ice-creams (caramel and walnut ice-cream with brandy-soaked prunes) and lots more temptations in between.

Very good and varied wine list (including some Ardetzenberger from Feldkirch – a local curiosity upon which hangs a romantic tale) and some interesting eaux-de-vie, including *Fraxner Kirsch*, a local speciality which you are unlikely to encounter outside Vorarlberg (and not always in Vorarlberg for that matter).

Advance booking is advisable.

How to get there: from Bregenz on 190 direction Feldkirch to Götzis and from there on unnumbered road through Klaus, Weiler and Röthis to Sulz. The restaurant is on the left, set back a little from the road.

Villach *Carinthia*

KRAPFENBACHER
Peraustrasse 39
9500 Villach
☏ 04242 24817
Open: 9.00–24.00 (kitchen: 11.00–14.00, 17.00–22.00)
Closed: Sundays
Prices: inexpensive/moderate

Krapfenbacher combines the best of two worlds: sturdy town elegance and a typical country inn garden well shaded by trees, a town setting and a country atmosphere. It is a good, solid Carinthian inn, well-known for local specialities and new owners have not only broadened the menu, but it is now available in English. I'd still choose at least some of the local specialities for you will not easily find them elsewhere: *Speck-Kraut Strudel, Lavantaler Mostbratl* and *Kärntner Ritschert* to quote but a few, and they change according to season. There's much to commend on the 'ordinary' menu as well, excellent home-smoked trout for instance, pork fillet cooked in beer and on my last visit there was a *Ripperlessen* (spare ribs) endearingly offered for 'as long as stocks last'. Good puddings too like blackberry 'gnocchi' with honeyed butter and I was much taken by the sight of a large baking sheet covered with freshly baked walnut and cherry cake, though in the end I returned to my favourite – *Grantenschleck* – a sort of superior cranberry fool (*Granten* being Carinthian for cranberries). Portions are of true inn generosity.

Good selection of Austrian and some Italian wines, also splendid eaux-de-vie from Pfau at Ruden (q.v.).

POST
Hauptplatz 26
9500 Villach
☏ 04242 261010
Open: 11.00–23.00
Prices: moderate

A hostelry since the eighteenth century – Empress Maria Theresa was one of the first 'paying guests', though by no means the first royal visitor. Charles V in whose empire 'the sun never set' and Henri III of France preceded her by two centuries when the house was a *Palais* belonging to the Khevenhüller family. Napoleon's brother Jerome Bonaparte stayed there as well, though whether he paid for his accommodation is not recorded, unlike his registration form which is still being kept in the archives. Now a Romantik Hotel it combines the best of several worlds: the seclusion and the elegance of a princely home and the cosyness of a country inn. Charming rooms and a delightful *Gastgarten* – a favourite place in which to dine in summer. Very good fixed-price meals and very seasonal menus – on my last visit I landed in the middle of asparagus week when there were no less than nine dishes based on local asparagus, including a particularly delicious asparagus *parfait*. Carinthian and Austrian *Schmankerl* (specials) are always on the menu, such as *Fleischnudeln* (pasta pockets with a savoury meat filling) with brown butter and salad or rabbit cooked with lots of herbs. Good wine list – many of which are available by the glass.

Excellent Viennese puddings, but you could be tempted by the footnote on their menu and adjourn to their *Postcafé* for coffee and luscious *pâtisserie* in order to, in the Post's own words, 'allow us to spoil you'.

Hotel Post Villaca

SEEGASTHOF SCHMID
Seestrasse 18
9500 Villach (am St Leonharder See)
☏ 04242 42149
Open: 10.00–24.00
Closed: Tuesday
Prices: moderate

At the last count there were 1,270 'official' lakes in the province of Carinthia and it should therefore come as no surprise that Seegasthof Schmid – though officially in the town of Villach – sits very prettily right above a small lake, well away from sight and sound of that town. A typical lakeside inn, with comfortable rooms, a charming garden and excellent food. The cooking is very rural, though not necessarily confined to Carinthia with a far more elegant touch than one would expect in a simple country inn. *Kärntner Festtagssuppe* (Carinthian 'festival' soup which is practically a meal in itself) is offered as well as Styrian wine soup. You'll always find good country dishes like Veal Gulasch, *Schinkenfleckerl* (pasta and ham) and a splendid *bollito misto* (*Allerlei Gekochtes vom Rind*) which includes several different cuts of beef, tongue and bone marrow, but there will also be specialities like duck's breast in aspic (*Entenbrüstchensülzchen,* excellent fish and particularly good pasta dishes, including a Carinthian pasta plate (*Kärntner Nudelteller*). Puddings are very Austrian and varied – from delicious home-made raspberry ice-cream to a marvellous *Bröselauflauf* (featherlight baked pudding) with wine sauce and include *Kletzen-Topfen-Nudel,* a Carinthian sweet pasta speciality which is worth ordering for the accompanying *Honigschmalz* alone – a whipped honey cream.

There is a superb wine list, almost entirely Austrian, but which also includes selected Italian and French wines at fair prices. If you stay longer than five days you'll be invited to a wine tasting in their own wine cellar, but you'll have to book well ahead as there are only a few rooms at the inn and they are much sought after.

How to get there: from Villach on 83 direction Velden, just outside Villach turn left for St Leonharder See and follow signs for Seegasthof Schmid.

Vomp *Tyrol*

KLOSTERGASTHAUS FIECHT
Fiecht
6130 Vomp
☏ 05242 71006
Open: 11.00–14.00, 18.00–24.00
Closed: Tuesday and last two weeks January
Note: During the Summer months the restaurant is open throughout the day.
Prices: moderate

Do not be deceived by the *Gasthaus* in the name and the appearance of a simple inn, Günther Sanin's cooking has all the 'simplicity' of a couture dress. He's a Chef after my own heart – enthusiastic and inspired, with an excellent palate and a fine flair for making the best of seasonal and regional produce. Best to arrive rather hungry – the menu is not too large, but it is one where I can recommend every single dish, besides which there's a small note saying *Sie wünschen – wir kochen* meaning 'Your wish is our command.' Start with the marinaded wood mushrooms with salad or *Fischvorspeisenteller* (fish platter) and go on to one of the delicious soups – *Frühlingskräutersuppe* (creamy herb soup) or the potato soup with marjoram and bacon, but whatever you choose as a main course, pick something that can be suitably accompanied by polenta. Sanin's polenta is the best I've ever eaten – light, creamy and good beyond belief. Leave room for a pudding – I was particularly taken by the chocolate mousse *mit schwarzen Nüssen* (walnuts preserved in liqueur). Not that you are expected to have an enormous meal: there are headings such as *Salatecke und kleines Feines* (salads and small delicacies) and *Zwischendurch und Überhaupt* ('in-between and anyhow') which include a platter of cruditees with fried mushrooms, there are *Pressknödel* 'zu Wasser oder zu Land' (cheese dumplings served either in broth or on their own) as well as home-made wholemeal noodles and *Rahmbeuschel* which, according to Günther Sanin, is *Vertrauenssache* (a matter of trust) which I can recommend wholeheartedly. (For definition of *Rahmbeuschel* look under *Kalbsbeuschel* in the glossary).

Excellent selection of wines, including some rarities you are not likely to find elsewhere (and certainly not in a simple country inn). Let Günther Sanin give you details or, better still, take you on a tour of his cellars!

How to get there: on 171 from Innsbruck to Schwaz. Turn left in Schwaz to cross bridge over Inn River, then right – you will see the monastery on a hill to your left. Follow road to monastery – the Klostergasthaus is to the right of the monastery, not too well signposted (unless they've taken my advice and invested in a larger poster).

Warmbad Villach *Carinthia*

KUCHER VULGO WIRT
Judendorfer Strasse 24
9504 Warmbad Villach
☏ 04242 56525
Open: 11.00–22.00
Closed: Mondays (October/April) and beginning January/ beginning February
Prices: moderate

'Kucher, commonly known as innkeeper' is the full name and a more typical inn – or innkeeper – it would be difficult to find. There's everything one would expect from a *Gasthof* just celebrating its centenary: spacious and comfortable dining-rooms, a large garden with old chestnut trees, good food (lots of Carinthian specialities) and an amiable host. Some of the dishes may need a little explanation, like *Brotherz'l* listed under soups. This would be any soup – usually *Knoblauchcremesuppe* (garlic soup) or *Käs-suppe* (cheese soup) served in a heart-shaped 'container' made with wholemeal dough, with the crumb removed to make room for the soup (you scrape up the inside crust with your spoon as you eat your soup). Delicious – but order the small portion! You will also notice that quite a number of dishes are available in small and large portions and unless you have worked up a huge appetite, order the small portion. These are good hearty dishes from game to *Gulasch* (which they reassuringly state is *aus'm Wadl* – 'from the shin' – as good *Gulasch* should be!). There are good salads like *Steirische Salatschüssel* with beef and *Riesenbohnen* (giant dried beans which taste like chestnuts) and a large range of hot and cold 'snacks' (enormous portions again) with home-made sausages and Glundner cheese. If you get as far as the special 'sweet' menu, there are some excellent traditional puddings (it is one of the few places where they'll accept orders for a single apricot dumpling!) and you could always have a slice of *Reindling* (Carinthian yeastcake) with your coffee. They'll also sell their cakes and *Strudel* to take away.

Good wines and in summer there's a separate beer counter in the garden. Also their own *Schnaps* – including one made from lovage, a herb much used in Carinthian cooking.

Simple, but comfortable rooms if you want to stay.

How to get there: from Villach direction Warmbad Villach, then branch off direction Spittal an der Drau. Drive for about 1 km on that road and Kugler is on the right, well signposted.

KURHOTEL WARMBADERHOF
9504 Warmbad Villach
☏ 04242 30010
Open: Kurcafe Konditorei: 10.00–18.00
Bürgerstube: 11.00–14.00, 18.00–24.00
Das kleine Restaurant: 11.30–14.00, 18.00–24.00
Prices: Kurcafe Restaurant: moderate
Bürgerstube: inexpensive/moderate
Das kleine Restaurant: moderate/upward

Thermal waters have bubbled out of the earth at Warmbad Villach since time immemorial – the Romans valued them, Paracelsus was the first to analyse the contents and Napoleon wanted to make Villach the spa to end all spas, starting with a huge park of which the Napoleonwiese (Napoleon's meadow) still exists today. In Imperial days Warmbad Villach was known as 'Excellenzen-Bad' – the spa of Their Excellencies who clearly appreciated that there's nothing like an Austrian spa hotel if you really want to be well looked after, not to say spoiled. The Warmbaderhof is the Excellenzen-Bad *par excellence* – large and comfortable with a great many of the rooms overlooking Napoleon's meadow and the swimming-pool where you can swim out-of-doors in hot thermal waters even in winter. All treatments are available in the house – the thermal waters pass through gravel directly into the large indoor swimming-pool and even the taps in the bathrooms spout hot spa water. It is a wonderfully restful place at which to stay – large enough to allow for solitude with well-spaced entertainment laid on should one feel in the mood for it. If you do not want to avail yourself of the spa treatments, there's a very efficient beauty centre.

Food at the Warmbaderhof is as good as the ambience and there are three restaurants open to non-residents: the Kurcafe Konditorei which is particularly pleasant, with its large outdoor terrace, serving not only coffee and pastries, but snacks throughout the day (and 'snacks' in this particular instance include fried spring chicken, veal or pork cutlets and *Wiener Schnitzel*) and – at lunch-time – a full range of Austrian specialities. Fully licensed, of course, with wines sold not only in ⅛l measures, but also in '*Stifterl*' bottles which in this particular case contain ¼l.

The Bürgerstube is a typically Austrian inn – solid and comforting – with a daily three-course lunch or dinner at S95.- and a fairly extensive à la carte menu with lots of seasonal specialities. As the name *Bürgerstube* (bourgeois) implies – good home cooking without having to dress up for it.

Das kleine Restaurant is the Warmbaderhof's showpiece – small, modern and elegant with a small and elegant à la carte selection as well as three set menus at different prices. I love their soups – *Kohlrabischaumsuppe* in particular which is very light and the watercress soup to which they add lightly poached sweetbreads. One of the other specialities which I particularly liked is the pink trout with creamed dill cucumber and on one occasion, arriving tired after a long journey I was tempted by '*Der Tafelspitz mit seinen klassischen Beilagen*' (the famous cut of boiled beef with 'classic' accompaniments – which incidentally is always on the menu). It was exactly as it should be – the beef tender and juicy, the accompaniments 'classic' and perfect, and it restored my faith in humanity. There's always at least one typically Austrian pudding on the menu. On the last occasion it was *Rahmdalken* – very light griddle cakes and in this particular case they are sandwiched together with dark plum jam laced with rum – clearly there's a master of this particular art in the kitchen.

Very good wine list comprising Austria, France and Italy (which is but a few kilometres distant).

Weissenkirchen (Wachau) ***Lower Austria***

JAMEK
Joching
3610 Weissenkirchen No credit cards
☏ 02715 2235
Open: 11.00–23.00 (hot food until 21.00) Tuesday/Saturday
Closed: Sunday and Monday, also mid December/mid February and first two weeks July
Prices: moderate

Jamek is a name to look for when studying the wine list in an Austrian restaurant; it stands for some of the best wines in the country. You can enjoy them on their home ground – the original *Weingut* of the Jamek family, where justice is done to fine wines by equally fine cooking. The menu is an absolute joy, concentrating on traditional dishes (to which some very special and original touches have been added) and local produce. Start with one of their terrines or a simple salad of lamb's lettuce and home-cured ham, served *im Brotkörbchen* (a hollowed-out large crusty roll) or smoked duck's breast with an apple and celeriac salad (their salad dressings are particularly commendable, using their own wine vinegar). Go on to a dish of locally gathered morels in a cream sauce and perhaps one of the best dishes I have encountered: fillet of beef with a sauce made with pickled walnuts – though the pork cutlet scented with coriander and served with spring onions in a herb sauce is memorable as well. Jamek's *Hechtnockerl* (*quenelles de brochet* which sounds so much better than pike dumplings) is the 'real thing' and their salmon trout comes wrapped in wafer-thin *Strudel* pastry. Puddings definitely belong to the 'higher regions' of culinary art – simple as they may sound – but I'd travel quite a long way for the marzipan cream with a purée of fresh fruit, or the poppy-seed pudding with morello cherries.

Jamek's also have an unusually good selection of 'small' dishes which go well with their beautiful wine – ideal fare if you want to sit in their terraced garden hung with vines and enjoy life. There's *Saumeise* (very much a speciality of Lower Austria, though Upper Austria stakes a claim as well: minced pork, wrapped in caul, smoked and then served either hot or cold), *Wachauer Jausenbrot* (a hearty snack served on dark country bread) and a good choice of home-made sausages, brawns and ham. It is also one of the few places where they still remember that *Grammeln* (the crispy bits which remain after rendering down pork fat) go splendidly with wine and where they serve them in various forms, last but not least on dark country bread spread with well-seasoned dripping.

Excellent eaux-de-vie and digestifs – try the Johannisnuss (walnuts matured in *marc* and very lightly sweetened with honey). All Jamek's wines can also be bought to take away (ask for the separate price list).

How to get there: On 3 from Vienna past Krems and Weissenkirchen. Joching is just past Weissenkirchen and Jamek's is on the right, set back from the road.

PRANDTAUERHOF
Joching
3610 Weissenkirchen
☏ 02715 2310
Open: 11.00–23.00 (kitchen 11.30–21.30)
Closed: Tuesday, Wednesday, also mid February/mid March
Prices: moderate

The building dates back to the seventeenth century, one of the earliest works of Jakob Prandtauer, grand master of the Baroque (magnificent Melk Abbey a little further along the river is one of his better known works). The arcaded courtyard is magic on a warm summer evening, though there's much to be said for the sturdy dining-room on a cold winter's night, when hearty local dishes come into their own: *Fischbeuschelsuppe* (the wonderful thick fish soup which is only served around Christmas as a rule – at the Prandtauerhof it is available at other times of the year as well), home-made black pudding (*Hausblutwurst*) with *Erdäpfelschmarrn* (more or less a cross between Swiss *Rösti* and its Austrian cousin *G'röste*), *Wildschweinsulz* (brawn made with wild boar) and a whole host of good puddings like *Topfenstrudel* as well as *Mohntorte mit Schlag* (a dark, rich poppy-seed gâteau). For less hearty appetites – and warmer days – there are, of course, lighter dishes like green beans with a yoghurt and garlic dressing and crispy bits of bacon, home-cured ham with asparagus, a delicate froth of Kohlrabi soup, exemplary fish and game, or simply a dish of home-made noodles with chicken livers and a fresh green salad. Delicious flummery with blueberries (*Maisgriessflammerie mit Heidelbeermark*) and a very good cake made with pumpkin seeds, served with cranberry cream (*Kürbiskernkuchen mit Preiselbeerobers*) – as well as all the 'classics' such as *Gulasch* and boiled beef (properly specifying the exact cut of beef), all impeccably prepared.

All the wines come from their own vineyards – and excellent ones at that – some sold in '*Stifterl* (⅓l). Their own Marillengeist (apricot eau-de-vie) and Trebener (*marc*) are also recommended. If you have enjoyed one of their wines particularly, most are for sale to take away.

How to get there: on 3 from Vienna, past Krems and Weissenkirchen. Joching is just past Weissenkirchen and the Prandtauerhof is on the right.

Prandtauerhof

Wels *Upper Austria*

GREEN HOUSE and INNVIERTLER STUBEN
Hotel Rosenberger
Adlerstrasse 1
4600 Wels
☏ 07242 62236
Open: 6.30–23.00
Prices: moderate

A modern, fairly new hotel with two restaurants, both pleasantly polished and comfortable, featuring identical menus with the typical Rosenberger touch plus a good bit of local colouring – all very commendable. There is an imaginative *Tagesmenü* as well as a good selection of standard dishes – good hearty soups like the *Innviertler Erdäfpelsuppe* (creamy potato soup with diced bacon) and *Gulaschsuppentopf*, after which you'll hardly have room for a main course, which would be a pity. Salads are particularly good – so much so that word has now got around and they are available in special containers for taking away. Special attention is given to *Schnitzel* in various forms (available in pork or veal) and there is always a good choice of vegetarian dishes. There are good pasta dishes too and lots of different pancakes (*Mozartpalatschinke* with a nougat-marzipan filling and pistachio sauce is worth every calorie!) and I am always particularly impressed by their cold snacks, like a platter of assorted hams. Most of the bread and rolls come from Rosenberger's own bakery and the *Vintschgerl* (crusty wholemeal rolls) in particular are a joy. Good choice of wines, many of which are available by the ⅛l glass and a particularly good selection of mineral waters.

Very comfortable rooms, reasonably priced – right in the centre of Wels which is not only an enchanting old town ('twas in Wels where the Muse supposedly kissed Hans Sachs after which he resolved to become a poet), but it ranks as 'tops' where shopping is concerned.

Werfen *Salzburg*

GASTHOF LEBZELTER
Hauptstrasse 46
5450 Werfen
☏ 06468 2120
Open: 8.00–24.00 and after (kitchen 12.00–14.00, 19.00–21.30)
Closed: Monday and Tuesday (variable, check when booking)
Prices: upward/expensive

You can't miss the huge and rather forbidding fortress of Hohenwerfen which all but overshadows the small town, but Werfen's real treasures are not obvious at first: forty-seven kilometres of gigantic underground ice caves, the largest in the world – and Gasthof Lebzelter, to all outward appearances a modest country inn, harbouring one of the best restaurants in Austria. Definitely worth a detour and even planning a special trip to suit the sometimes erratic closing days (the restaurant gets taken over by private parties from time to time and closing days can vary accordingly). The small restaurant is delightful, having kept its country inn character with lots of wood in the furnishings (though rather elegantly appointed) and there's a typical *Gastgarten* well-shaded by ancient trees. The food is nothing short of superb – a splendid mixture of genuine creative cooking and Austrian favourites to which the Obauer brothers have added their own special touch. Most of all, there's a genuine enthusiasm for good food which turns every meal into a feast. The menu changes frequently, of course, but I have established some favourites which I can recommend and which should not be missed (but please be advised as to the specialities of the day): their incomparable *Forellenstrudel* (*Strudel* with a trout filling) with *Veltlinersauce* and purée of mushrooms, local lamb with a sauce of wild garlic and *Schottentascherl* (small pasta envelopes filled with curd, for which *Schotten* is but another name) calves liver with chestnuts and black truffles. Puddings are as delightful as the rest of the menu – there's a poppy-seed *Strudel* (*Mohnstrudel*) with a Williams' pear sorbet, a chestnut pudding with mocca sauce, or order the *Dessertteller* if you feel you could possibly manage it – it's sensational. At lunch there's a three-course menu at S275.- as well as two more expensively priced ones which are also available in the evening. (It is one of the restaurants where I would not hesitate to recommend the six-course menu, knowing that each course will be a revelation.)

Excellent and extensive wine list – predominantly Austrian where white wines are concerned, French and Italian for the reds (with Austrian support).

There are some very comfortable, reasonably priced guest-rooms at the Lebzelter and an even more moderately priced guest-house owned by the same family a few doors further up the road.

How to get there: on Motorway or 159 from Salzburg. Follow directions for Werfen which lead straight into Hauptstrasse where you can park – if not in front of the house, a little further up the road.

Ybbs/Danube *Lower Austria*

VILLA NOWOTNI
Trewaldstrasse 3
3370 Ybbs an der Donau
☏ 07412 2620
Open: 12.00–14.00 Tuesday/Saturday, 12.00–14.00 Sunday
18.00–22.00
Closed: Sunday evening and all day Monday
Prices: upward

Ybbs – built in a half-circle on a rock above the Danube – always strikes one as rather grim and grey, lacking the soft charms of other Danube towns. Villa Nowotni more than makes up for this: an enchanting turn-of-the-century villa, with a wide terrace overlooking garden and swimming-pool (open to guests), a charming hostess and absolutely superb cooking by her husband. For a long time it was an almost 'secret' address well-guarded by discriminating Viennese, but word has now got around and advance booking is absolutely essential. Food and ambience will well reward you for your pains and their special aperitif of fresh orange-juice and local apricot brandy should put you in the right mood straight away. You may find – as I have done – that some of the starters make a very good light main course, preceded perhaps by one of the light and creamy soups. On my last visit starters included a delicious smoked tongue aspic, asparagus mousse with smoked salmon and – a speciality of the house – boned and fried quail with an asparagus salad (at which point I must admit that I am also very partial to Franz Nowotni's rather homely dish of lentils with bacon and '*Brezn'knödel*' which also ranks as a starter), but do not let that deter you from sampling some of the 'real' main courses like rabbit roasted '*im Kräuternetz*' (wrapped in caul with fresh herbs). Accompaniments to main courses are particularly good – like a savoury semolina soufflé, baked chicory, white cabbage cooked with crispy bacon or a salad of potatoes and radishes. Puddings are as delicious as one would expect after the foregoing, but *Zwetschkenvariationen* (variations on a theme of plums) and their chocolate pudding with iced vanilla cream deserve special mention.

Very good Austrian wines, many of which are sold by the glass.

There is no accommodation at the Villa Nowotni, but this can be arranged at the equally charming Villa Vogelsang (☏ 07412 46810) a little further up the hill.

How to get there: from Vienna on A.1 direction Salzburg for the quickest route (exit for Ybbs) or on 3 if you want a beautiful drive through the Wachau. Coming into Ybbs from the Motorway through Bahnhofstrasse turn left at the traffic lights into Reiteringerstrasse and first left into Trewaldstrasse. Villa Nowotni is immediately on the left. (Travelling on 3 cross the Danube at Ybbs and turn left which should bring you to Stauwerkstrasse and the same traffic lights where you turn right into Reiteringerstrasse and first left into Trewaldstrasse as before.)

Zell am See *Salzburg*

CAFÉ FEINSCHMECK
Dreifaltigkeitsgasse 10
5700 Zell am See
☏ 06542 2549
Open: 6.30–24.00
Prices: moderate/slightly upward

This is where I must plead prejudice as a good many of my childhood holidays were spent at Zell am See and my tastes in *pâtisserie* were largely formed by the Café Feinschmeck. In those days lunch would often consist of two courses at one of the nearby inns and we would then repair rather quickly to the Café Feinschmeck where a freshly arranged buffet of delicacies would await us. 'Better than Demel' my aunt would murmur (a great connoisseur in matters of *pâtisserie* particularly, who would take great care to arrive early at the Feinschmeck lest one of her favourite pastries should be no longer available). Certainly the selection was impressive and to this day I can still savour the taste of the special roulade filled with a wonderful cream into which tiny wild strawberries had been folded. I remember also the excitement of trying to guess which ice-creams (home-made, of course) would be on offer on that day – caramel ice-cream was a special and rare treat, but there was also a water-ice (they didn't call them sorbets in those days) made with vineyard peaches. I am delighted to say that the Feinschmeck is still there in its full glory – spruced up and modernized almost beyond recognition, though there's a nice nostalgic *Kaiserstüberl* with the old Austrian double eagle and a bust of the Emperor Franz Josef keeping close guard that nothing untoward should happen – and the pastries are as good as ever. The list of drinks has expanded considerably – you can now order six kinds of Scotch and four kinds of Bourbon, but they'll still serve a glass of milk, freshly squeezed lemon or orange juice or raspberry syrup if you want it. I cannot remember whether the Feinschmeck served snacks in the old days, but they certainly do so now – you could have a light lunch and wallow in pastries afterwards or have a warming *Gulaschsuppe* on a cold winter's night.

The upstairs part has now been turned into a very elegant small hotel – most rooms have a small terrace or balcony. Prices are reasonable, and I'm sure you get all the delicious scents from the *pâtisserie* wafting upwards at no additional charge!

HOTEL ST GEORG
Schillerstrasse 32
5700 Zell am See
☏ 06542 3533
Open: 11.00–14.00, 18.30–21.30
Closed: beginning October/mid December, after Easter/mid May
Prices: upward

One would expect one of the best hotels in Zell am See to be on the shores of the lake – not this one though, which is all but hidden in the valley, with some of the rooms overlooking (and overhearing) the rushings of the Schmittenbach. It is a very elegant hotel – spacious and comfortable and scented with pinewood which has gone into much of its panelling. There are other bonuses too, not apparent at first sight, like a 20% green fee reduction at the local golf course and a strip of beach solely reserved for hotel guests. The restaurant is particularly attractive; the sort of place frequented by local worthies, not only if they want to dine out in style, but to which they take their guests which alone speaks volumes for the quality of the food. It is exactly like that of a *soignée* private house with the hostess taking inordinate trouble to pander to her guests. Thus you'll find good soups as well as home-made goose-liver terrine, exemplary boiled beef (specifying the exact cut) with all the time-honoured accompaniments such as chive sauce and apple-horseradish relish, chicken roasted with rosemary and good game when in season. There are some good light puddings – fluffy curd dumplings sprinkled with hazelnuts instead of breadcrumbs and a sauce made of fresh strawberries (*Topfenknöderl im Haselnussmantel*).

Very good selection of Austrian and South Tyrolean wines with excursions to Germany, France and Italy, as well as some good wines offered by the glass (ask for the *Kleine Weinkarte* and the *Weinempfehlung* – the special wine recommendation).

ZUM HIRSCHEN
Dreifaltigkeitsgasse 1
5700 Zell am See
☏ 06542 2447
Open: 11.00–23.00
Closed: usually mid November/mid December and mid April/mid May
Prices: moderate/upward

How to pick a restaurant by studying the menus displayed outside is quite an art and my aunt was an unsurpassed mistress of that art. I started learning under her expert guidance rather early in life – as soon as I was able to read – mostly by being made to study the menus at the various restaurants and inns in Zell am See. In those days there were always at least three different fixed-price lunch menus displayed at each establishment and deciding which place should be 'honoured' with our custom took quite a bit of time, deliberation and some brisk walking during which one worked up a healthy appetite, but in the end the Hirschen usually won. Not quite as grand (in those days) as the Lebzelter down the road, and not quite as rustic as the Auerhahn round the corner, the Hirschen was then a small country inn with modest accommodation and what was known as *gute Hausmannskost* (good home cooking). Times have changed – the Hirschen has expanded, with very comfortable, not to say luxurious, accommodation, but the dining-rooms are as cosy as ever – and the set-price meals are still excellent value: Creamy soup with ceps, sautéd calves liver with fresh herbs and rice and finishing with a red-currant sorbet sharpened with vodka – for a commendable S185.- on a recent visit, though nowadays I prefer to choose from the à la carte menu more often than not. There's still all the good *Hausmannskost* with *Zwiebelrostbraten, Tafelspitz* and ceps as well as chanterelles prepared any way you choose (all conveniently listed under *Österreichische Spezialitäten*), but there are also some successful excursions into the higher regions of culinary art including goose liver and thyme-scented rack of lamb. Good selection of Austrian as well as French and Italian wines, good beer from the barrel, and the Hirschen is also one of the few remaining restaurants where they'll sell *Soda mit Himbeer* (thick raspberry syrup with soda water) – a soft drink much favoured by children.

I have not forgotten about puddings, but when in Zell am See I revert to childhood habits, one of which was to choose a two-course menu for lunch (or have two à la carte dishes only) and then repair to one of the *pâtisseries* for 'afters' – Moshammer at Stadtplatz, Köpfl in Seegasse, and Café Feinschmeck just across the road from the Hirschen being a favourite choice.

Zirl — *Tyrol*

GOLDENER LÖWE
6170 Zirl
☏ 05238 2329 and 2330
Open: 11.00–14.00 and 17.30–22.00
Hot food throughout the day
Prices: moderate

The Goldener Lôwe has been an inn for over 700 years. It was certainly well-established in the fifteenth century when Archduke Sigmund whom they called 'the one rich in coins' and a frequent visitor, conveniently 'forgot' the necessary coins with which to pay his bill.

Apparently the Löwe's landlord was wise to these tricks and would take out loans from his archducal customers first, then writing off any debts they might have incurred against such loans. Zirl and the Goldener Löwe have been recorded as *neunmal verbrunnen* (nine times burned down), yet despite all this there's still a 'Goldener Löwe' with many of the original walls intact. A good, solid and very traditional country inn, with good comfortable rooms, good traditional cooking, and particularly attentive service. You can always rely on the Goldener Löwe – no hungry traveller will remain thus for long. Even if he happens to drop in between meal-times, there'll be a warming bowl of soup, freshly prepared *Wiener Schnitzel* and comforting *Gulasch*, plus a whole host of other small and not so small snacks for immediate sustenance. There will always be *Stockfischgröstl* (made with air-dried cod) on Good Friday, but traditional as the menu at the Goldener Löwe may be, there are many 'plus points' which put it into a higher category altogether: the excellent selection of game (from venison to chamois), the good home-baked country bread, the lightness of the spinach gnocchi, the nice caramel finish on the *Apfelküchel* (apple fritters) served with cranberries and the good, home-made *Graukäse* (a Tyrolean speciality) as well as the trout smoked to order.

Good selection of beer (including Guinness!) and the fairly short but selective wine list has the wines from the South Tyrol under a separate heading – not under Austria, not under Italy (of which the South Tyrol is now part), but separately. Tactful and considerate, as is everything at the Goldener Löwe.

How to get there: on 171 (or A.12) direction Arlberg. Zirl is about 10 km west of Innsbruck.

Zug — *Vorarlberg*

RESTAURANT KLÖSTERLE
6764 Zug – Lech am Arlberg
☏ 05583 3190
Open: 14.00–17.30, 19.30–23.00
Mid December/one week after Easter
Prices: upward

During the summer months the centuries-old farmhouse reverts to its original use – come winter and it is transformed into the elegant Klösterle Restaurant (owned by the Schneider family of Almhof Schneider in Lech). Life at the Klösterle starts in the early afternoon when it opens for '*Jause*', this very Austrian afternoon meal which can vary from quite a substantial snack including hot savouries to coffee and cream cakes. The '*Jausenkarte*' at the Klösterle caters for all eventualities – from a bowl of thick pea soup to sustain returning skiers to even more sustaining *Germknödel* (yeast dumplings with dark plum jam and poppy seeds), good country ham on dark bread or delicate venison sausages served hot to elegant *Sachertorte 'mit Schlag'* and coffee with more whipped cream if you so desire.

In the evening the mood changes again – the Klösterle's candle-lit tables are a favourite place for gathering round a fondue – Bourguignon, Chinoise or Cheese – they will also provide *Raclette* (as a first or main course), but if you follow my advice you'll order roast duck. Nothing wrong with the fondues – on the contrary – but you'll not find a more perfectly roasted duck in a hurry. Or roast knuckle of veal (*Kalbshaxe*). The *Topfenknödel mit Zwetschkenröster* (very light curd cheese dumplings with plum compote) are delicious – if you can still manage them!

How to get there: simply follow the road for Zug from Lech (turn left past Almhof Schneider) and you will find Klösterle on your right at Zug.

Introduction to Glossary

A German/English dictionary will be of limited use in a typically Austrian restaurant featuring Viennese or regional cooking, for most of the definitions (ingredients as well as the finished dish) will be purely Austrian and not found in an ordinary dictionary (they will also be incomprehensible even to a German from further west than Bavaria). Others could be misleading – you will certainly find '*Gerste*' (barley) in an ordinary dictionary and you could therefore expect '*geriebenes Gerstl*' to be finely ground or grated barley (it is in fact pasta left to dry and grated to the size of a barleycorn, in addition to which *Gerstl* is Viennese slang for money). What about '*Kaisergerstl*' then, listed as an addition to clear soup? (a savoury custard scooped out in tiny portions and 'fit for an emperor'!). You may have managed to discover that *Grammeln* are crisp bits of crackling (*Grieben* in German, *grattons* in French, *cicciole* in Italian), but what are you to make of *Grammelpogatscherln*? (delicious savoury biscuits made with dark flour, crackling and yeast).

The following glossary should not only see you through the maze of Austrian culinary terms (with 'proper' German names in brackets where applicable), but it should also help you to select some delicious meals and to discover and enjoy dishes which you would not have found or ordered otherwise (adding a bit of Austrian history and background where I thought this appropriate for further enjoyment). You will find that there is often more than one name for the same thing (cranberries are *Preiselbeeren* in most parts of Austria, but *Granten* in Carinthia. *Chervil* is kerbel except for certain regions where it is known as *Keferfil* etc.), but there are some peculiarities of Austrian culinary life which need additional explanation. There is a fairly recent trend for long descriptive terms like *Bodenseezanderfilet* or *Rosmarinknoblauchsafterl* (I swear that these were taken at random from a menu – there are countless others). The best way to 'unravel' those is to start translating at the far end as a rule, e.g. Filet (fillet), plus *Zander* (pike/perch) plus *Bodensee* (Lake Constance) and you have filet of pike/perch from Lake Constance. Or *Safterl* (sauce) plus *Knoblauch* (garlic) plus *Rosmarin* (rosemary) equals sauce scented with garlic and rosemary. This brings me to another 'speciality' – the Austrian love for diminutives which manifests itself in the 'r' inserted at the end of a name which is not always an indication of size. Certainly *Knöderl* (as in *Leberknöderl*, a frequent addition to clear beef broth) is a small dumpling (*Knödel* being medium to large size), but when you find menus abounding with *Schnitzerl* and *Safterl* and *Krebserl* (crayfish) it does not mean that the *Wiener Schnitzel* (described as *Kalbswienerschnitzerl*) is smaller than normal or that there's a lack of good sauce or that the crayfish (*Krebserl*) is particularly minute (in fact I have even seen it used in conjunction with *Solo-Krebserl* which have to be of a certain minimum weight). The diminutive 'r' so beloved by the Austrians and particularly the Viennese is very often used almost as a term of endearment, denoting that a dish has been cooked with special loving care. How to differentiate and what to expect? If it is an addition to soup or an accompaniment to a main dish, the diminutive usually applies in the true sense, otherwise take it as a term of endearment and loving care. *Topfenknöderl* (particularly delicious curd cheese dumplings), *Marillenknöderl* (apricot dumplings) and other sweet dumplings are borderline cases – they are smaller than ordinary dumplings fully justifying the 'r' (which does however often denote the loving care as well). Cautionary warning: occasionally a surplus of diminutive 'r' denotes a tendency towards pretentious cooking. I found '*Wildhenderl Brüsterl*' (small breast of small free range chicken) on a recent menu which was surely intended as loving care in rearing as well as cooking the chicken and not as a diminutive breast portion of a diminutive chicken. As it happens, it was excellent (the chickens were specially bred for the restaurant and the preparation faultless), but you have been warned!

Glossary

Aal: eel
Achtl, Achterl: an eighth of a litre (125 ml, about 4½ fl. oz, a large wineglassful). Measure by which house wine (*offener Wein*) is sold.
Abendmenü: fixed-price dinner menu.
Agrasl (*Stachelbeere*): gooseberry.
allerhand: all sorts/kinds, an assortment of – as in *allerhand hausgem. Würste* – an assortment of home-made sausages.
an: on. Not edible, but a word of which to beware if it appears instead of *mit* (with) on menus other than in the province of Vorarlberg (where it is perfectly permissible), since it denotes more often than not pretentious cooking. (The worst example was found in an otherwise excellent restaurant where the owner swore that he would never allow this to happen and where I had to point out that his *Topfenknödel* were offered 'on' plum sauce, but 'with' fried breadcrumbs).
Ananas: pineapple, but sometimes also used for strawberries which should then be qualified as *Ananaserdbeeren*.
Äpfel im Schlafrock: apple fritters, literally 'apples in a dressing gown'.
Apfelkren: horseradish and apple sauce, one of the classic accompaniments to *Tafelspitz* and all the other cuts of boiled beef.
Apfelküchle: apple fritters in the province of Vorarlberg.
Apfelschlangl, Apfelschlankerl: an oblong cake filled with apples and sprinkled with sugar, speciality of the Traunviertel in Upper Austria and the Ybbs valley in Lower Austria – in fact a Strudel made with *pâté brisé*.
Apfelstrudel: should not need an explanation, except that *Apfelstrudel* as against some other types of Strudel (*Mohnstrudel*, Nuss Strudel, etc., q.v.) is always made with proper Strudel pastry (if it is made with other pastry, it is not called *Apfelstrudel* – see *Apfelschlangl* above) which should be so thin that you can read a love letter through it (an ordinary letter will not do!). Best eaten warm straight from the oven. *Apfelstrudel* rates as pudding, not a tea-time pastry, and it should not, repeat not, ever be served with anything except a thick dusting of icing sugar. I am fully aware of the fact that some restaurants serve it with whipped cream, vanilla custard and even ice-cream 'because that is what our foreign visitors expect'. Don't encourage it!
Amurkarpfen: vegetarian, i.e. grass-eating carp bred at Waldschach in Styria. Similar to ordinary carp and very good. Available only in a few restaurants such as Steirerland at Kitzeck in Styria (where they have a smoked version sometimes) and at Am Spitz at Purbach in Burgenland. Try it.
Aschanti, Aschantinuss (Erdnuss): peanut.
auf Wunsch: on request. Anything from *Kernöl* dressing (pumpkin-seed oil dressing for a salad) to *Stoffserviette auf Wunsch* (cloth napkin) for which you may have to pay extra in certain restaurants.

Glossary

Aufschnitt: selection of cold meats, sausages etc. which you buy at butchers, delicatessen and good supermarkets. Ask for *zehn Deka* (100g) or *viertel Kilo* (250g). If served in a restaurant, it is called *kalte Platte* (cold platter) and usually also includes some cheese, a hard-boiled egg, chopped aspic jelly and a pickled cucumber.
ausgelöst: boned.
Austern: oysters.
Auszügla: Carinthian for *Krapfen* q.v.

Bachforelle: river trout.
backen: to deep-fry, but when applied to cakes and pastries it also means to bake. Fried pastries such as *Krapfen, Strauben*, etc. are usually qualified as *herausgebacken* – fried.
Backerbsen: 'fried peas'. Thick batter pushed into hot fat through a coarse sieve when it fries immediately into crisp golden morsels. A favourite addition to clear beef broth (*Backerbsensuppe*), but alas, nowadays originating more often than not from a packet!
Backhendl: fried Spring chicken, an Austrian classic, particularly wherever new wine (*Heuriger*) is being sold, for *Backhendl* and new wine go together like – well, new wine and *Backhendl*. Spring chicken – and the emphasis is on 'Spring', not an old boiling fowl – cut into portions, dipped into egg and breadcrumbs and crisply fried. *Backhendl* can usually be ordered *ausgelöst* (boned before frying) and in some places also *ohne Haut* (skin removed before frying). Some of the best *Backhendl* can be found at Zimmermann in Vienna and Schimanszky at Berndorf. *Backhendl* station is a place where they serve practically nothing else (except wine of course) and where you eat your *Backhendl* with your fingers (as you do at a *Heuriger*). *Backhendlzeit* is the glorious golden past and *Backhendlfriedhof* the large paunch sported by gentlemen who have eaten too many fried Spring chickens!
Baiser mit Schlag: two meringue halves sandwiched together with whipped cream.
Bärlauch, Berlaich: wild garlic, used for soups and sauces.
Bauernschmaus: large platter of smoked pork, sausages, ham, usually also a pork cutlet or a slice of roast pork served with sauerkraut and a featherlight dumpling.
Baumstamm: chocolate log cake.
Baunzerl: bread roll with a cut across the top.
Bein: bone.
Beinfleisch: meat on the bone, a term often – and erroneously– used for a cut of beef used for the famous boiled beef, known as *Beinscherzl*.
Beinschinken: ham on the bone.
Beiried: sirloin.
Bertram (Estragon): tarragon:
Beuschel (Lungenhaschee): lights, lungs (see *Kalbsbeuschel*).
Biegel (Keule): poultry leg as in *Gansbiegl* (leg of goose) or *Hühnerbiegl* (chicken leg).
Bienenstich: yeast pastry with *crème pâtissière* filling and caramelized almonds or nuts on top.
Birnenmost: pear wine.
Birnensekt: sparkling wine made from pears.
Bischofsbrot: light sponge cake with dried fruit, glacé cherries, chunks of chocolate and nuts, baked in a loaf tin.
Biskotten (*Löffelbiskuit*): boudoir biscuits, sponge fingers. Austrian sponge

fingers are larger than their French or English equivalent and they widen at each end.

Biskuit: sponge cake (more or less).

Biskuitschöberl: savoury sponge cut into rhomboids and served with clear soup (sometimes just called *Schöberl*).

Blunzen, Blunz'n (Blutwurst): black pudding.

Blunzeng'röstl, G'röstl (q.v.): made with lightly fried black pudding, potatoes, etc. Varies according to restaurant.

Blunzenparfait: speciality of Karl Eschlböck's at Plomberg, Mondsee (q.v.), based on black pudding.

Bodensee: Lake Constance.

Bohnen: beans, but *Bohnensalat* could be made from French beans (*Fisolen*) or dried beans.

Bohnenkraut: literally 'bean herb', summer savoury.

Bohnenstrudel: savoury Strudel, typical of the Burgenland, with a type of cassoulet filling, highly spiced – with or without meat.

Bosniakerl: bread roll made with wholemeal flour, spiced with caraway seeds.

Bouillon mit Ei: clear beef broth with egg or egg yolk. The egg (or egg yolk) is placed into an individual soup bowl and the hot broth poured over it which just sets the outer layer of the egg. You stir the practically raw egg into the broth as you eat it.

Bouteillenwein per Glas: vintage wines (specified) sold per glass (holding about ⅛l – 4½ fl. oz), usually marked separately on the wine list or listed on the menu. House wine is usually not sold by the glass, but in litres and fractions thereof (⅛l, ¼l, 1½l) – see *offene Weine*.

Brand: spirit, another name for eau-de-vie and always used in conjunction with the fruit from which it is distilled, e.g. *Marillenbrand*, etc.

Braten: should indicate roast meat and frequently does as when applied to pork (*Schweinsbraten*), veal (*Kalbsbraten*), chicken (*Brathuhn*), etc., but it can also refer to pot roast, mostly in the case of beef (*Rindsbraten*) when it should however be prefaced by *gedünsteter*. Roast beef – for which the Austrians have a healthy respect and which they roast beautifully as a rule – is almost invariably described by its proper name.

Brathuhn, Brathendl, roast chicken, often prefaced by *Steirisches* since Styrian chickens are considered the *Poulardes de Bresse* of Austria.

Bratkartoffel, Braterdäpfel: roast potatoes.

Bratwurst: frying sausage, *boudin blanc*.

Brein, Prein (Hirse): millet.

Bries (Kalbsmilch): sweetbreads, usually calves.

Brösel, Semmelbrösel (Paniermehl): fine white breadcrumbs, not toasted or horribly coloured – as used for *Wiener Schnitzel* and a variety of sweet and savoury dishes.

Bröselknöderl: small dumplings made with fine breadcrumbs and more often than not bone marrow which gives them a particularly good flavour. Used in soups and white stews and more or less identical with *Markknöderl* (q.v.).

Brot: bread.

Brust, Brüsterl: breast of, as in *Kalbsbrust* (breast of veal) or *Brüsterl von …* (breast of …).

Bruckfleisch: Viennese speciality. Ragout including heart, liver, melts, sweetbreads, aorta and *Kronfleisch* (a special cut of beef) cooked with herbs, grated root vegetables and red wine.

b'soffene Kathi, Liesl, Kapuziner: 'drunk Kathi, Lizzie, Capucine' the last name varying according to region. Delectable steamed or baked pudding liberally doused in mulled wine.

Buchteln, Wuchteln: small yeast buns filled with jam, baked closely together and separated after baking. Best eaten whilst still warm when they are at their most delicious (and alas, their most indigestible). A speciality of the Café Hawelka in Vienna in the early hours of the morning.

Buderl: small bottle and measure for *Schnaps*, usually containing $\frac{1}{16}$ l, 60ml or 2 generous fl. oz.

Burgenland: Austrian province near the Hungarian border, famous for its wines and where food has a strong Hungarian flavour.

Buschenschenke: place in a vineyard where wine from that particular vineyard is sold. Marked by a fir branch (*Buschen*) and frankly a *Heuriger* (q.v.) outside Vienna. Light refreshments – usually based on pork – are often served as well.

Busserln: literally 'little kisses'. Small, very light biscuits, usually based on egg-white and named after the main ingredient, e.g. *Nussbusserln* (with walnuts), *Kokosbusserln* (with coconut), etc.

Butterbrösel: breadcrumbs fried in butter.

Butternockerln: particularly light little gnocchi which may be served in soups, but also as an accompaniment to meat.

Butterschnitzel: sometimes prefaced by *faschiertes* (minced). No relation of *Wiener Schnitzel* and – sometimes – alas, no relation to butter. *Butterschnitzel* are in fact meat cakes which can be extremely good when ordered at places like Pfudl in Vienna. As my friend Günther Sanin says about *Kalbsbeuschel* (q.v.), *Butterschnitzel* are 'a matter of trust'!

Chaudeau: see *Weinchaudeau*.

Cevapcici: Yugoslav speciality often found in Austrian menus. Highly spiced minced meat shaped into sausages and grilled, preferably over charcoal. No skin, but the meat is sometimes wrapped in caul.

Cremeschnitten: *mille-feuilles* filled with *crème pâtissière*.

Cremesuppe: cream soup, either prefaced by the main ingredient as in *Selleriecremesuppe* (cream of celery soup) or with the main ingredient added at the end as in *von frischen Eierschwammerln* (of fresh chanterelles).

Dalken, böhmische Dalken: thick yeast cakes cooked on top of the stove like griddle cakes, in a special pan with small hollows. Usually two and two of these cakes are sandwiched together with a sweet or savoury filling.

Dampfnudeln, Dukatennudeln: small yeast buns, like *Buchteln*, but smaller (the size of an old Ducat coin) and without the jam filling, baked closely together and served with a thick Vanilla sauce as a pudding.

Debreziner: Hungarian cousin of Frankfurter sausage, coarser chopped and more highly spiced.

Dialog von ...: pretentious way of saying 'a selection of ...' (usually puddings) served on a plate'.

Dobostorte: gâteau made of layers of sponge cake sandwiched together with chocolate butter cream which should be of the exact thickness as the sponge layers. Topped with caramelized sugar. Invented by *pâtissier* Josef Dobos in 1887 in Budapest where its 100th birthday was duly celebrated.

Donauland-Carnuntum: wine region along the Danube to the immediate East and West of Vienna.

Doppelschlag: a double portion of whipped cream.

edel: noble. Used in connection with anything from fish (*Edelforelle*) to paprika (*Edelsüss*) where it denotes a degree of sharpness.

Eier im Glas: soft-boiled eggs, shelled and served in a glass goblet.

Eierkren: chopped hard-boiled eggs, freshly grated horseradish and sour cream or mayonnaise, mixed together and served as an accompaniment to cold meat or fish.

Eiernockerln: small gnocchi, usually *Butternockerln* (q.v.) tossed in butter with lightly beaten eggs scrambled into it. A sort of Austrian *à la carbonara* version without the bacon. Excellent if properly made. Cucumber salad makes the perfect accompaniment.

Eierschwammerl (Pfifferlinge): chanterelles.

Eierspeis(e): Viennese speciality, a cross between an omelette (not folded) and very lightly scrambled eggs. Served in the pan in which it was cooked (*Eierspeispfandl*). A good dish to order in a coffee house where they will usually ask you how many eggs should be used and whether you want the *Eierspeis* fried in butter or dripping. Salt and pepper are the only seasonings, though I like an additional light sprinkling of paprika. Chopped chives are the almost obligatory garnish.

Einbrenn (Einmach): roux.

eingemachtes Kalbfleisch: white veal stew (*blanquette de veau*) with vegetables and (usually) *Markknöderl*.

Eingetropftes: batter poured through a coarse sieve into hot clear broth where it poaches gently.

Einmachsuppe: soup based on good veal or chicken stock, thickened with eggs and cream.

Einspänner: tall glass of hot black coffee topped with a great mound of ice-cold whipped cream. Careful when ordering though – *Einspänner* also stands for half a pair of Frankfurter sausages (i.e. a single sausage) as well as for a carriage drawn by one horse!

Eiskaffee: thick, creamy iced coffee topped with whipped cream.

Ente: duck.

Erdäpfel (Kartoffel): potatoes.

Erdäpfelgulasch: thick, spicy potato stew, usually with the addition of sliced sausage. Particularly good at Rosenberger Motorway Restaurants (q.v.) where it is served piping hot (temperature as well as spicing).

Erdäpfelkren: potato and horseradish relish, accompaniment to boiled beef.

Erdäpfelschmarrn: potatoes boiled in their skins, peeled, sliced and fried with onions. Mashed whilst frying and served as an accompaniment to meat, not to be confused with *G'röste* (q.v.).

Erdäpfelnudeln: dough made with cooked potatoes, shaped – not into noodles as the name implies, but into oblong gnocchi about the thickness of a small finger. Cooked in boiling salt water and usually served with breadcrumbs fried in butter, as an accompaniment to meat or with fruit compote and sugar as a pudding.

Erdäpfelsuppe: potato soup which more often than not has mushrooms and bits of smoked ham added. Sometimes called 'Wiener' *Erdäpfelsuppe*.

Erdäpfelknödel: dumplings made with potato dough, sometimes wrapped round a meat filling. Dough varies according to region – some contains raw as well as cooked potatoes. Filled dumplings are usually served as a main dish, often with sauerkraut.

Erdbeere: strawberry.

Essig: vinegar. Unless stated otherwise (e.g. sherry vinegar) this is always wine vinegar. Malt vinegar is practically unknown in Austria, except possibly for adding to the water when washing the insides of refrigerators.

Essiggurke: cucumber pickled in vinegar.

Essigkren: horseradish vinaigrette.
Esterházy Rostbraten: steak with sauce containing julienne of root vegetables, spiced with capers and sour cream.
Esterházy Schnitten: delicious cream slices, recognizable by the 'feathered' design on the icing. Available at most good *pâtisseries*, but best ones probably at Merzendorfer at Fischamend (q.v.) where they are made from a secret recipe handed down by grandfather (who – as rumour has it – was chef to Prince Esterházy).
Esterházy Torte: same as above, but presented as gâteau.
Estragon: tarragon.
Extrawurst: sausage with consistency and taste rather like Frankfurter, but sold in thick rounds. Appears on menus as *Extrawurst mit Essig und Öl* (sliced with a vinaigrette dressing and sprinkled with finely chopped onions) and makes a good starter, typical inn food. *Extrawurst braten* has no culinary connotation whatsoever and suggests a special favour as an exception to the rule.

fangfrisch: freshly caught. Watch out: I saw a huge notice at an inn in the depth of the Tyrol, proclaiming *fangfrischer Kabeljau* (freshly caught cod) about a thousand miles from the nearest sea!
Farferl, Farfarle, Ferberl: noodle or Strudel dough left to dry and then grated coarsely and dried again, sometimes lightly browned in the oven. Used in soups or as an accompaniment to meat when it is treated like rice, sometimes with the addition of green peas like *Risi Bisi*. Same as *Reibgerstl*.
Fasan: pheasant.
Faschiertes, faschierter Braten: minced meat, usually a third each of veal, beef and pork, shaped into a loaf, with hard-boiled eggs (and sometimes also a Frankfurter sausage or two in the centre). Roasted and served sliced with sauce made from the juices in the pan to which chopped capers and sour cream have been added.
faschierte Laberln: meat cakes. Mixture as for faschierter Braten, shaped into patties and fried.
Faschingskrapfen: carnival doughnuts, a Viennese speciality. Respectable *Faschingskrapfen* are light, fluffy, filled with jam and noted for the pale band which runs right round their plump middles. In the old days a *Faschingskrapfen* broken in half and handed to a girl was equal to a proposal of marriage, but in those days *Faschingskrapfen* were strictly seasonal, the season extending to the last four days of the *Fasching* (carnival) only. Later on the season for *Faschingskrapfen* was extended to cover the period between New Year's Day and Ash Wednesday and nowadays they can often be found at dates throughout the year. At 'serious' *pâtisseries* and bakers, yesterday's doughnuts are displayed on a separate dish marked *von gestern* and sold at a discount.
Feinschmecker, Feinspitz: gourmet.
Fenchel: fennel.
Fiakergulasch: *Gulasch* made with beef, served with a fried egg on top, as well as with a pickled cucumber and half a pair Frankfurter sausages.
Fischbeuschelsuppe: rich fish soup made with roes, traditional at Christmas (Merzendorfer at Fischamend are one of the few restaurants who make it practically throughout the year). Thick and delicious and almost a meal in itself.
Fisolen (grüne Bohnen) Prinzessbohnen): French beans, also called *Strankerln, Strankalan* in Carinthia.
Flädle: pancakes or *Frittaten* (q.v.) in Vorarlberg.
Flaxen: gristle.

Fleckerln: pasta cut into small squares (*Fleckerln* means little patches) used in soup, but mostly to make *Schinkenfleckerln* (q.v.). *Contrariwise*.

Flecksupp'n: is not soup with *Fleckerln*, but tripe soup.

Fledermaus: cut of beef as well as a dish made from that cut. Boiled beef covered with a creamy horseradish sauce, *au gratin*.

Fleischknödel: meat dumplings which could be dough wrapped round a meat filling or all meat dumplings, according to region.

Fleischlaberln: same as *faschierte Laberln* (q.v.).

Fleischpalatschinken: pancakes with a savoury meat filling.

Fleischstrudel: strudel with savoury meat filling, boiled or baked, cut into portions and served as an accompaniment to clear beef broth. Baked *Fleischstrudel* is also served as a main course.

Fochaz: wheat loaf (in the Tyrol).

Fogos, Fogosch, Fogas: pike/perch.

Forelle: trout.

Frankfurter mit Saft: Frankfurter sausages served with thick *Gulasch* gravy. Good old-fashioned inn food, much favoured by impecunious travellers. Make sure that the bread basket on the table is well filled with crisp rolls with which to mop up the gravy! (My father-in-law always maintained that in his youth his favourite greeting by fellow students was 'tonight there's lots of gravy' which meant that they'd all sup well, particularly if the inn made no extra charge for the enormous amount of rolls they consumed.

Fridatten, Frittaten: pancake cut into strips.

Frittatensuppe: clear beef broth with finely cut strips of pancakes. Chopped herbs are sometimes added to the pancake batter, in which case the proper name is *Kräuterfrittatensuppe* (don't try to pronounce it!).

Früchtebrot: fruit loaf.

Frühling: Spring, as in *Frühlingsgemüse* (spring vegetables, usually referring to *primeurs*), *Frühlingszwiebel* (spring onions) etc.

Frühstück: breakfast. *Wiener Frühstück* as offered by many coffee houses in Austria consists of tea, coffee, chocolate, a selection of breads and crisp rolls, butter, jam or honey and a soft-boiled egg. And as many newspapers as you may care to read. Sometimes – and as a new-fangled concession – fruit-juice is also offered, but this is not obligatory.

Frühstücksgulasch: when the Viennese talk about the times when a 'breakfast *Gulasch*' cost a mere few Kreuzer (before the First World War) they do not mean breakfast, but *Gabelfrühstück* (q.v.).

Gabelfrühstück: literally 'fork breakfast'. Since Austrians rise early and breakfast is somewhat meagre, a substantial mid-morning snack is called for, best described by Austrian poet Josef Weinheber (translated from the Viennese by John Trench):

Elevenses – I don't deny
Myself some meat and beer, and why,
Occasionally, not include
A Goulash? (*Bruckfleisch* too is good),
And juicy beef, though not too greasy
Lest midday find one feeling queasy.

Gabelfrühstück is now being reintroduced by some rather elegant restaurants; the Steirereck (q.v.) in Vienna started the trend, followed by others and at the Korso in Vienna *Gabelfrühstück* is 'celebrated' on Fridays only (after which everybody goes away for the weekend, I presume). Good old-fashioned inns never stopped the custom though and you will often find that they offer small portions of *Gulasch, Kalbsbeuschel* and the like during the morning.

Gabelkraut: Sauerkraut cooked with caraway seeds and *Speck*, sometimes with a little wine as well. Loosened with a fork (*Gabel*) as it is arranged in the serving dish, hence the name.

Gailtaler Kirchtagssuppe: speciality from the Gail valley in Carinthia. Rich broth with meat, thickened with egg yolk and practically a meal in itself.

Gans, Gansl, Ganserl: goose (the greater the diminutive, the larger the goose as a rule, but I wouldn't bank on it, since the diminutive ('r') is sometimes also used to suggest how delicious a dish it is – practically as a term of endearment!

Gansleber, Gänseleber, Gänsestopfleber: goose liver.

Gansleberpastete: goose-liver pâté.

ganztägig warme Küche: hot food served throughout the day. Does not mean, however, that the full menu is available, quite often it means a shortened menu outside normal meal times.

Gasthaus: inn.

Gastgarten, Gasthausgarten: garden for the guests/garden belonging to an inn, though often not so much a garden as a paved or gravelled area with tables set under chestnut, walnut or linden trees (oleanders in the Burgenland). A sign outside a restaurant saying *schattiger Gasthausgarten* (garden well shaded by trees) is usually worth following, even if only for a cool drink.

geb., gebacken: fried, usually deep-fried and often dipped in egg and breadcrumbs first, though in that case the word *paniert* is usually added.

gebackene Mäuse: 'fried mice'. Thick yeast batter with raisins and rum, deep-fried in spoonfuls, dusted with icing sugar. Sometimes served with raspberry syrup or purée.

Gebäck: rolls, bread, etc.

gebeizt: pickled.

gebr., gebraten: shallow-fried, as in *gebratene Forelle* (shallow-fried trout).

Gedeck: literally 'table setting', but in fact cover charge which should include bread/rolls and butter, sometimes also a spread such as herb cheese etc. In some – mostly inexpensive – restaurants you will find the words *Gedeck auf Wunsch* on the menu which means that on request (*auf Wunsch*) and for a charge you get bread/rolls, butter and a cloth napkin (alternately you pay for rolls etc. according to number consumed and get a paper napkin).

ged., gedünstet: braised or stewed.

Geflügel: poultry.

Gefrorenes: ice-cream.

gef., gefüllt: stuffed, as in *gefüllte Paprika* (stuffed green peppers) or *gefülltes Kraut* (stuffed cabbage leaves).

gefüllte Paprika: unless otherwise stated, this always means green peppers with a savoury meat and rice filling, cooked in a thick tomato sauce.

Geist: spirit. Another name for eau-de-vie and always used in conjunction with the fruit from which it is distilled, e.g. *Himbeergeist, Marillengeist*. Never order *Geist* on its own, particularly in a lonely castle hotel – you could be calling for the resident ghost!

gek., gekocht: boiled, though the word simply means 'cooked'.

gem., gemischt: mixed as in *gemischter Salat* (mixed salad) which in Austria is usually not really a mixed salad at all, but an assortment of different salads set side by side on a salad dish or in a bowl.

geräuchert: smoked.

gerieben: grated.

geriebenes Gerstl: 'grated barley', another name for *Farferl* (q.v.) because the dough is grated to the size of a barleycorn.
gepöckelt: pickled.
Germ (Hefe): yeast.
Germknödel (Hefeklösse): yeast dumplings, usually filled with thick dark plum jam and served with melted butter, sugar and poppy seeds. An old-fashioned pudding enjoying renewed popularity, particularly in ski resorts where these dumplings – usually huge in size – provide good, cheap and filling nourishment for hungry youngsters.
ger., geröstet: sauté.
ger. Knödel mit Ei: a good, simple dish: sliced dumpling – usually a *Semmelknödel* (q.v.) – gently fried in butter or good dripping, with an egg scrambled over it. Sometimes served in the pan in which it was prepared and usually accompanied by a green salad.
Gerste, Gerstl: barley. (Careful here: *Gerstl* is also Viennese slang for money!)
geschäumt: frothy.
Geselchtes: smoked meat, usually pork, otherwise the meat is specified as in *geselchte Gansbrust* (smoked goose breast).
gesotten: boiled.
gespickt: larded.
gesulzt: jellied, in aspic.
gezupft: pinched, as in *gezupfte Nudeln, Nockerln* etc. – pasta pinched off by hand into requisite gnocchi etc.
Glundner, Glundna, Gelundener: cooked soft farmhouse cheese, often served with herbs and an oil/vinegar dressing.
Goderl: chin, usually denotes meat from pork chin. *Goderlspeck* is pork fat taken from the chin, but the term *Goderl kratzen* is not a culinary one – it means trying to flatter someone.
Golatschen, Kolatschen: large square yeast pastries filled with plum jam or sweetened curd cheese in which case they are called *Powidlgolatschen* and *Topfengolatschen* respectively.
Grammeln (Grieben): *grattons* in French, *ćicciole* in Italian. The crispy bits of crackling left after rendering down fat. Mostly pork, but also goose and duck (both a delicacy). Sometimes sold loose at butchers (sign says *frische Grammeln*). Delicious eaten whilst still warm, with coarse salt and hunks of dark bread. Used in many dishes, sprinkled over salads, particularly white cabbage salad and as filling for dumplings (*Grammelknödel*). At their most delicious in
Grammelpogatscherln (do not try to pronounce, just pounce if you have the opportunity), incredibly delicious thick savoury biscuits made with dark flour and yeast, sometimes available at a *Heurigen* and also in the bread basket of some restaurants like the Kellerwand at Kötschach.
Grammelschmalz (Griebenfett): dripping, usually pork, but could be goose (in rare cases) which includes small bits of crackling, well spiced and sometimes put on the table together with the butter or as an *amuse-gueule*.
Granten (Preiselbeeren): cranberries in Carinthia.
Grantenschleck: Carinthian speciality, purée of cranberries with sweet and sour cream – a sort of cranberry fool.
Graupen: pearl barley.
Grazer Zwieback: light sponge baked in loaf tin, cut into slices, dried in the oven and dusted with icing sugar. Good on its own, but also used to make *Triet* (q.v.).
Griess: semolina made from durum wheat.
Griessknödel: very light dumplings made with semolina. Served with various

sauces (*Griessknödel* with dill sauce was a favourite Friday dish of my childhood). *Griessknöderl* are a diminutive version of the above, a popular addition to clear beef broth (*Griessknöderlsuppe*).

Griessnockerl: a gnocchi version of *Griessknöderl*, very light and fluffy, used in clear beef broth.

Griess Schmarrn: a very delectable version of *Schmarrn* (q.v.) based on semolina.

Griesszucker: granulated sugar.

G'röste: in fact *geröstete Erdäpfel*, but never called that, always *G'röste*. A Viennese speciality, obligatory accompaniment to *Tafelspitz* and all the other boiled beefs. A close relation of the Swiss *Rösti*, but don't tell that to the Viennese – they think they have the copyright!

Gröstl: called *Tiroler Gröstl* everywhere except the Tyrol where it is called *Gröschtl*. Very finely chopped onions fried lightly with meat and potatoes – in a good *Gröstl* the meat should be succulent, the potatoes crisp – a pinnacle of perfection that's not always achieved. *Gröstl* can be made with beef or pork and the meat should be fresh, but unfortunately left-overs are sometimes used. There are many versions such as *Blunzengröstl* (made with black pudding), *Herrengröstl* (with an egg on top and sometimes a pickled cucumber is added as well), *Stockfischgröstl* (a Good Friday special in the Tyrol, made with dried salt cod).

grüner Salat: green salad, usually lettuce only, also called *Häuplsalat*.

g'schmackig: tasty. Sometimes used on menus when trying to accentuate the genuinely rural aspect, etc. *g'schmackiger Salat* and can denote slight pretentiousness!

G'spritzter, Gspritzter: never *Spritzer*. Half wine (red or white), half soda water. Should appear under *offene Weine* on the list, but this is not always the case, though it is always available.

Guglhupf (Napfkuchen): yeast cake with raisins, always baked in a special fluted ring mould which is well buttered and sprinkled with slivered almonds before cake mixture is put into the mould. Dusted with icing sugar whilst still warm. Occasionally a non-yeast mixture is used, in which case it is called *Backpulverguglhupf* (made with baking powder, a particularly delicious miniature version of which is presented with coffee at the Villa Schratt in Bad Ischl). Variations on the *Guglhupf* theme are *Schokoladeguglhupf* (with chocolate icing), *Marmorguglhupf* (marbled – half plain, half chocolate), *Patzerlguglhupf* (different mixtures including one with poppy seeds arranged in small portions = *Patzerl*, in the mould before baking).

Gulasch, Gulyas, Gollasch: in Austria (not in Hungary) a stew spiced with paprika and – for *Rindsgulasch* (beef *Gulasch*) also with marjoram, garlic and caraway seeds. For variations on the *Gulasch* theme look under the following: *Szekely (Szegediner), Kalbsgulasch, Znaimer Gulasch, Erdäpfelgulasch, Herrengulasch, Schwammerlgulasch.*

Gulaschgewürz: *Gulasch* spice, usually a finely ground mixture of marjoram, caraway seeds, garlic – available with or without the paprika.

Gulaschsaft: Gulasch gravy, served with Frankfurter sausages (see *Frankfurter mit Saft*).

Gulaschsuppe: *Gulasch* soup in Austria (*Gulyas* in Hungary). Very often – and none the worse for that, for Gulasch improves on being warmed up – left-over *Gulasch* stretched by addition of stock and cubed potatoes. Favourite late-night snack, but with a crisp *Salzstangerl* (q.v.) also makes a good in-between meal (Rosenberger Motorway restaurants, most coffee houses). During the carnival season it is usually available in the early hours of the morning.

Gurkerl: typically Austrian diminutive used for smallish pickled cucumber. Just when a pickled cucumber (*saure Gurke*) becomes a *Gurkerl* is not easy to define – probably when it is too small to be selected for specialized pickling. There are many different ways of pickling cucumber, such as *Senfgurke, Essiggurke* (found under their respective names), but *Gurkerl* usually refers to a small cucumber pickled in brine or vinegar.

Gurkensalat: cucumber salad. Cucumber is cut wafer-thin, sprinkled with salt and then drained of all moisture. Vinaigrette dressing, sometimes containing garlic, but sour cream/yoghurt dressing usually available on request.

Gustostückln: choice pieces. Could refer to selected pieces of almost anything, but more often than not *Gustostückln* denote the special cuts of beef particularly suitable for the famous boiled beef, such as *Tafelspitz, Beinscherzl, Hieferschwanzl, Hieferscherzl, schwarzes Scherzl*. If you find one or more of these on the menu instead of just *gekochtes Rindfleisch* (boiled beef) you know that the restaurant takes the boiled beef very seriously indeed, as they do at the Hietzinger Bräu in Vienna (q.v.).

g'wuzelt, handgewuzelt: rolled by hand, as in *gwuzelte Erdäpfelnudeln* (oblong gnocchi made from potato dough, rolled by hand).

Haferflocken: porridge oats.

Halazlé: Hungarian fish soup, often served in Austria. Clear fish broth with paprika in which pieces of fish are poached at the last minute. Best eaten near the Hungarian border in the Burgenland or near a lake where there is good fish.

Hammel: mutton.

Harder Koteletten: *Vorarlberg Schübling* sausage halved and fried, served with fried eggs and salad.

Hase: hare.

Hasenpfeffer: jugged hare.

Haselnuss: hazelnut.

Häuplsalat (Kopfsalat): lettuce salad. When the words are reversed, i.e. *Salathäupl*, it means head of lettuce.

Hausbrot: literally 'bread of the house' which one would take to be home-baked bread. Not so – it stands for bread made from mixed flour, sometimes also called *Graubrot*.

hausgem, hausgemacht: home-made, as in *'hausgemachte Würste'* (home-made sausages).

Hausmannskost: home cooking, sometimes found heading a separate section on the menu. Always worth considering because it usually means that someone takes pride in their home cooking and has probably unearthed a few old family recipes. Often includes dishes which one would really only find in private homes.

Haussulz: home-made brawn, usually served with vinaigrette dressing.

Haxn, Haxl, Haxerl: leg (as in *Hendlhaxl* – chicken leg) or feet (as in *Schweinshaxl* – trotters), depending on the animal in question.

Hecht: pike.

Hecht mit Sardellenbutter: pike with anchovy butter.

Hechtnockerln, usually *nach Wiener Art*: frankly pike dumplings except that *quenelles de brochet* sounds much more elegant. A time-honoured Viennese speciality, usually served with fresh dill sauce.

Heiden, Hadn (*Buchweizen*): buckwheat.

Heidenmehl (Buchweizenmehl): buckwheat flour.

Hendl (Huhn): chicken.

Heringschmaus: literally herring feast. Enormous hot and cold buffet presented on Ash Wednesday evening by practically every restaurant and inn in Austria. Fixed price and eat as much as you like. Herrings are included in the buffet (of course) which varies from the very elegant with oysters and caviar (the *Heringschmaus* at Zu den 3 Husaren in Vienna is particularly splendid) to a rural feast at the village inn. Not to be missed if you are in Austria on Ash Wednesday – it is usually advertised in newspapers well before that date.

Herrengulasch: beef *Gulasch*, served with a fried egg on top and a pickled cucumber.

Hexenschaum: light froth made of apples, egg-white, sugar and a dash of wine (or lemon juice) served in a glass.

Herrenpilz: Boletus mushroom, also known as *Steinpilz*. Ceps.

Hetschepetsch, Hetscherl (Hagebutten): rosehips.

Heurige: new potatoes, not to be confused with *Heuriger*.

Heuriger: new wine, i.e. wine from grapes gathered the previous year. Also the place – usually surrounded by vineyards – where the new wine is sold. In the old days the only food served at a *Heurigen* were salt *Pretzels* or spiced honeycakes – you brought your own food. Nowadays most *Heurige* have a full restaurant licence. A fir branch suspended from a pole is the 'trademark' of a *Heuriger* and they are also listed in a special column in newspapers, usually headed *Ausgsteckt* (fir branch displayed). Confusingly, the plural of *Heuriger* is *Heurige*, but then, you would not want to visit more than one in one evening, would you?

Hieferschwanzl, Hieferscherzl: special cuts of beef, used mostly for boiled beef.

Himbeer: raspberry.

Hirn mit Ei: a very Austrian speciality: calves brains very lightly fried – almost scrambled – together with egg, so that you get a luscious, creamy mixture, completely integrated. Served sprinkled with chives.

Hirnpofesen: slices of bread with crust cut off, sandwiched together with lightly cooked ragout of calves brains. Dipped into milk, egg and breadcrumbs and crisply fried – a sort of savoury (and rather rich) 'poor knights'.

Hirsch: hart, venison.

Holler, Hollunder: elderberry, but the name is sometimes also applied to lilac.

Hollersekt: sparkling elderberry wine.

Hollunderblüten, gebackene: elderberry flowers, dipped in batter and fried.

Hortobagy Palatschinken: pancakes with a savoury meat filling.

Hummer: lobster.

Husarenkrapferl: small mounds of pastry, sprinkled with slivered almonds before baking, decorated with a blob of jam in the centre (usually part of *Teebäckerei* (q.v.).

Hühnerleberpastete: pâté of chicken livers.

Indian (Pute): turkey, also known as *Truthahn* in Austria. In fact you will find the word *Pute* quite often on Austrian menus – it is about the only concession to 'proper' German.

Indianerkrapfen: two mounds of very light sponge, covered with chocolate icing and sandwiched together with sweetened whipped cream.

Ingwer: ginger.

Innereien: offal such as liver, heart, kidneys – sometimes listed under separate heading on menus.

Ischler Törtchen: a speciality of the *pâtisserie* Zauner in Ischl. Rounds of *pâté brisé* sandwiched together with chocolate butter cream, covered with chocolate icing. Variations can be found in *pâtisseries* throughout Austria – the pastry sometimes includes hazelnuts or walnuts and the rounds are sandwiched together with jam.

Ischler Oblatten: also a speciality of Zauner's. Large round wafers (sold in tins) with a nougat filling, used for making *Zaunerstollen* (q.v.).

Jägerbraten: usually another name for *faschierter Braten* (q.v.).

Jägerschnitzel: can be virtually anything, but more often than not it is beef cooked with bacon, onions and mushrooms, with a wine sauce.

Jägerwecken: a baguette hollowed out so that only the crust remains. Filled with a delicate mixture of spiced butter into which chopped ham, salami, pickled cucumber, hard-boiled egg and anchovies have been folded. Chilled and cut into thin slices and absolutely delicious.

Jause (Vesper): in-between meal, more often than not referring to afternoon meal which invariably centres around gâteau or cake. *Zehnuhrjause* (ten o'clock *Jause*) which is the equivalent of elevenses (they get up earlier in Austria) is really a light *Gabelfrühstück* (q.v.).

Junges: usually prefaced by the name of the animal from which it derives, e.g. *Ente, Gansl*, etc. Giblets, including neck, made into soup or stew. Liver is not usually included – at least not goose liver – but chicken liver might be. Neck of goose is usually skinned, the skin is stuffed and roasted, served separately.

Jungfernbraten (Schweinslungenbraten): whole pork fillet, roasted. Sometimes wrapped in caul before roasting.

k. & k.: stands for *kaiserlich und königlich* (imperial and royal). Sometimes found on menus as in *nach k. & k. Rezeptur* (according to imperial and royal recipes) meaning as cooked at the Court (usually that of Franz Josef) and perfectly genuine as a rule, particularly when found in places such as Attwenger's at Bad Ischl.

Kaffeecremekrapfen: like *Indianer* (q.v.) but with coffee-flavoured icing and filling.

Kaffeestriezel: plaited yeast loaf with raisins or sultanas. There's no coffee in the dough, but *Kaffeestriezel* is a favourite accompaniment to coffee.

Kaiser ... Emperor: Used in conjunction with many dishes from soups to puddings and indicates that a dish is fit for an emperor – the emperor in question being Franz Josef more often than not (whose tastes were paradoxically modest, not to say frugal). Often an improved and more elegant version of a more mundane dish (see *Kaisergerstl, Kaiserschöberl*).

Kaiserfleisch (geräuchertes Schweinefleisch): smoked belly of pork served thinly sliced. Often part of a *Brettljaus'n* (q.v.).

Kaisergerstl: a more elegant version of ordinary *Gerstl* or *Reibgerstl* (q.v.) which are made with left-over *Strudel* or noodle paste. *Kaisergerstl* is really a savoury custard cooked in a *Bain Marie*, from which small portions are scooped out and served in clear broth.

Kaiserschmarrn: pancake batter with raisins or sultanas into which whipped egg-whites have been folded. It is then cooked like any other *Schmarrn* (q.v.) from very moist to almost crisped to a frazzle. Thickly dusted with icing sugar and traditionally served with *Zwetschkenröster* (stewed blue plums) or *Preiselbeerkompott* (cranberries). Always cooked to order in restaurants (allow about twenty minutes) and one portion is usually more than enough for two. Although legend has it – and legends die hard – that *Kaiserschmarrn* was the favourite pudding of the Emperor Franz Josef, the *Kaiser* in this particular case probably stems from *Koaserer* (cheese-maker).

Kaiserschnitzel: veal escalope with a sauce of sour cream and capers.

Kaiserschöberl: richer version of ordinary *Schöberl* or *Biskuitschöberl* (q.v.) with butter and grated Parmesan cheese added to the basic sponge mixture.

Kaisersemmel: 'Emperor's roll'. Bread roll made from wheat flour with five cuts, the edges of which are drawn towards the centre to form a rosette. 'Bold, well-shaped Kaiser rolls with small, round bottoms' in the correct definition according to Victor F.A. Richter in *Vienna Bread* – the definitive work on that subject.

Kalbfleisch: veal.

Kalbsbeuschel (Lungenhaschee): *Beuschel* are calves lights (lungs), but the actual dish, whether called *Kalbsbeuschel, Kalbsrahmbeuschel, Rahmbeuscherl,* or *Salonbeuscherl* contains heart as well as lights. Perhaps I should have just said 'delicious ragout made with herbs and cream' and left it at that. (Some years ago a famous food writer was invited to Vienna, duly introduced to all sorts of culinary delights and finally a dish of *Kalbsbeuschel* was set before her. 'Delicious,' was the verdict, 'but what is it?' At which courage failed her hosts. 'Mushrooms,' mumbled one. 'Sort of liver,' said another. Eventually the dish got an enthusiastic review in the glossiest of glossies, complete with – invented – recipe. '*Kalbsbeuschel*' it said and in brackets underneath, 'Soured liver and mushrooms'.

At one time *Beuschel* was considered a poor people's dish – typical inn food, now it is more often found at the more expensive restaurants (sometimes as *Amuse gueule*) because preparation takes so much time and care. Still available in really good country inns though. '*Beuschel ist Vertrauenssache,*' says Günther Sanin of Klostergasthaus Fiecht which means to say that you have to trust the cook because virtually anything can be put into a *Beuschel*.

Kalbsbries (Kalbsmilch, Kalbsmilken): veal sweetbreads.

Kalbsbriesrose: choice piece of veal sweetbreads.

Kalbsbrust, gefüllte: stuffed breast of veal, sometimes called *nach Wiener Art* – Viennese style.

Kalbsgulasch: veal *Gulasch* to which sour cream may have been added.

Kalbsherz, gespicktes: larded calves heart, cooked with root vegetables and usually served with a piquant sauce.

Kalbskopf, gebackener: calves head cooked, then cooled, cut into slices, dipped into egg and breadcrumbs and fried.

Kalbsleber, gebackene: calves liver cut into slices, dipped into egg and breadcrumbs and fried like *Wiener Schnitzel*.

Kalbsnierenbraten: roast loin of veal with kidneys.

Kalbsrahmgulasch: veal *Gulasch* to which sour cream has definitely been added.

Kalbsstelze: knuckle of veal, usually roasted and sold according to weight.

Kalbsvögerl: sometimes called *gespickte* (larded) *Kalbsvögerl*. Cut of veal taken from the shin, rolled up and larded and either roasted or pot-roasted.

Kalbszüngerl: calves tongue, usually cooked with vegetables.

Kalbszüngerlsulz: brawn of calves tongue.

kalte Platte: cold platter, usually a collection of ham, various sausages, tongue, roast beef, with hard-boiled eggs, pickled cucumber and chopped aspic jelly.

Kamptal-Donauland: wine region in Lower Austria, north east of the Wachau.

Kanarienmilch: light creamy custard served with puddings.

Kaninchen: rabbit.

Kapaun: capon.

Karbonadl: cutlet or chop, with bone.

Karfiol (Blumenkohl): cauliflower.

Karotten: carrots.

Karree: loin.

Kärntnen: Carinthia, Southern province in Austria, bordering Yugoslavia as well as Italy. The name probably stems from the Celtic *Carantum* or *Caranta*, meaning 'friend'. As the Carinthians are quick to point out, theirs was the only province not conquered by the Romans, but became part of the Roman Empire by way of trade agreement.

Kärntner Nudeln: sometimes known as *Kärntner Kasnudeln*. Noodle paste rolled out thinly, cut into rounds and filled with a mixture of curd cheese, potatoes (which are sometimes replaced by bread and/or millet) and herbs, mostly mint and chervil, though lovage has also been known to play a part. Paste rounds are folded over to form half-moons, sealed and cooked in boiling salt water. Served with melted butter. Could be called an Austrian cousin of Parma's *Tortelli di Erbette*.

Kärntner Reinling: yeast cake with raisins and powdered dried pears and originally baked in a short-handled saucepan called *Rein* (hence the name *Reinling*), though it can of course be baked in a large cake tin. For festive occasions such as weddings etc. the *Reinling* is baked with a hole in the centre in which flowers and other decorations are arranged.

Karpfen: carp.

Karpfen, gesulzter: carp in aspic.

Karte (Speisenkarte): the Menu. (If you ask for *das Menü* in an Austrian restaurant, you will be given details of that day's set-price meal or meals.) If you want to see the Menu, ask for *die Karte* or *'die Speiskarte – Speisenkarte* being the 'proper' German name!

Kasnocken: not to be confused with Carinthian *Kasnudeln* (see above). Tyrolean speciality: small dumplings made with potatoes, flour and *Graukäs* (a local cheese) which are fried.

Kaspressknödel: a speciality of Salzburg: fried dumplings with cheese, usually served in clear broth.

Kastanien: chestnuts.

Kastanienreis: purée of chestnuts pushed through a coarse sieve or potato ricer and served with mounds of whipped cream. Also known as 'Mont Blanc'.

Kastanientorte: chestnut gâteau.

Kavalierspitz: cut of beef (shoulder) particularly suited to boiling.

Keferfil (Kerbel): chervil.

Keks: derived from 'cakes', but in fact refers to biscuits.

Kerbel: chervil.

Kernöl: sometimes prefaced by *Steirisches*. Oil derived from green pumpkin seeds. A Styrian speciality, now used throughout Austria. Delicious in salads, and sometimes blended with other oils for a lighter texture. Some menus state *Kernöl dressing nach Wunsch* (on request) and you may have to ask for it.

Kessel: as in *Kesselgulasch*. Small cauldron, usually made of copper in which certain dishes such as *Kesselgulasch* are brought to the table.

Kipfel, Kipferl (Hörnchen): Austrian version of croissant, much drier and crisper. If *Kipferl* is prefaced by another noun it denotes the type of filling (as in *Nusskipferl* – with walnut filling) or extra ingredients (as in *Butterkipferl* – with rich pastry, or *Vanillekipferl* – small crescents rolled in Vanilla sugar).

Kipfelauflauf, Kipfelkoch: a particularly delectable old-fashioned pudding based on *Kipfel* (in one of Nestroy's plays a character is called 'Lord Kipfelkoch' – naming a person after a dish rather than the other way round).

Kipferlschmarrn: a *Schmarrn* (q.v.) based on *Kipferl*.

Kipfler: special kind of waxy potato, about the thickness of a finger, often crescent-shaped, hence the name. Particularly good for potato salad and certain potato dishes. Hitler banned the planting of *Kipfler* as a luxury and it took years after the war to get them to grow properly again.

Kirschen: cherries.

Kirschenstrudel: cherry Strudel, sometimes filled with morello cherries when it should really be called *Weichselstrudel* but seldom is.

Kitz: kid, young goat. Often served at Easter, usually fried like *Backhendl*.

Klachlsuppe: rich soup made from pig's head and trotters and probably an acquired taste, but there was a high-ranking civil servant (retd.) who made a weekly trek from Vienna to Graz just to eat *Klachlsuppe* at the (now alas defunct) Steirerhof.

klar: clear.

klare Rindsuppe: clear beef broth, bouillon.

Klarer: eau-de-vie which can be distilled from practically anything from fir tips to Gentian roots. Should be preceded by its origin, but if you are offered a measure of *Klarer* in a rural or mountain region, go very carefully indeed – it is usually a pretty fierce home-distilled spirit strong enough to raise the dead.

kleine Karte: small menu, usually the menu offered out of regular restaurant hours, such as afternoon or late at night.

Kletzen: dried pears.

Kletzenbrot: sometimes called *Tiroler Kletzenbrot*, though it exists practically all over Austria. Rich fruit loaf which is practically all fruit in which *Kletzen* play a prominent part. There are many regional variations and often the fruit is wrapped in very thin dough before baking.

knackig: an expression only fairly recently applied to matters culinary, meaning crisp. Perfectly in order when used to denote crispness in salads – though I am slightly wary of it even then. Watch out, however, if used in conjunction with vegetables (*knackiges Gemüse*), meaning not only severely undercooked vegetables, but more often than not heralding pretentious 'cuisine'!

Knackwurst: like *Extrawurst* (q.v.) but sold in short lengths and like *Extrawurst*, often served with a vinaigrette dressing (*Knackwurst mit Essig und Öl*). Also excellent when fried. Sometimes lovingly referred to as *Beamtenforelle* (trout of the white-collared workers) and as such a favourite cheap lunch or supper dish in the old days.

Knoblauch, Knofel: garlic.

Knoblauchcremesuppe: creamy soup with lots of garlic, claimed by several regions and often named after that region, e.g. *Waldviertler Knoblauchcremesuppe*. Sometimes served *im Brottöpferl* – in a hollowed-out round of bread or large bread roll.

Knödel (Klösse): dumplings. Austrian dumplings are usually featherlight and delicious and there are literally hundreds of varieties, some of which are listed under their respective names.

Knöderl: small to very small dumplings such as those used in soup which is then named according to the dumpling, e.g. *Leberknöderlsuppe* (soup with small liver dumplings).

Knurrhahn: gurnard.

knusprig: crisp, crispy, as in crackling and in *knusprig gebacken* (crisply fried). I am still puzzled by a menu description at the Altes Gericht at Sulz in Vorarlberg which offered a dish *mit knuspriger Sahne* (with crisp cream). Quite apart from the fact that they used Sahne instead of Obers which is understandable since Sulz is close to the Swiss and German borders, I would not even hazard a guess as to what this could mean. (There was no chance to ask since it happened to be their busiest day with three large family parties in full swing and a host of other visitors, but I am determined to find out!)

Kochsalat mit grünen Erbsen: braised lettuce with green peas. Delicious, even if you lose a few vitamins in the process.

Kohl: savoy cabbage.

Kohl nach Wiener Art: savoy cabbage in a creamy sauce, often spiced with garlic.

Kohlsprossen (Rosenkohl): Brussels sprouts.

Konditorei: *pâtisserie*, pastry shop – which is an over-simplification as well as an understatement. A good *Konditorei* should be permeated by that undefinable scent of which vanilla forms a strong but not overpowering part (for details see under Strehly at Graz). The late Hans Weigel once wrote that those of us who had grown up to the sound of the Vienna Philharmonic strings were 'forever damning, forever damned'. The same could be said for the scent of an Austrian *pâtisserie* – or the contents.

Körberl: literally 'small basket', referring to the basket containing bread and rolls which is usually placed on the table as a matter of course. Apparently in recent years a number of restaurants in Austria got rather slack about this and the Austrian Master Bakers mounted a large advertising campaign calling for its return. Asking for *das Körberl* is therefore not only perfectly justified, but also shows that you are well up in internal restaurant politics, and have watched Austrian TV!

kräftig: strong, hearty – as in *krättige Rindsuppe* (strong beef broth) which always makes me suspect that it has come out of a packet. This is very unjustified and unfair of me and only shows my suspicious nature.

Krainer Würstl: particularly good, spicy sausages from Styria, the best ones being *Sulmtaler* (Sulm valley) *Krainer* of which the best ones are made by Messner at Stainz.

Kranewett, Kranebitten, Krammetbeer (Wacholder): juniper berries.

Krapfen: more often than not refers to *Faschingskrapfen* (q.v.), but basically to all fluffy yeast buns – filled or unfilled – fried in deep fat.

Kraut (Weisskraut): white cabbage, rarely called *Weisskraut* in Austria. Red cabbage is however always called *Rotkraut*.

Kräuter: herbs.

Kräuternockerl: small or large gnocchi to which chopped herbs have been added – used mostly for clear soups.

Krautfleckerln: definitely an acquired taste, but very good indeed for the combination of different textures and flavours: small pasta squares (*Fleckerln*) cooked in salted water and then combined with what is almost a sauce with a definite sweet/sour flavour made of finely shredded cabbage (it is cooked so delicately that you will barely recognize it as such). A speciality of Lower Austria and the Burgenland. Served as a dish on its own or as an accompaniment to meat. The further south east you get in the Burgenland, the sweeter the seasoning – in fact *Krautfleckerln* are sometimes served as a pudding of the 'sweet pasta' variety.

Krautfleisch: almost identical to *Szegediner* and Szekely *Gulasch*, occasionally containing potatoes as well.

Krautsalat: finely shredded white cabbage salad, served warm, usually with a sprinkling of crispy bits of crackling. Sometimes described as 'warmer' *Krautsalat* on menus which does not mean that every *Krautsalat* merely described as such is served cold.

Krautsuppe: also described as *Ungarische Krautsuppe (Korhelyleves)*. Soup made with *Sauerkraut*, sour cream and smoked pork and – like Essence of Tokay, only cheaper – credited with curing anything from a broken leg to a broken heart. Best in the Burgenland near the Hungarian border – like at Raffel in Jennersdorf or the Café Sommer in the Hauptstrasse at Mörbisch in the early hours of the morning.

Krebse: crayfish, sometimes called *Flusskrebse* or *Bachkrebse* (river crayfish), the most superior ones being described as *Solokrebse* which have to be of a minimum weight.

Kremser Senf: a slightly sweet mustard, particularly good with Frankfurther sausages.

Kren (Meerrettich): horseradish. *'Kren oder Senf?'* (horseradish or mustard?) the waiter will ask when you order a pair of Frankfurter sausages – freshly grated horseradish being the customary alternative to mustard for serving with cold meat and certain sausages. Horseradish is also much used in sauces, particularly those used as accompaniments to the famous boiled beef, e.g. *Apfelkren, Semmelkren* and you will find those listed throughout the glossary. N.B. Should anyone have the audacity to suggest that you are much needed 'to grate horseradish' (*Kren reiben*), this is *not* a compliment!

Krenfleisch: a hearty dish of boiled pork liberally sprinkled with freshly grated horseradish. Different cuts of pork are used as well as vegetables.

Kriasi: superb cherry eau-de-vie from Vorarlberg.

Kronfleisch: nothing at all to do with *Krenfleisch*, but a cut of beef which should always be included in *Bruckfleisch* (q.v.). Also used for the lesser type of *Gulasch* as it does not require hanging.

Krotzbeer: blackberry.

Krügel: measure by which beer is sold, ½ litre. If you ask for a large beer (*grosses Bier*) you are likely to get a *Krügel*.

Kruspelspitz: special cut of beef.

Kukuruz (Mais): maize, corn-on-the-cob.

Kümmel: caraway seeds, much used in Austrian cooking. Also the name of the liqueur.

Kümmelbraten: roasted pork which has been rubbed with paprika and caraway seeds prior to toasting (sometimes first ground to a fine powder) which gives a distinctive flavour to gravy and meat.

Kümmelfleisch: a splendid ragout or stew – depending on the cut of meat – of lean pork, flavoured with caraway seeds, often cooked with beer.

Kümmelsuppe: very lightly thickened soup based on good veal or beef stock to which caraway seeds (ground or whole) have been added, served with crisp *croûtons*. Considered an excellent remedy for 'delicate' stomach conditions, such as after drinking too much wine, but unlike most remedies, it tastes delicious (depending on the stock). Not a reviver or a cure for hangovers like *Krautsuppe*, however!

Kürbis: vegetable marrow.

Kürbiskerne: green pumpkin seeds from which the special oil (*Kernöl*) is pressed. The pumpkins – which have very little flesh – are grown only for the seeds. In fact the seeds – lightly roasted – taste delicious on their own and it is only a question of time before someone takes this a step further when pumpkin seeds will probably vie very successfully with other salted nuts in popularity. At present quite a number of restaurants serve pumpkin seeds with cheese and they are also used in several sweet and savoury dishes.

Kürbiskraut: nothing at all to do with *Kraut* (cabbage): finely shredded vegetable marrow cooked with sour cream, paprika and fresh dill, occasionally also with tomatoes and beef stock added – speciality of Burgenland, Styria and Lower Austria, with regional variations.

Kutteln, Kuttelfleck (Kuhmagen): tripe.

Kuttelkraut (Thymian): thyme, literally 'tripe herb' because it is usually added to tripe dishes.

Lachs: salmon.
Lachsforelle: salmon trout.
Lamm: lamb.
Lammnüsschen: noisettes of lamb.
Landjäger: hard, flat and highly spiced dried sausage.
Leber: liver.
Leberkäs: literally 'liver cheese' though it contains neither. A highly commendable sort of cross between hot meat loaf and pâté, made of various kinds of meat. Available at good butchers – some have a notice *'warmer Leberkäs'* in the window, others are known for the time of its arrival and they have fresh rolls in readiness into which they slip the hot *Leberkäs* for a mid-morning snack (sometimes a pickled cucumber is added as well). *Leberkäs* is occasionally available in restaurants (particularly those with their own butchery) where it appears on menus as *geb.* (fried) *Leberkäs* though it is more often grilled than fried and served with an egg on top. A splendid snack, always reasonably priced which few visitors to Austria ever order, simply because the name puzzles them. Try it – you may well become an addict!
Leberknöderl: small liver dumplings, served in clear broth.
Leberreissuppe: a mixture not unlike the one used for liver dumplings is pushed through a coarse sieve straight into hot clear broth where it sets into 'grains' slightly larger than rice grains – hence the name.
Lebkuchen: honeycakes.
Leberpastete: liver pâté.
Liebstöckl, Lustock (Maggikraut): lovage, much used in Carinthia where there's even a lovage eau-de-vie.
Linsen: lentils, in Austria always brown lentils.
Linsen, saure: lentils cooked preferably in ham stock, with thyme and bay leaf and definite sweet/sour taste, i.e. seasoned with vinegar and sugar.
Linsenspecksalat: lentil salad with bits of *Speck* or crackling. Highly commendable.
Linzertorte: basically a cake made with pastry to which almonds or nuts as well as spices have been added. About two-thirds of the pastry are used for the base, the remainder is used to form a criss-cross pattern on top, the space between being filled with raspberry jam. There are many variations, like 'white' *Linzertorte* made with blanched almonds and *gerührte Linzertorte* where the basic mixture is stirred as for a cake and there are also small pastries, all prefaced with *Linzer* like *Linzer Augen* which are usually rounds of pastry sandwiched together with jam and holes ('eyes') cut out of the pastry so that the jam is visible.
Liptauer: cream or cottage cheese mixed with an equal quantity of butter and spiced with paprika, caraway seeds, capers, mustard, anchovies and finely chopped onion. In some restaurants it is served on a large plate with the cheese/butter mixture in the centre, surrounded by the other ingredients and you can then 'compose' your *Liptauer* according to your taste.
Liwanzen: very superior cheesecake on a yeast base, spread liberally with curd cheese and sour cream mixture before baking.
Lorbeer: bay leaf (careful: in Austria the same word is used for bay leaf and for laurel!)
Löwenzahn: dandelion.
Lunge: lights, lungs, known as *Beuschel* in Austria.
Lungenbraten (Filet): whole fillet of beef.
Lungenstrudel: a mixture of lights, cooked with onions and herbs and wrapped in *Strudel* pastry, then baked or boiled (more often the latter) and served with or in clear beef broth (*Lungenstrudelsuppe*).

mager: lean, as in *mageres Meisl* (a particularly lean cut of meat).
Maisgriess: cornmeal, Polenta.
Maismehl: maize flour, finely ground cornmeal.
Mandarinen: tangerines.
Mandeln: almonds.
Mandelkren: freshly grated horseradish mixed with cream and finely ground almonds, chilled and served as an accompaniment to meat or fish.
Marillen (Aprikosen): apricots.
Marillenbrand, Marillenschnaps: apricot eau-de-vie, particularly good in the Wachau region and in Burgenland.
Marillenknödel: apricot dumplings served sprinkled with breadcrumbs browned in butter, sugar and sometimes a dusting of powdered cinnamon as well. *Marilleneisknödel* are a 'modern' version of the above and either ordinary *Marillenknödel*, the apricot in the centre having been replaced with an apricot sorbet or 'dumplings' made entirely of ice-cream – vanilla outside with apricot centre and probably rolled in toasted nuts. (If you find them on a menu, ask before ordering for I cannot possibly tell you which to expect.)
Marillenröster: exactly the same as *Zwetschkenröster* (q.v.) but made with apricots.
mariniert: marinaded.
Majoran: marjoram.
Majoranerdäpfel: potatoes in a light cream sauce, flavoured with fresh marjoram.
Mark: bone marrow.
Markknöderl: small dumplings made with fine breadcrumbs and bone marrow, practically identical with *Bröselknöderl* (q.v.). Favourite addition to *eingemachtes Kalbfleisch* (*blanquette de veau*) and *Einmachsuppe* (creamy soup based on veal stock).
Markscheiben: slices of cooked bone marrow, served on top of steaks or with boiled beef.
Marmelade: not marmalade, but Austrian generic for jam. If the fruit is not specified, e.g. *Ribislmarmelade* (redcurrant jam) and it just says *Marmelade*, you can be fairly sure – though by no means certain – that the jam will be apricot.
Maroni (Kastanien): chestnuts.
Maschinrostbraten: basically, braised whole steak with onions, capers, pickled cucumber, cooked in a closely covered pan. The sauce is usually thickened with cream or sour cream.
Matrosenfleisch: close relation, possibly forerunner of *Boeuf Stroganoff*. Finely sliced fillet beef in a sauce of sour cream with capers, but the recipe varies, according to the restaurant.
Mayonnaise-Ei: hard-boiled egg sitting on top of Russian salad, masked with mayonnaise. Usually rather elegantly garnished – sometimes with strips of smoked salmon. Often at its best in a *pâtisserie*!
Mehlspeis(e): pudding, sweet, dessert, literally 'dish made with flour' though many Austrian and particularly Viennese puddings contain no flour at all and one of the reasons – to quote Hans Weigel again – 'why Freud had to be Viennese'.
Meisl: sometimes described as *mageres Meisl*, a special cut of beef and a so-called *Gustostückl* (q.v.).
Melanzani: aubergines, egg-plant.
Menu, Menü: sometimes prefaced with *Mittag* or *Abend*. Fixed price meal, *not* the Menu which is called *Speiskarte* or *Speisenkarte* or simply *Karte*. Some restaurants have several fixed-price menus from which to choose, including *Feinschmecker*, *Degustation* and *Gourmet* menus.
Milch: milk.

Milchbrot: raisin or sultana bread, milk having been used for the dough.
Milchrahmstrudel, Millirahmstrudel: to my mind the ultimate in *Strudel*. Filled with curd cheese, raisins and sour cream and baked in a light egg custard. Served warm, not hot. Sometimes called Breitenfurter *Milchrahmstrudel* – Breitenfurt being a small village in Lower Austria where the *Milchrahmstrudel* was legendary at one time – now available throughout Austria. Usually excellent at a *pâtisserie* and if you spot the sign *'warmer' Milchrahmstrudel* in a *pâtisserie* window, think seriously about forgoing pudding at lunch in a restaurant and moving over to the *pâtisserie* for 'afters'.
Milz: melts, often used in a spread on toast with clear soup (*Milzcroutons*), also in savoury dishes.
mitgebraten: roasted with.
Mittag: noon.
Mittagsmenü: set-price lunch.
Mittelburgenland: central Burgenland, wine region known particularly for its red wines.
Mohn: poppy seeds, grown mostly in the Waldviertel region of Lower Austria.
Mohnbeugel: often called Pressburger *Mohnbeugel* since the ones from Pressburg (now Bratislava, formerly Poszony) are the 'classic' ones. Small crescents made of yeast pastry with a filling of ground poppy seeds, raisins and noted for their marbled exterior (the crescents are brushed with egg, then left to rise before baking which creates the marbled effect). *Nussbeugel* (q.v.) are the same but with a walnut filling. To differentiate between the two at a baker's or confectioner's: *Nussbeugel* are narrower, *Mohnbeugel* wider.
Mohnkipferl: basically like *Mohnbeugel*, but without the marbled effect.
Mohnnudeln: typical example of 'sweet pasta' dish popular in Austria where – particularly in country regions – a meal may well consist of 'soup and pudding'. Ordinary broad noodles cooked in boiling salt water as usual and served with melted butter and a mixture of finely ground poppy seeds, sugar and cinnamon. In the Waldviertel region of Lower Austria where poppy seeds are grown, *Mohnnudeln* are made of a special potato paste – short, thick and plump, and *gewuzelt*, i.e. rolled by hand.
Mohnstriezel: a large plaited loaf made of ordinary white bread dough and sprinkled with poppy seeds before baking.
Mohnstriezerl: miniature version of above. Should be in every self-respecting selection of breakfast rolls and breads.
Mohnstrudel: yeast dough with a filling of ground poppy seeds, raisins etc., rolled up, formed into horseshoe shape and baked. Favourite with afternoon coffee.
Mohntorte: delicious moist cake made with poppy seeds, particularly good in Salzburg (where they add raisins and sometimes chopped glacé fruit) and in the Burgenland (where it is often served warm with hot chocolate sauce as a pudding).
Mohr im Hemd: the ultimate in chocolate puddings: very light, almonds or walnuts often partly replacing flour. Served hot with ice-cold whipped cream and hot chocolate sauce.
Mondseer: pungent cheese from the Mondsee region of the Salzkammergut.
Morcheln: morilles, morel mushrooms.
Most: in and around Vienna *Most* stands for unfermented grape juice (the lightly fermented grape juice which is slightly cloudy, is called *Sturm*), but in some regions, particularly in Upper Austria with its *Mostviertel* whose inhabitants are sometimes – rather unkindly – referred to as *Mostschädel* (thick-headed). *Most* is basically apple wine, though it can be made with fruit other than apples – sometimes a mixture of apples and pears is used. You may also find

quite a number of dishes – particularly in orchard areas – with the preface *Most* which means that they were either cooked or marinaded in apple wine or have a sauce or sabayon based on it.
Muskat: nutmeg.
Muskatblüte: mace.

Nagerl (Nelken): cloves.
Naturschnitzel: veal escalope, very lightly dusted with flour on one side, fried in butter with gravy made from the juices in the pan.
Netzbraten: meat wrapped in caul before roasting.
Neusiedler See: Lake Neusiedl, huge shallow lake in the Burgenland the southern tip of which is in Hungary.
Neusiedler See Hügelland: wine region to the west of Lake Neusiedl which includes the famous wine town of Rust.
Neusiedler See Seewinkel: wine region to the east of Lake Neusiedl.
Niederösterreich: Lower Austria, largest Austrian province. Vienna which is situated in Lower Austria is a province in its own right of which Vienna is the capital. The capital of Lower Austria is called St Pölten.
Nierndl (Nieren): kidneys.
Nocken: basically a dumpling by another name, or large gnocchi. Named after the main ingredient e.g. *Griessnocken* (semolina *Nocken*). Can be sweet or savoury and should be listed in the relevant section on the menu.
Nockerln (Spätzle): generally a smaller version of the above. *Nockerln* are scooped out with a teaspoon (or snipped off with a knife from a *Nockerlbrett* – a slanted bevelled board which is held in one hand whilst the *Nockerl* are cut straight into boiling salt water). Plain *Nockerl* are often served with stews (*Gulasch mit Nockerln*) or in soup (*Griessnockerlsuppe*). Exception: *Schneenockerl* (q.v.) and *Salzburger Nockerln* (q.v.) which defy the diminutive and are huge.
Nuss: nut, usually walnut.
Nussbeugel: like *Mohnbeugel* (q.v.) only slimmer and with a walnut filling.
Nussener, Nuss Schnaps: digestif made with green walnuts. There is also a liqueur version which should be called thus but seldom is – if in doubt, ask (*Nuss Schnaps* tastes not unlike *Fernet Branca* and is attributed the same curative qualities).
Nusskipferl: like *Mohnkipferl* (q.v.) but with walnut filling.
Nusslan: *Medaillons* (mostly in Carinthia) usually prefaced by the meat in question e.g. *Kalbsnusslan* (*Medallions* of veal).
Nussnudeln: like *Mohnnudeln* (q.v.) but served with ground walnuts, sugar and cinnamon. Unlike some *Mohnnudeln* however, they are hardly ever made with potato paste.
Nuss Strudel: like *Mohnstrudel* (q.v.)

Obatzter: cream cheese mixed with butter and well spiced – a speciality of the Sänger Blondel at Dürnstein.
Oberösterreich: Upper Austria – Austrian province to the west of Lower Austria and containing a large section of the Salzkammergut, the famous lake region.
Obers (süsse Sahne): thick cream. If just described as *Obers* it usually means in liquid form – (*Schlagobers* is whipped cream – in name and in fact), but I would not necessarily rely on this. *Kaffeeobers* is – or rather, should be – single cream, but alas, it now sometimes denotes some type of longlife or other plastic horror.
Oberskren: horseradish cream.
Oblaten: could mean rice paper or wafers, but generally refers to large round

wafers with sugar (*Karlsbader Oblaten*) or sugar and nut (*Ischler/Zauner Oblaten*) filling.

Obst: fruit.

Obstler: eau-de-vie distilled from mixed fruit, usually apples, pears and plums.

Ochsenmaulsalat: salad made with thinly sliced ox cheek and mouth, served with a vinaigrette dressing and finely chopped onions.

Ochsenschlepp, Ochsenschwanz: oxtail.

Ofenkatze: Vorarlberg speciality: yeast pastry sprinkled with dried fruit and rolled up, covered with melted butter and baked 'like a cat curled up near a tiled stove'. Not unlike *Kärntner Reinling*, but don't tell that to anyone in Carinthia, where they have something called *Ofenkater* (male counterpart of *Ofenkatze*) which is totally different from *Ofenkatze* and sometimes called *Trenten*, just to confuse matters.

offene Weine: 'open wines', i.e. house wines sold in fractions (eighth, quarter, half) of a litre (an eighth of a litre is about a glassful), Usually several kinds are on offer and – particularly in wine regions – very drinkable. Slight warning: beware of *französischer Landwein* (French *vin du pays*) sold under *offene Weine* – it is usually no better (and often much worse) than good local Austrian wines, but very much more expensive (Austria is not a member of the EEC – yet!).

Olivenöl – olive oil.

Omelette Stephanie: named after the unfortunate Crown Princess Stephanie whose husband, Crown Prince Rudolf, sought his untimely death at Mayerling. Crown Princess Stephanie's lot at the Austrian Imperial Court was not a happy one, but she did have an unfortunate knack of saying the wrong thing such as complaining that Austrian cooking and particularly Viennese pastries and puddings – were too coarse for her delicate Belgian palate. By way of response Austrian Chefs invented Omelette Stephanie, the lightest, fluffiest baked omelette, in her honour – just to prove a point. They also invented *Stephanie-torte* (q.v.) – the richest, most complicated (and to my mind, most overdone) gâteau ever!

Palatschinken (Pfannkuchen): pancakes. Austrian pancakes are much larger – and usually also thicker – than ordinary pancakes and they are always filled. Listed on the menu under the filling which can be sweet or savoury, e.g. *Schokolade-palatschinken* (with chocolate), *Fleischpalatschinken* (with a savoury meat filling).

Falffy Knödel: glorified version of *Serviettenknödel* (q.v.) created at the beginning of the century in honour of a visit by Prince Palffy (those were the days!). Incredibly light dumpling mixture wrapped in a napkin and cooked suspen-ded in boiling water. Served sliced like *Serviettenknödel*.

Panadlsuppe: soup made with bread rolls and based on good veal or beef stock, thickened with eggs.

Panamatorte: soft moist chocolate cake made with almonds, with chocolate cream filling and topping and sprinkled with finely ground blanched almonds.

Panier: coating of flour, eggs and breadcrumbs as for *Wiener Schnitzel*.

Paniermehl: very fine breadcrumbs.

paniert: dipped first into flour, then into egg and finally into fine breadcrumbs and fried.

Paprika: green, yellow or red peppers, also the spice.

Paprika, gefüllte: see *gefüllte Paprika*.

Paprikahendl, Paprikahuhn: chicken in rich paprika sauce, often thickened with cream or sour cream. Sometimes described as *ausgelöst* (boned). Usually served with *Nockerl*.

Paradeis (Tomate): tomato.

Paradeiskraut: finely shredded white cabbage cooked with tomatoes.

Paradeissuppe: tomato soup.
Pariser Schnitzel: veal dipped first into flour and then into lightly beaten egg and fried – moist, succulent and altogether excellent.
Pariser Wurst: like *Knackwurst* or *Extrawurst* (q.v.), but minced finer and larger in diameter.
Parmaschnitzel: escalope first dipped into flour, then into lightly beaten egg and finally into grated Parmesan cheese and fried.
passiert: sieved. You will quite often find Roquefort (or Gorgonzola) *passiert* or *passierter Roquefort* on the menu. This means that the cheese is pushed through a sieve and arranged in a mound on a plate (one portion is usually enough for two). Sometimes the cheese is first mixed with butter – in which case the menu should say *passiert mit Butter*, – at other times the butter is served separately. N.B. *Passiert* also means 'something's happened' – avoid using it on its own unless you want to create a slight panic!
Pastete: pâté.
Pastete, Wiener: usually a vol-au-vent with savoury filling.
Paunzga: large beans.
Perlhuhn: guinea fowl.
Perlhuhnbrüstchen: breast of guinea fowl.
Perlzwiebel: button onions.
Petersilie: parsley.
Petersfisch: John Dory.
Pfandl: pan, frying pan (*im Pfandl* usually means pan-fried).
Pfau – peacock, also the name of a restaurant at Ruden (q.v.) where excellent eau-de-vie of the Pfau brand are being distilled, – now available at selected restaurants.
Pfeffer: pepper.
Pfefferkarpfen: carp cooked in a casserole with fish stock, peppercorns and potatoes.
Pfeffernüsse: a type of honeycake, small and round, highly spiced and at one time one of the few things one could buy at a *Heurigen* (other than wine, of course) since it greatly increases one's thirst!
Pfiff: 'whistle', old Viennese measure, ⅛ litre, now used for beer in some restaurants and snack bars.
Pfirsich: peach.
Pfefferoni: small and sharp red or green peppers, always pointed (the more pointed the sharper as a rule), often preserved in brine and served with cold meat.
Pilze, Pilzlinge: mushrooms.
Plenten: '*Knödel, Nudel, Nocken, Plenten sind die vier Tiroler Elementen*' (Dumplings, noodles, gnocchi and *Plenten* are the four Tyrolean 'basics') goes an old saying. Cooked Polenta – but it could be made with buckwheat flour instead of cornmeal.
Pöckeltes: meat pickled in brine.
Pöckelzunge: pickled tongue, usually ox-tongue.
Pofesen: same as poor knights – slices of crustless bread sandwiched together with a sweet or savoury filling from which the dish then takes its name, e.g. *Hirnpofesen* (filled with a ragout of calves brains), dipped in milk and egg and fried. If not prefaced with anything, the filling is usually jam. Despite the fact that some version of *Pofesen* can be found in practically every country in Europe, they are considered typically Viennese (in other parts of the country they are usually called *Arme Ritter* – poor knights) and there's a charming nursery rhyme which goes something like this:

Pofesen, Pofesen, wo bist so lang g'wesen?
Im Himmel sechs Wochen,
Die Teuferln tun kochen
Die Engerln tun lachen
dass d'Buckerln tun krachen

(Pofesen, where have you been for so long? In heaven for six weeks, where the little devils are cooking and the little angels are doubled up with laughter.)

Polenta: sometimes refers to the ingredient (cornmeal – *Maisgriess*), at other times to the cooked dish.

Polsterzipfel: 'cushion corners'. Pastry triangles filled with jam and either baked or fried in deep fat. Served dusted with icing sugar.

Pörkölt: In Austria *Pörkölt* is usually a type of *Gulasch* to which tomato purée has been added. In Hungary where *Gulyas* is more of a soup than a stew, *Pörkölt* is what the Austrians call *Gulasch*. Therefore if you order *Pörkölt* near the Hungarian border in the Burgenland you are likely to get the Hungarian version, i.e. an Austrian *Gulasch*.

Porree, Purri: leeks. Viennese adaptation of the French *Poireaux*.

Potitze: Yeast pastry is rolled out, spread with a filling of poppy-seeds, raisins, sugar etc (*Mohnpotitze*) or walnuts (*Nusspotitze*) and then both sides of the pastry are rolled towards the centre which gives the *Potitze* its distinctive shape.

Powidl (Pflaumenmus): very thick plum jam made with blue plums (*Zwetschken*) cooked with cloves, cinnamon, ginger and lemon rind but without sugar, literally for days – until a wooden spoon will stand up in it unaided. Used in many puddings such as *Germknödel* (q.v.). The Empress Maria Theresa ordered that her children be served good, filling puddings with *Powidl* at least twice a week and the *Powidl* was sent to the Imperial Court in huge tubs from Bohemia.

Powidltascherln, Powidltatschkerln: small pasta envelopes with a filling of *Powidl* (see above), served with melted butter, cinnamon, sugar and crisp browned breadcrumbs (some restaurants serve browned walnuts instead of breadcrumbs which is particularly delicious).

Preiselbeeren: cranberries.

Presskopf: brawn, head cheese.

Presswurst: brawn in a sausage skin.

Punschkrapferln, Punschtorte: small pastries or large gâteau made of sponge cake, centre layer consisting of cake (usually offcuts from pastries and even fine biscuit crumbs) soaked in rum punch. Always covered in pink icing. The better the *pâtisserie*, the better the *Punschkrapferln/Punschtorte*, since offcuts and biscuit crumbs for the filling will be of the finest.

Quendel (Thymian): thyme.

Quitten: quinces.

Radieschen: small radish.

Rahm (Sauerrahm): strictly speaking thick cream, but in Austria it usually means sour cream.

Rahmbeuschel: see *Kalbsbeuschel*:

Rahmdalken: *Dalken* (q.v.) using sour cream instead of yeast as raising agent. Very delicate.

Rahmsuppe: delicious soup made with sour cream. There are many regional versions, *Waldviertler* being one of the most popular.

Rasnici: Balkan speciality. Pieces of meat, usually pork, often previously marinaded, threaded onto a skewer interspersed with onion, paprika, bacon and bayleaf and grilled over charcoal.

Räucherlachs: smoked salmon.

Rebhuhn: partridge.

Rechnung: bill.

Reh: venison.

Rehrücken: saddle of venison if listed under meat or game on the menu, otherwise delicious moist chocolate cake baked in special oblong and ridged cake tin. Covered with chocolate icing and studded with slivered almonds to simulate larding. Like *Sachertorte*, sometimes served with whipped cream.

Rehschlögel: haunch of venison.

Reibertatschi: potato pancakes made with grated potatoes.

Reibgerstl: exactly the same as *Farferl* and *geriebenes Gerstl* (q.v.) namely pasta dough left to dry, coarsely grated and cooked.

Rein, Reindl (Pfanne): saucepan.

Reisauflauf: very commendable rice pudding baked in a soufflé or deep *gratin* dish with a fruit filling and usually topped with meringue. Served with vanilla custard or raspberry syrup.

Reisfleisch: sometimes called *Serbisches Reisfleisch* – fairly highly spiced Austrian version of risotto, containing meat. Usually pressed into timbales and inverted onto plate or serving dish. Served with grated Parmesan cheese.

Rettich: large radish, sometimes called *Bierrettich*.

Ribisl (Johannisbeere): red currant. Black currants are called *schwarze Ribisl*.

Ribislrotkraut: delicious way of cooking red cabbage with redcurrants, first encountered at the Barth Stuben, Neusiedl (q.v.).

Ribislschaumtorte: gâteau topped with redcurrants in a cloud of meringue.

Riebel: Vorarlberg version of *Sterz* (q.v.). Should not be too dry, otherwise the cry will be 'close the windows lest the Riebel fly out!'

Rigo Janczi: pastry squares with a thick filling of chocolate cream. Created in Paris in honour of a gipsy musician (Rigo Janczi) who won the heart of a fair princess which is why this particular cream filling is sometimes known as *Pariser Crème*.

Rind, Rindfleisch: beef.

Rindfleisch, gekochtes: the famous boiled beef of Vienna: fresh not salted, cooked with infinite care (you could call it the roast beef of Vienna since it is traditional for Sunday lunch). The cut of meat of which the best-known is *Tafelspitz* – should always be specified (at the Hietzinger Brâu in Vienna they list no less than ten different cuts). Should be served with *G'röste* (q.v.) or *Erdäpfelschmarrn* (q.v.) and a choice of at least two sauces (usually chive and apple/horseradish) and creamed spinach or other creamy vegetable. In good old-fashioned restaurants and country inns you may still find *gekochtes Rindfleisch, fein garniert* – the beef will appear on a special dish in the centre division, surrounded by smaller divisions into which lots of hot and cold accompaniments are placed – different sauces, vegetables, relishes, etc.

Rindsgulasch, Rindssaftgulasch: *Gulasch* made with beef.

Rindsbraten: could be roast beef (which is more often than not described as roast beef however) or pot roast, in which case it should be described as *gedünsteter Rindsbraten*, but I wouldn't bank on it!

Rindslungenbraten: whole fillet of beef.

Rindspöckelzunge: pickled ox-tongue.

Rindsrouladen: beef olives.

Rindsuppe: clear beef broth.

Rindszunge: ox-tongue.

Ringlotten: greengages (Viennese for *reineclaudes*!).
Ripplerts: spare ribs.
Risi Bisi, Risipisi: from Risi e Bisi, rice with green peas.
Ritschert: sometimes called *Steirisches* or *Kärntner Ritschert*, depending on where you are and nationality of the chef. There are a great many regional variations, but basically a hearty stew containing pearl barley (often also dried beans, lentils and other pulses), smoked pork and other meats, flavoured with lovage and sage (favourite herbs) and celeriac.
roh: raw.
Rohschinken; air-dried ham.
Rogen: fish roe.
Rollgerstl: pearl parley.
Rosmarin: rosemary.
Rostbraten: steak in one piece, braised with different additions and named accordingly, e.g. *Esterhazyrostbraten, Maschinrostbraten, Zwiebelrostbraten*, all of which are listed under their respective name in this glossary. Sometimes the cut of meat e.g. *Beiried* is also stated. At no time does *Rostbraten* stand for what you would expect it stands for, namely roast beef!
Röster: as in *Zwetschkenröster* (q.v.) – fruit stewed with very little water, but plenty of spices such as cloves, cinnamon etc. and served with a variety of dishes, mostly puddings such as *Kaiserschmarrn*. Theoretically *Röster* can be made with practically any soft fruit, but until recently *Zwetschkenröster* appeared to rule in splendid isolation, or perhaps it is a case of 'forgotten favourites' as lately there have been sightings – or rather tastings – of *Marillenröster, Ribislröster, Kirschenröster* and the long-forgotten *Hollerröster* (elderberry) – no doubt others will follow.
Rote Rübe (rote Beete): beetroot.
roter Rübenkren: relish made from cooked and shredded beetroot and horseradish.
Rotkraut (Rotkohl): red cabbage.
Russisches Ei: practically the same as *Mayonnais-Ei* (q.v.).

Sachertorte: legendary chocolate cake created in 1832 by the sixteen-year-old Franz Sacher when in the employ of Prince Metternich (the equally legendary Madame Sacher was Franz Sacher's daughter-in-law and later heard to say 'personally, I find it too dry' which may or may not be the reason why *Sachertorte* is served with whipped cream – upon request). Copied all over the world and never quite equalled (it has been murmured that the secret lies in the chocolate which is made especially for Sacher). There was a lawsuit – known as the *Tortenkrieg* (war of the cakes) between Sacher and Demel (q.v.) which lasted for years about the authenticity of the 'real' *Sachertorte* (Demel fill theirs with apricot jam). Sacher won, and one of the stalwart waitresses at Demel's swore that the owner of Sacher's would go to hell for this 'to be boiled in hot chocolate'. Basically a not-too-moist (to quote Madame Sacher) chocolate cake, spread with apricot jam and thick, wonderful chocolate icing. Available in several sizes for sending all over the world. *Sacher Konfekt* is a very small – as against miniature – version with almost more icing than cake mixture.
Sacherwürstl: extra-large Frankfurter, served at the Café Sacher in Vienna.
Saft, Safterl, Saftl (Sosse): gravy.
Saftgulasch, Wiener Saftgulasch: *Gulasch* with particularly good, natural and practically unthickened gravy.
Saibling: type of pink trout (char) found in Austrian rivers and lakes.

Salbei: sage.
Salonbeuscherl: see *Kalbsbeuschel* (with a ladleful of Gulasch gravy).
Salzburger Koch: very good pudding based on bread with filling of fresh fruit.
Salzburger Nockerl(n): spectacular and showy dish of eggs, egg-whites and sugar to which literally the merest flick of flour has been added. Shaped into great mounds and baked in the oven, then rushed to the table where they have to be eaten at once, lest they collapse. Why they are called by the diminutive of *Nockerln* instead of *Nocken* according to their size remains a mystery, but legend has it that Napoleon, when presented with a Salzburg version of a soufflé, sneered that this was not a soufflé but a *Nocken,* hence the creation of *Salzburger Nockerln* and the diminutive. An unlikely tale since there were 'original' *Salzburger Nockerl,* based on choux pastry since the early eighteenth century and in my opinion a superior, if less showy, dish. (Tennerhof at Kitzbühel serves particularly delectable *Salzburger Nockerl* – smaller than usual, but caramelized).
Salzburg: town and province in Austria.
Salzerdäpfel: boiled potatoes.
Salzgurke: cucumber pickled in brine, with dill. Sometimes served *geschält* (peeled).
Salzkammergut: literally 'Salt Chamber Estate'. Lake district which spreads into the provinces of Salzburg, Upper Austria and Styria. Salzkammergut lakes provide excellent fish.
Salzstangerl: small batons sprinkled with coarse salt and caraway seeds before baking.
Sardellen: anchovies.
Saubohnen: large broad beans also known as *Paunzga, Paunzen.*
Sauerkirschen: morello cherries.
Sauerrampfer: sorrel.
Saumeise: a speciality of Lower and Upper Austria (and claimed as their very own by both provinces.) Pork is minced, seasoned, portioned to the size of a goose's egg, wrapped in caul and lightly smoked. Eaten hot or cold.
saure Linsen: see *Linsen, sauer.*
saures Rindfleisch: thinly sliced boiled beef with a vinaigrette dressing.
Sautanz: 'pork feast' and sometimes advertised as such at country inns, particularly those with their own home-farm and/or butchery. A feast of pork products – ham, sausages, brawn, etc. from freshly slaughtered pig.
Schafskäse: ewe's milk cheese.
Schanigarten: pavement café or restaurant, the area being marked by shrubs planted in tubs. '*Schani, trag den Garten aussi*' (Johnny, bring out the garden') are the orders when spring has arrived and it is warm enough to sit outside – Schani being the name for the youngest employee, hence 'Schani's garden'. Listed frequently as an extra attraction of a restaurant or café, like a speciality of the house.
Schaum: froth.
Scheiterhaufen: 'stake' pudding. Austrian version of bread-and-butter pudding in which bread is arranged like a stake. Usually layered with sliced apples and served with vanilla sauce.
Scherzl: crusty end of loaf.
Scherzl, schwarzes: cut of beef, *Gustostückl* (q.v.).
Schilcher: wine from the Wildbach grape, a speciality of Western Styria. Colour varies from pale to dark pink.
Schilchersekt: sparkling version of above.
Schill, fogas: pike/perch.

Schindelbraten: roast or pot-roast with slices of meat arranged like overlapping roof tiles (*Schindel*). Am Spitz at Purbach (q.v.) does a particularly delectable one.

Schinken, Schunken: ham.

Schinkenfleckerl: small squares of pasta (*Fleckerl*) cooked and mixed with sour cream, egg and chopped ham and baked.

Schlagobers: whipped cream.

Schlegel, Schlögel (Keule): leg, as in *Lammschlegel* (leg of lamb).

Schlickkrapferln, Schlutzkrapferln: small pasta envelopes with a savoury meat filling, cooked in salt water and then either served with melted butter or in clear broth. In some parts of Austria they are deep-fried.

Schlosserbuben: prunes soaked in tea or rum, the stone replaced with an almond or with marzipan, dipped into batter and deep-fried. Served dusted with sugar and grated chocolate.

Schmalz: rendered fat, dripping. Should be qualified as in *Ganslschmalz* (goose), *Schweinsschmalz* (pork), etc. *Grammelschmalz* also contains small bits of crackling.

Schmankerl: a selected titbit, a delicacy, something very special. (You will sometimes find a separate section headed *Schmankerl* on the menu, listing specialities of the house or the region.) There is, however, a recipe for *Schmankerl* – a light sponge mixture spread thinly on a baking-sheet, baked and then scraped off when it will more or less crumble into thin slivers. The slivers are then used for puddings, *parfaits* and the like to which they give their name, e.g. *Schmankerlparfait, Schmankerlcreme, Schmankerlpudding*.

Schmant: sour cream.

Schmarren, Schmarrn: means a mere nothing, a trifle, a favour denied (if the answer to a request is a curt *'ein Schmarrn'*, it is the most definite 'No' imaginable). Culinary *Schmarrn* were first mentioned in 1563 – basically a batter poured into hot butter, baked or fried (according to recipe and region) and then torn into small pieces and finished in the oven. The batter can be made with flour, semolina, lightened with egg-whites and there are savoury as well as sweet versions, of which *Kaiserschmarrn* (q.v.) is probably the best known. *Erdäpfelschmarrn* (q.v.) is not based on batter, but still belongs to the same family. All *Schmarren* are close relations of *Sterz* (q.v.) and *Tommerl* (q.v.), and *Ofenkater* (not *Ofenkatze*) also belongs to the same family.

Schnaps: sometimes called *Brand*, prefaced by the fruit etc. from which it is derived, eau-de-vie. *Bauernschnaps* is usually identical to *Klarer* (q.v.) or *Obstler* (q.v.), home-distilled and very potent. (Incidentally, the plural of *Schnaps* is *Schnäpse*.)

Schnecken: a) snails, particularly good in Styria, except that they are mostly exported.
b) yeast pastry, sprinkled with raisins, sugar and spice, rolled up, cut into rounds and baked. Not unlike Chelsea buns, but flat.

Schneeballen: 'snowballs'. Pastry cut into squares and then cut through once or twice almost to the edge, loosely threaded on to a wooden cooking spoon and dropped into hot fat. Crisply fried, dusted with icing sugar and served warm, sometimes with raspberry syrup as a pudding. Demel (q.v.) make huge, featherlight and particularly good ones.

Schneenockerln: floating islands, *oeufs à la neige*. Huge poached meringues served with vanilla sauce and/or chocolate sauce or raspberry purée. A portion of *Schneenockerl* at the Hietzinger Bräu in Vienna consists of three large *Schneenockerl*, each served with a separate sauce.

Schnepfe: snipe.

Schnittlauch, Schnittling: chives, used abundantly (some say too abundantly) in Austrian cooking.
Schnitzel escalope which can be veal, pork, beef, etc., though this is usually stated. Not every Schnitzel is a *Wiener Schnitzel* (q.v.), however. For variations look under *Naturschnitzel, Pariserschnitzel, Kaiserschnitzel, Parmaschnitzel. Butterschnitzel* (q.v.) is not an escalope.
Schöberl: see *Biskuitschöberl*. Sometimes extra ingredients – like liver, herbs, etc. – are added to basic sponge mixture and the *Schöberl* (and soup to which they are added) are named accordingly e.g. *Leberschöberlsuppe, Kräuterschöberlsuppe*.
Schokolade: chocolate.
Schokoladebrandteigkrapfen: small choux pastry buns filled with whipped cream and served with hot chocolate sauce.
Schokoladebusserln: small chocolate meringues (literally 'chocolate kisses') to which almonds or walnuts may have been added.
Scholle: plaice, flounder.
Schöpsernes (Hammelfleisch): mutton.
Schotten: another name for curd or *Quark*.
Schottensuppe: creamy soup based on above, served with black bread and sprinkled with chives. Similar to *Rahmsuppe* (q.v.).
Schübling: special sausage in Vorarlberg.
Schunken (Schinken): ham.
Schupfnudeln: there are many regional variations, but basically elongated gnocchi (or finger-thick noodles, pointed at the end) made of potato paste, cooked and then tossed (*schupfen*) in hot butter or fat.
Schwammerl (Pilze): mushrooms.
Schwammerlsuppe: mushroom soup, very often clear soup with sliced mushrooms in it. In Styria served with *Sterz* (q.v.). Cream of mushroom soup is usually listed as *Champignoncremesuppe* or *Schwammerlscremesuppe* on the menu.
Schwammerlgulasch: mushroom *Gulasch*. Boletus mushrooms are the most usual for this dish, but other mushrooms can be used or a mixture of several kinds.
Schwarzfisch: fish – usually carp or pike – in a thick rich sauce with grated honeycake, walnuts and prunes.
schwarzes Scherzl: (see *Scherzl, schwarzes*).
Schwein: pork.
Schweinsbraten: roast pork.
Schweinsfischerl: long, lean fillet of pork.
Schweinsöhrl: pig's ears, but also folded puff pastry, sprinkled with sugar, rolled up from both sides, cut into thin slices and baked flat.
Seeteufel: sea-bass.
Seewinkel: (see *Neusiedlersee, Seewinkel*).
Seezunge: sole.
Seidel, Seidl, Seitel: measure by which beer is sold, ⅓ litre. If you ask for a small beer (*kleines Bier*) you are likely to get a *Seidel*.
Sekt: sparkling wine.
Selchfleisch: smoked meat, usually pork – otherwise the type of meat should be specified.
Selchfleischknödel: dumplings containing smoked pork.
Selchspeck: smoked fat pork.
Sellerie: usually refers to celeriac (also known as *Zeller*), but could mean celery (which is usually qualified as *Stangensellerie*). If in doubt, ask!
Semmel (Brötchen): bread roll.
Semmelbrösel (Paniermehl): fine breadcrumbs (literally crumbs made from rolls,

though they can of course be made from white bread).

Semmelknödel: very light dumplings made from cubed rolls.

Semmelkren: one of the classic accompaniments to *Tafelspitz* and all the other boiled beefs. Sauce made with bread or rolls, beef broth, milk or cream and horseradish. Not unlike bread sauce spiced up with horseradish, but don't tell that to the Viennese – they think they invented it!

Senf: mustard. There are lots of different kinds, but try *Kremser Senf* for a change, a rather pleasant slightly sweet mustard.

Senfgurke: cucumber pickled with mustard seeds. Should always be served *geschält* i.e. peeled after pickling.

Serviettenknödel: dumpling cooked in a napkin. (The dumpling mixture is shaped into a long roll, wrapped in a napkin, cooked and sliced). *Palffy Knödel* (q.v.) is a variation on that theme. Josef Wechsberg once told me that in his family the dumplings were so delicate that a violin string was used instead of a knife for slicing them.

Skubbanki, Skubanken: gnocchi made with potato paste, fried in butter and served with ground poppy seeds (or ground honeycakes) and sugar.

Slibovitz, Slibowitz: plum brandy.

Soda mit Himbeer: raspberry syrup topped up with soda water to make a long drink. (*Himbeerwasser* which can only occasionally be found on menus these days is a 'poorer' relation, using water instead of soda). Children's version of *G'spritzter*.

Solo- ...: as in *Solo-Krebse* – denotes large and select specimen.

Somloer, Szomloer Nockerl: light and delicate confection consisting of sponge, chocolate cream and whipped cream. Originated in Hungary, but often served in the Burgenland and could be considered a forerunner of Tiramisu.

Soss (Sauce): sauce.

Spagatkrapfen: fried pastry tied to its special mould with string (*Spagat*) which leaves distinctive marks.

Spanferkel: suckling pig.

Spargel: asparagus.

Spargelschaumsuppe: frothy cream of asparagus soup.

Spätzle: not an Austrian definition, but sometimes used in Vorarlberg and regions frequented by German and Swiss tourists for small dumplings or gnocchi.

Speck: air-dried fat pork (if smoked it should be called *Selchspeck*, – if rubbed with paprika *Paprikaspeck*).

Speckknödel: there are many variations on that theme of which *Innviertler Speckknödel* (spicy filling of chopped *Speck* enclosed in noodle paste) and *Tiroler Speckknödel* (flour dumplings containing chopped *Speck*) are the best known.

Speckkrautsalat: salad made with shredded white cabbage sprinkled with crisp pork cracklings, usually served warm.

Speckkrusteln: bits of crackling, often *Grammeln* (q.v.).

Specklinsen: brown lentils cooked in ham stock, with pork crackling or fried *Speck*.

Speisenkarte, Speisekarte, Speiskarte: the menu.

Spinat: spinach.

Spinatnocken, Spinatnockerl: large or small spinach gnocchi, usually served with brown butter.

Spritzkrapfen: choux pastry pushed into hot fat with a forcing bag, fried and served dusted with icing sugar. If very large they are filled with vanilla cream.

Stanitzl, Starnitzel: cornets. Usually made of fine crisp pastry and filled – just before serving – with whipped cream and fresh fruit, preferably wild strawberries.

Staubzucker (Puderzucker): icing sugar.

Steiermark: Styria, province in Southern Austria.
Steinpilze (Herrenpilze): boletus mushrooms, ceps, porcini.
Steirisches Kernöl: see *Kernöl*.
Steirische Klachlsuppe: see *Klachlsuppe*.
Steirisches Rebhuhn: tender cooked beef, sliced thinly, with a vinaigrette dressing made with pumpkin-seed oil.
Steirisches Schöpsernes: delicate ragout of mutton with lots of root vegetables, well seasoned with herbs.
Steirisches Wurzelfleisch: hearty dish of boiled pork, a Styrian version of *Krenfleisch* (q.v.) – and may all Styrians forgive me for thus simplifying matters!
Stelze: knuckle – as in *Kalbsstelze, Schweinsstelze*.
Stephanietorte: like Omelette Stephanie (q.v.) named in honour of the unfortunate Crown Princess Stephanie. Although I have no proof for this assumption, I think that this is where the *pâtissiers* of Vienna took their 'sweet' revenge on the Crown Princess for saying that Austrian cooking was too coarse for her delicate Belgian palate: *Stephanietorte* (also known as *Stephaniecremetorte*) is just about the richest and to my mind the most unsubtle combination of flavours, each perfectly delicious and delicate on its own, but unbearably rich when served up in one gâteau. The basic gateau contains chocolate and hazelnuts, is cut through three times and filled with layers of hazelnut cream, raspberry cream and chocolate.
Sterz: often called *Steirischer Sterz*, probably more for the alliteration than for its origin, for most Austrian provinces can lay claim to their own version (called *Riebel* in Vorarlberg). There are many variations, but basically flour is cooked in water until it forms a large lump. This is then thrown into hot fat and torn into tiny shreds with a fork (*Sterzgabel*) and fried until crisp. The procedure may sound revolting, but the result is delicious, particularly if served with clear mushroom soup (and incidentally, you do not sprinkle *Sterz* on to soup, you scoop up separate portions with your spoon for each spoonful of soup). There are many versions of *Sterz*, according to the flour – if made with buckwheat it is called *Heidensterz*, with cornmeal *Türkensterz* – and many additions such as crisp crackling (*Grammelsterz*) or dried beans (*Bohnensterz*) when it becomes a dish in its own right.
Stockfisch: flattened, salt and dried cod, used in the Tyrol (land of the *G'röstl*) for *Stockfischgröstl* on Good Friday.
Stoffserviette: cloth napkin. You will sometimes find the words '*Stoffserviette* S.=' on the menu of the more modestly priced inns where they'd normally hand you a paper napkin. If you want a cloth napkin, you pay for it.
Stoss Suppe: see *Rahmsuppe*, usually with caraway seeds.
Strankalan, Strankerln: French beans, same as *Fisolen* (q.v.).
Strauben: deep-fried pastry, thickly dusted with icing sugar.
Striezel (Hefezopf): plaited yeast loaf.
Strudel: denotes the type, not the dough: dough rolled out or pulled out (depending on the dough), filled, rolled up and then either baked or boiled. Different *Strudel* are listed under their respective names, e.g. *Apfelstrudel, Fleischstrudel*, etc.
Strudelteig: Strudel dough. Special dough pulled out to wafer thinness (you should be able to read a love letter through it). Dough can be used for savoury *Strudel* (*Fleischstrudel, Lungenstrudel*, etc.) which are more often boiled than baked (usually portioned off first) or for sweet *Strudel* which are always baked.
Suppennudeln: vermicelli, very fine noodles used in clear beef broth.
Suppentopf: sometimes called *Wiener Suppentopf*, literally 'soup pot', *pot au feu*.

Surfleisch: pickled meat, usually pork.
Szegediner, Szekely Gulasch: pork *Gulasch* with *Sauerkraut* and – usually – sour cream.

Tafelspitz: Viennese speciality, denoting cut of beef primarily used for the famous boiled beef. ('A Viennese legend' they describe it at the Hietzinger Bräu in Vienna where they list ten different cuts for their boiled beef.) Unfortunately restaurants have been known to use the term *Tafelspitz* as a generic for boiled beef and not every *Tafelspitz* listed as such on the menu is that particular cut (since there's a limit to the number of portions a *Tafelspitz* will yield, this is understandable, if not pardonable.) There is of course no reason why *Tafelspitz* should always be boiled – except for the smallness of the cut and the Viennese predeliction for their (admittedly excellent) boiled beef, and thus it can be found prepared in other ways as well, as in '*gedünsteter* (braised) *Tafelspitz*'. The cut is sometimes applied to other meat such as in *Tafelspitz vom Hirsch* (venison).
Tafelspitzsülzchen: brawn made with *Tafelspitz* (q.v.), one of the specialities at Schickh, Klein-Wien (q.v.).
Tageseinlage: clear beef broth with varying additions (*Griessnockerl, Leberknöderl* etc.) is featured on most Austrian menus and the soup is named according to the addition (*Griessnockerlsuppe etc.*). Some restaurants, instead of stating 'soup of the day' state *Tageseinlage* meaning that day's addition to clear beef broth and you have to ask for details.
Tageskarte: *carte du jour*, dishes of the day.
Tagesmenü: fixed price meal of the day which is sometimes split into *Mittagsmenü* (lunch) and *Abendmenü* (dinner). You may also find that there are several *Tagesmenüs* at different prices, depending on the number of courses. Always worth considering, particularly at lunch when many otherwise quite expensive restaurants offer positive bargains!
Tagesspezialitäten: specialities of the day, often identical with *Tageskarte*.
Tarhonya: Hungarian pasta, about the size of a barleycorn (and similar to *Farferl*).
Taschenfeitl, not edible, but a sharp folding knife which some country restaurants and *Buschenschenken* (q.v.) provide with a *Brettljaus'n* (q.v.). Particularly good for slicing through *Speck*, sausages and smoked meats (to be wiped on leather shorts for real rural touch). Some restaurants encourage you to take it with you as a souvenir since it usually also bears the name of the restaurant.
Tascherl: 'little pockets' more often than not made with pasta, with a sweet or savoury filling and named according to the filling.
Taube: pigeon.
Tellerfleisch: Viennese speciality: boiled beef served in a soup plate with clear beef broth, root vegetables and a few slices of bone marrow, sprinkled with chopped chives. Freshly grated horseradish is the usual accompaniment, as well as beetroot and horseradish relish. Favourite for *Gabelfrühstück* (q.v.) in the olden days, but now quite often available for lunch.
Tellergericht: basically a *plat du jour*: 'served on a plate', i.e. not on a serving dish from which second helpings are usually offered when ordering à la carte. Frequently available at lunch in restaurants catering for a clientele in a hurry and portions are usually fairly large.
Teebäckerei: selection of biscuits like *Husarenkrapferl* (q.v.), small meringues, etc. either home-made or bought at a good *pâtisserie* or bakers.
Thermenregion: wine region south of Vienna in Lower Austria, producing some excellent reds as well as whites (Baden, Sooss, Gumpoldskirchen are some of the place names for which to look).

Thymian: thyme.
Tirol: Tyrol, Austrian province.
Tiroler Knödel: *Semmelknödel* (q.v.) with bits of ham or smoked pork incorporated in the mixture.
Tiroler Leber: sautéd liver with onions and a piquant sauce.
Tiroler Ofenleber: liver pâté wrapped in caul and baked in the oven.
Tommerl: Styrian speciality, but also claimed by Carinthia (*Tomele*). Thick batter with sweet or savoury additions which is baked – basically a *Schmarrn* (q.v.) which is not torn. *Türkentommerl* (q.v.) is probably the best-known *Tommerl*.
Topfen (*Quark*): curd, cottage cheese, but usually less moist and smoother. Used in innumerable dishes, some of which are listed below.
Topfenauflauf: baked pudding based on curd or cottage cheese.
Topfengolatschen: *Golatschen* (q.v.) with a sweet curd and raisin filling.
Topfenhaluschka: pasta dough which is not cut but pinched into small shapes, cooked and then mixed with curd cheese and bits of crackling. Hungarian, but often found on Austrian menus, particularly in the Burgenland.
Topfenknödel: small featherlight dumplings made with curd cheese and served as a pudding, with breadcrumbs (or ground walnuts) crisply fried in butter and accompanied by a fruit compote or purée.
Topfennockerl: variation on the above, even lighter.
Topfenpalatschinken: pancakes with a filling of sweetened curd cheese, raisins and egg, lightly rolled up and baked, very often with a vanilla custard. At their most magnificent at Häupl's, Seewalched (q.v.) where they come – to quote Mr Häupl – *'mit vüll Füll'* (with a lot of filling).
Topfenstrudel: close relation of *Milchrahmstrudel* (q.v.) and what is termed *Topfenstrudel* in one restaurant may well turn out to be another restaurant's *Milchrahmstrudel. Topfenstrudel* is drier, however, and should be served without vanilla sauce. The best *Topfenstrudel* I have ever eaten – beyond shadow of a doubt – was at the Post at Lech in Vorarlberg.
Topfentascherl: small pasta envelopes with a sweet curd filling. Boiled and served with melted butter, sugar and cinnamon – a typical 'sweet pasta' dish.
Topfentorte: baked sweet cheesecake.
Torte: gâteau. In Austria *Torten* are not only named after the principal ingredient (*Schokoladetorte, Haselnusstorte*) or the person who created it (*Sachertorte*), the place of origin (*Linzertorte*), but also after the person in whose honour it was created (*Esterhazytorte, Stephanietorte*) or even a title (*Hofratstorte*).
Trauben: grapes.
Traunkirchner Torte: a regional speciality (*Traunkirchen* is a small, enchanting village on a lake in the Salzkammergut). Basically a gâteau made of layered pâté *brisé*, filled with whipped cream (or egg-white) and fruit, covered with whipped cream.
Trebern, Treberner: *marc.*
Triet: *Grazer Zwieback*: (q.v.) put into a deep plate and liberally moistened with *Glühwein*. There are regional variations – *Triet* (or *Tried*) exists all over Austria – probably best in Styria where it is always made with *Grazer Zwieback* (in other regions raisin bread may be used instead).
Trinkgeld: tip.
Truthahn (Pute): turkey, also known as Indian in Austria.
Türken: literally 'Turks', but in Southern Austria often used for maize. (It was thought that the Turks brought maize to Austria. This is not correct, but the name has stayed and the hot summer wind is sometimes called *'Türkenwind'* – beneficial for the growing of maize.)
Türkengriess: cornmeal.

Türkenmehl: maize flour.
Türkentommerl: delicious pudding made with cornmeal batter and fresh fruit such as cherries or apples. Served dusted thickly with icing sugar.

überbacken: *gratiné*, covered with a sauce and baked or put under the grill.
Ulmergerstl: pearl barley.
ungarisch: Hungarian.
unterspickt: marbled (for meat).

Vanillekipferl: small pastry crescents (containing walnuts or hazelnuts) rolled in vanilla sugar whilst still hot. Good *pâtisseries* sell them and so do most branches of Julius Meinl (which can be found all over Austria). Buy a bagful and take them back to your hotel – you will not regret it!
Vanillirostbraten: not vanilla-scented meat as one might expect from the name, but braised steak or pot roast heavily larded with garlic. Vanilla in this case being a euphemism for garlic. In the old days when vanilla was very expensive and considered a great luxury, garlic was called 'poor man's vanilla'.
Verhackerts: a speciality claimed by Styria as well as Carinthia and no doubt several other Austrian provinces as well. Lightly smoked pork fat with the rind removed, chopped up (*Verhackert*), packed tightly into earthenware receptacles – garlic and possibly other seasonings added – and covered with a layer of melted fat to seal off the air. Delicious with dark country bread and often served as part of a *Brettljaus'n* (q.v.) with copious draughts of Styrian wine or *Obstler*. Sometimes a dollop of *Verhackerts* is added to cooked pasta and to vegetables or boiled potatoes instead of butter. *Verhackerts* is also added to pasta fillings and used for making roux.
Verhackerts Würste: *Verhackerts* in a sausage skin.
Viertel: quarter (as in Waldviertel – forest region of Lower Austria), but also – and most importantly – the measure (quarter litre) by which you order house wine (a quarter litre equals about two glasses). You could, of course, start off by ordering the smaller measure – ⅛ litre (*ein Achterl*) – but a number of restaurants only start selling house wine from a quarter litre upwards!
Vintschgerl: delicious crusty roll made with mixed flour, usually with caraway seeds – *Vintschgerl* being a name used mainly in the Salzburg region and Tyrol.
Vogerlsalat (Feldsalat): lamb's lettuce, corn salad, *Salade Mâche*. Sometimes mixed with potato salad and sprinkled with crackling.
Vorarlberg: most Western (and smallest) Austrian province and part of Austria since the fourteenth century. However: 'Vorarlberg is an independent state,' it says in the constitution, 'which joined the Austrian Federal Republic of its own free will.' (True, but only after a plebiscite in 1919 in which 80% of the population had voted in favour of joining Switzerland instead – an offer graciously declined by the Swiss). Anything outside that 'independent state' is considered foreign – even neighbouring Tyrol (when they built the Arlberg Tunnel over a hundred years ago which was to make access to and from the rest of Austria easier, the Vorarlbergers were very put out and said 'what God has put asunder by a mountain, let no man join by a tunnel'). All of which by way of explanation as to why some of the restaurant and menu descriptions are often different in Vorarlberg – closer to the Swiss and the Alemannic ties which link Vorarlberg as much to the Valais as to Vienna. Gastronomically speaking, however, Vorarlberg has the greatest concentration of excellent restaurants in the smallest area. And Ernst Huber at the

Deuring Schlössle in Bregenz (q.v.).
Vorarlberger Marend: Marend is the Vorarlberg term for *Jause* (q.v.) which in turn is Austrian for mid-morning or mid-afternoon snack. *Marend* consists of a platter of *Speck*, local cheese, dark bread, butter and *Most* (q.v.) made from apples. Wine is allowed instead if you insist!
Vorarlberg Würstle: not really a traditional dish, but a fairly recent Viennese invention graciously accepted by Vorarlberg: Frankfurter sausages (known lovingly as *Zizele*) cut into half lengthways, the halves sandwiched together with a sliver of cheese. Streaky bacon is wrapped round sausages which are then grilled.
Vorspeis, Vorspeisen: *hors-d'oeuvres*, starters.
Vorspeisteller: a selection of different *hors-d'oeuvres*.

Wachau: region between Krems and Melk in Lower Austria, one of the loveliest stretches of the Danube. Famous wine region, but also known for its apricots from which eaux-de-vie and liqueurs are distilled.
Wachauer Laberl: particularly good crusty bread roll – a speciality of the Wachau, but also available in other parts of Austria.
Wachauer Torte: according to the book a rich chocolate gâteau, but you may well be offered a gâteau with apricot halves, liberally doused in apricot brandy or liqueur, called by this name.
Wacholder: juniper.
Wachtel: quail.
Wadl, Wadschunken: shin (shin of beef is much favoured for *Gulasch*).
Waffeln: until fairly recently *Waffeln* meant thin wafers served with ice-cream, but nowadays more often than not it refers to waffles (Rosenberger Motorway restaurants serve delicious ones with various toppings) and ice-cream wafers are usually described as *Eiswafferln* or *Wafferln* (the diminutive for once being correctly applied). You can tell by the price as a rule – ice-cream wafers should be part of an ice-cream serving and if a charge is made, it should be small. Waffles are listed separately, with details of the various toppings.
Wald: forest, woods.
Waldbeeren: 'berries of the woods' which usually means just a selection of berries.
Waldmeister: woodruff.
Waldviertel: forest quarter, region in Lower Austria, north of the Danube and bordering Czechoslovakia, where the best carp comes from. (Also other good things like poppy-seeds from Zwettl, excellent beer and some splendid regional dishes.)
Waldviertler Rahmsuppe: delicious soup made with sour cream, sometimes known as *Stoss Suppe*.
warmer Krautsalat: finely shredded white cabbage salad, served warm with bits of crisply fried bacon (often identical to *Speckkrautsalat*). Sometimes the pan in which the bacon was fried is swilled out with the vinaigrette dressing giving a slightly smoky flavour. Not at all the *nouvelle cuisine* invention which it may appear to be at first sight, but a very old traditional dish.
Weckerl: oblong bread roll.
weich: soft.
Weichsel (Sauerkirschen): morello cherries.
Weichselcremetorte: gâteau with morello cherries (no relation to Black-Forest Gâteau!).
Weichselkuchen: sponge cake – sometimes including chocolate into which whole

fresh morello cherries have been folded.

Weihachten: Christmas.

Weihnachtsbäckerei: different biscuits, small meringues, honeycakes, etc. which are baked before Christmas, carefully stored in airtight tins which are ransacked immediately so that fresh batches have to be baked. Every family has its own treasured recipes and some of the *Weihnachtsbäckerei* is also used for hanging on the Christmas tree. Some of the biscuits etc. can also be found as part of *Teebäckerei* (q.v.) whilst others – like small honeycakes – are only made at Christmas.

Wein: wine.

Weinbauer: vintner.

Weinbeisser: type of honeycake which used to be sold at Heurigen (similar to *Pfeffernüsse*). Not very sweet, but highly spiced.

Weinbergschnecken: vineyard snails.

Weinberln: small raisins or currants.

Weinchaudeau, Weinchadeau: Viennese sabayon. Much lighter and fluffier than *Zabaglione* (mixture contains some egg-whites as well as yolks) served in glasses. Supposedly has restorative powers and suitable for any age. I was always fed on glasses of frothy *Weinchaudeau* when recovering from measles and the like – a sure sign that I was well on the way to recovery (to anyone worried about a child being fed wine by the spoonful – to say nothing of barely cooked egg – it's too late now to worry!).

Weingarten: vineyard.

Weingartenpfirsich: vineyard peaches – usually green or white, never yellow – and the best peaches of all!

Weinkraut: finely shredded white cabbage, cooked very gently with lightly caramelized sugar and onions, with a dash of wine vinegar or wine (not necessarily the latter). Definite sweet/sour flavour.

Weintrauben: grapes.

Weinviertel: largest Austrian wine region, in Lower Austria, stretching from North of the Danube to the Czech border in the north and east.

Weststeiermark: wine region in Western Styria to the west and south of Graz, known for the pink *Schilcher* wine.

Wien: Vienna, capital of Austria as well as a province of which Vienna is the capital. Also a wine region (excellent white wines).

Wiener Koch: delicious light and creamy pudding. Absolute heaven if you can get it – otherwise get the recipe and cook it yourself when you get home – it's easy.

Wiener Saftgulasch: *Gulasch* with particularly good gravy – like *Saftgulasch* (q.v.) only more so. It has been said that you can only get a real *Wiener Saftgulasch* in a *Gasthaus* or *Wirtshaus* (q.v.).

Wiener Savarin: usually rum babas with orange zest (or liqueur) added to the rum and crowned with whipped cream. There are, however, variations and chocolate has been known to make an appearance.

Wiener Wäschermädl: apricot fritters (stone replaced by an almond) served with vanilla sauce. Highly commendable.

Wiener Schnitzel: should be made with veal, though nowadays it is often made with pork. Some restaurants offer both, with the veal at a higher price. (Figlmüller's – reputedly the largest *Wiener Schnitzel* in captivity – is made with pork). *Wiener Schnitzel* (preferred cut is leg) must be freshly made to order. It should be golden brown and the coating 'blistered' or 'ruched' (beware of a *Wiener Schnitzel* with a straight coating like a board) and you should be able to slip your knife easily between the coating and the meat.

The coating should be crisp and the meat succulent and there should be no garnish other than a decent-sized wedge (never a coyly crimped slice) of lemon. A *Wiener Schnitzel* should also be of commendable size, i.e. it should just about cover the plate. (I feel that Figlmüller go a little over the top – literally – with their *Wiener Schnitzel* which are usually larger than the plate). If the *Wiener Schnitzel* you have ordered lacks seriously in one or more of these qualities, send it back. They will respect you for knowing your *Wiener Schnitzel*! (A *Wiener Schnitzel* should not be the least bit greasy, the test for this being that you should be able to sit on the *Wiener Schnitzel* or the plate on which it was served wearing a silk dress without staining it, but I would not suggest trying that in a restaurant!) Salads are the best accompaniments – cucumber being my own preference.

Wiener Suppentopf: *pot-au-feu* which usually contains a piece of beef, some chicken, sometimes tongue, vermicelli and green peas, but there are variations and the menu should list whatever is included. More often than not a meal in itself, leaving room only for a pudding or cheese to follow.

Wiesenkräuter: meadow herbs such as dandelion, wild garlic, often used in salads.

Wild: game.

Wildbachtraube: grape from which pink *Schilcher* wine is made, a speciality of the West Styrian wine region.

Wildpastete: game pâté.

Wilderer: poacher, as in *Wildererragout*, usually denoting that the dish contains game.

Wildschwein: wild boar.

Wildschweinschinken: smoked and/or air-dried wild boar.

Wirtshaus: inn, not necessarily a country inn (there are *Wirtshäuser* in Vienna as well), considered one step beneath a *Gasthaus* – a term sometimes also used in a derogatory sense. Careful though: – the term is occasionally used as an understatement, a typical example of which is 'Hasi' Unterberger who insists on calling his very elegant and exclusive (and excellent) restaurant in Kitzbühel (q.v.) a *Wirtshaus*.

Wirsing: savoy cabbage.

Witwenküsse: 'widow's kisses', small meringues which usually have chopped walnuts and/or chopped peel folded into the mixture.

Woazenes: Carinthian term for white bread made with wheat flour.

Würstl mit Saft: see *Frankfurter mit Saft*.

Wurzelwerk: root vegetables, including carrots, celeriac, parsley root, etc.

Wurzelfleisch: can be lamb or mutton, beef or pork – meat cooked with root vegetables. *Steirisches Wurzelfleisch* always denotes pork, often served with grated horseradish.

Wurzelkarpfen: carp cooked with root vegetables.

Wurzelrahmsauce: a sauce based on root vegetables (sometimes roasted with the meat) and the juices from the pan, bound with sour cream.

Zapfen: special cut of beef.

Zander: pike/perch.

zart: tender.

Zeller: celeriac (*Sellerie* can be either celeriac or celery).

Zieser of Riegersburg: has been called the 'Rolls Royce' of eaux-de-vie. Expensive but once tasted, never forgotten. Some very good restaurants (Raffel at Jennersdorf) stock it, though it is not always listed. (Riegersburg is in Styria on the Burgenland border – known for its grim fortress.)

Ziege: goat.

Ziegenkäse: goat's cheese.
Zigeuner: gipsy (if prefacing a dish it usually denotes that paprika and/or green peppers play a prominent part).
Zigeunerschnitten: usually identical with Rigo Janczi (q.v.), but cut into slices instead of squares.
Zillertaler Krapfen: pasta rolled out and cut into squares, filled with potatoes, curd and *Graukäse*, also chopped chives. Folded, sealed and deep-fried.
Zimt: cinnamon.
Zimtparfait: *parfait* flavoured with cinnamon which at one time appeared rather too frequently on menus.
Zimtsterne: star-shaped biscuits flavoured with cinnamon, part of *Weihnachtsbäckerei*.
Zizele: Vorarlberg for Frankfurter sausages.
Znaimer Gurke: particularly good cucumbers pickled in brine, named after the town of Znojmo (formerly Znaim) home of the best pickled cucumbers.
Znaimer Gulasch: beef *Gulasch* with sliced pickled cucumber as garnish.
Zucchini: courgettes.
Zucker: sugar.
Zuckerl: strictly speaking a boiled sweet (*zuckerlrosa* is sugar pink) but often applied to other sweets, including chocolates. (If somebody says that he/she has saved up a '*Zuckerl*' especially for you, it could mean something extra-special, – more often than not a particularly juicy bit of gossip!)
Zunge: tongue.
Zwetschken (Pflaumen): blue plums.
Zwetschkenfleck: yeast pastry covered with sliced blue plums and baked.
Zwetschkenknödel: dumplings made with potato paste wrapped round a plum (stone having been replaced by a lump of sugar – sometimes first dipped into *Slibowitz*). Served sprinkled with breadcrumbs fried in butter, sugar and cinnamon.
Zwetschkenröster: blue plums stewed with little or no water and cinnamon, cloves, sugar until the skin starts to wrinkle. Favourite accompaniment to *Kaiserschmarrn, Topfenknödel*, etc.
Zwiebel, Zwiefel: onions.
Zwiebelrostbraten: braised whole steak with onions.

Index

Vienna